RATIONING EDUCATION

RATIONING EDUCATION

Policy, practice, reform and equity

**David Gillborn and
Deborah Youdell**

Open University Press
Buckingham · Philadelphia

Open University Press
Celtic Court
22 Ballmoor
Buckingham
MK18 1XW

e-mail: enquiries@openup.co.uk
world wide web: http://www.openup.co.uk

and
325 Chestnut Street
Philadelphia, PA 19106, USA

First Published 2000

A catalogue record of this book is available from the British Library

ISBN   0 335 20361 2 (hb)   0 335 20360 4 (pb)

Library of Congress Cataloging-in-Publication Data
Gillborn, David.
    Rationing education: policy, practice, reform, and equity / David Gillborn and Deborah Youdell.
        p.   cm.
    Includes bibliographical references (p.) and index.
    ISBN 0-335-20361-2 (hard). – ISBN 0-335-20360-4 (pbk.)
    1. Educational equalization–Great Britain–London–Case studies.
    2. Education and state–Great Britain–London–Case studies.
    3. Education, Secondary–Social aspects–Great Britain–London–Case studies. I. Youdell, Deborah, 1970– . II. Title.
    LC213.3.G73L664   1999
    379.421'2–dc21   99-13290
                                                                                  CIP

Typeset by Graphicraft Limited, Hong Kong
Printed in Great Britain by St Edmundsbury Press Ltd, Bury St Edmunds, Suffolk

Dorn, Jim, Joyce, Rebecca and Sarah, for their love and patience (DG)

Angela, for making my life (DY)

Contents

Acknowledgements

This study would not have been possible without the help and cooperation of the teachers and pupils in our two case-study schools, Taylor Comprehensive and Clough Grant Maintained. The need to preserve anonymity prevents us thanking individuals separately, but hopefully our analysis will begin to repay the debt that we owe all the participants in the project.

The research was funded by a grant from the Nuffield Foundation. We would like to thank the foundation for its support and, in particular, gratefully acknowledge the assistance and encouragement we received from Anthony Tomei and Helen Quigley.

Many individuals have contributed to our work. In some cases they have helped us think through problems differently; on occasion they have provided invaluable support and encouragement; there are some without whom this book would simply not have been completed. They include Michael Apple, Stephen Ball, Len Barton, Nazir Carrim, Lois Davis, George J. Sefa Dei, Sean Demack, David Drew, Jannette Elwood, Greta Gibson, Caroline Gipps, Anne Gold, Harvey Goldstein, Mike Grimsley, Graham Hobbs, Alison Kirton, Cate Knowles, Máirtín Mac an Ghaill, Louise Millward, Heidi Mirza, Tariq Modood, Louise Morley, Shona Mullen, Peter Mortimore, Desmond Nuttall, Diane Onyango, Sally Power, Peter Ratcliffe, Sheila Riddell, Tami Ryan, Pam Sammons, Roger Slee, Christopher Smith, Gordon Stobart, Sally Thomas, Sally Tomlinson, Barry Troyna, Carol Vincent and Geoff Whitty.

David would especially like to thank Deborah, who took a modest, small-scale project and turned it into an ambitious, wide-ranging journey that was exciting, frightening, depressing and exhilarating (though not necessarily in that order). Special thanks to my family who, in the interests of my research, put up with too many absences, late nights and tight deadlines.

Mum and Dad, you have always been there for me and I cannot describe the debt I owe you. Dorn, Becky and Sarah, you bring new happiness and new surprises to my life. Thank you for everything.

Deborah would like personally to thank a number of people. Dave Gillborn for his guidance, support and friendship throughout this research. He has made writing this book an incredibly enjoyable learning experience. It has been fabulous to work (and drink) with him. David Woodhead for his interest, debate and eternal friendship. Nicola Douglas for all of the lunch-times given up to the ongoing pleasure and pain of fieldwork and writing. All of my family, in particular my mum Pat and sister Linny who have always had immense faith in me. Finally, I would like to offer my love and appreciation to my partner Angela, who shared the unfolding of this analysis and provided valuable medical knowledge of triage. I am honoured by her love, care and patience as well as the many cups of tea offered and late suppers prepared during the writing of this book.

Key to transcripts

---

italicized text	Denotes emphasized speech or raised voice.
. . .	Pause.
(. . .)	Material has been edited out.
[square brackets]	Paraphrased for sake of clarity.

List of figures and tables

1

Education and equity

Education is not, as older social science pictured it, a mirror
of social or cultural inequalities. That is all too still an image.
Education systems are busy institutions. They are vibrantly
involved in the production of social hierarchies. They select
and exclude their own clients; they expand credentialed labour
markets; they produce and disseminate particular kinds of
knowledge to particular users.

(Connell 1993: 27)

This study is concerned with educational inequality and how it is made.
We seek to identify the mechanisms that have simultaneously delivered
year-on-year increases in the headline indicator of educational 'standards'
and prompted ever-widening inequalities associated with gender, ethnic
origin and social class. Through an analysis of the major reforms and their
impact at the school level, we explore and expose the everyday, routine
practices by which these inequalities are reproduced, extended and legitimized. Our argument is that schools are *rationing education*. This process is the
culmination of many factors, the full effects of which often remain hidden
from public scrutiny. Where teachers are aware of the divisive nature of their
actions, 'pragmatism' is frequently offered as a justification – pragmatism
within a system whose values and priorities are antithetical to equity.

Our analysis suggests that this situation has worsened regardless of the
political party in government; despite the rhetorics of inclusivity and em-
powerment; and irrespective of the motivation of pupils. The British school
system is increasingly selective, disciplinary and discriminatory.[1] In the classroom and staffroom these processes can be subtle, complex and hidden:
their effects are simple and devastating. Equality of opportunity is denied
many pupils, especially Black young people and their peers from working-
class backgrounds. The obsession with measurable and elite 'standards', the
publication of school 'league tables', heightened surveillance of schools, and
increased competition for resources (all central to the reforms) are part of
the problem, not the solution.

Researching equity

One of our driving concerns in this book is to examine the consequences of contemporary education reforms in relation to inequalities of opportunity and experience. The terms 'equity', 'inequality' and 'opportunity', however, are open to markedly different interpretations and uses. Before examining our sources of data, therefore, we wish to begin by commenting briefly on these debates and the understandings that inform our analysis.

The concept of *equality of opportunity* has a long and contested history on both sides of the Atlantic (cf. Apple 1993; Foster *et al.* 1996; Gipps and Murphy 1994; Halsey *et al.* 1980; Valli *et al.* 1997). In the USA, in particular, the notion of *equity* has come to prominence in recent debates:

> equity has replaced the older concept of equal educational opportunity. Both are related to 'egalitarian concepts of liberty, democracy and freedom from bias' [Grant 1989: 89]. But equity places more emphasis on notions of fairness and justice, even if that requires an unequal distribution of goods and services.
>
> (Valli *et al.* 1997: 254)

This is an important shift in the terms of debate. It represents a further strand in the varied and sometimes conflicting interpretations that are mobilized around the concept of equal opportunity. Indeed, it is possible to identify at least four different uses of the term.[2]

- *Formal equality of access and provision.* Writing about the British educational scene, Halsey *et al.* (1980) identify several separate but related understandings of equality of opportunity. The most limited approach stresses a concern with formal and explicit barriers to access and participation, such as restrictions on the gender or religion of participants in an organization. Hence, inequality by this definition would rest on members of one or more social or ethnic groups openly being denied access to particular schools or examination systems on the basis of their ascribed identity. This is the most conservative definition of the concept and is frequently asserted as the *only* viable definition by critics of the right (cf. D'Souza 1995; Flew 1986).
- *Equality of circumstance.* Halsey *et al.* go on to identify a second understanding, which emerged before the 1944 Education Act. This perspective is concerned with the inequalities of circumstance that can bar certain groups from participation in practice (especially via poverty) despite the abolition of any formal barrier to access. The existence of a separate private education system, and limits on the availability of student 'loans' and other forms of support, mean that the contemporary British education system does not satisfy the requirements even of this relatively limited definition.
- *Equity of participation (treatment).* Writing in relation to the North American literature, Linda Valli and her colleagues subsume the former two categories,

but isolate an understanding (in terms of participation and treatment) that does not receive explicit attention in the British literature.[3] Included in this definition are 'the structures and processes that define everyday life in schools' (Valli *et al.* 1997: 254). This includes both the formal and 'hidden' curriculum and would lead schools to 'eliminate tracking, biased testing, and other arrangements' that give structural force to inequalities of 'race', gender and class (Beane and Apple 1995: 11, cited in Valli *et al.* 1997: 254).

- *Equity of outcome.* In both the British and North American literatures, a final understanding of equity concerns the substantive outcomes of education – what has also been called the 'strong' or 'radical' understanding. In Britain this perspective came to prominence in debates concerning selective public education (in the 1960s and 1970s) and was enshrined in the approach of the Rampton (1981) and Swann (1985) reports on the education of children from minority ethnic backgrounds. According to Valli *et al.* (1997: 225):

Equity of outcomes refers to the result of educational processes: the equitable distribution of the benefits of schooling. Equitable outcomes of schooling would decrease, if not eliminate, group differences in school achievement, attitudes, dropout rates, college attendance, and employment.

It is this 'radical' understanding that has been most prominent in critical education research in Britain and which informs the present study. Such an approach has the advantage of moving beyond individualistic notions of conscious intent and focusing on concrete questions concerning those defined as 'winners' and 'losers' by the system. As Andy Dorn (1985: 21) has argued, in relation to research on racism and education, this approach

rests on collectivist and impersonal notions of justice and equality and is concerned with the structural exclusion of racial groups. It is concerned to look beneath the surface of formal treatment and identify the discriminatory effects of institutional practices.

It is important to recognize that, in adopting this perspective, researchers are making particular assumptions about the nature of the social groups in question. Namely, that there is no inherent reason why members of one socially defined group should not achieve average results on a par with any other such group. This is not to say, of course, that every member of the group will achieve at the same level. It simply means that, on average, and all other things being equal, it is reasonable to assume that members of each group are equally capable of success. Consequently, if the average achievements of one group (based on class, gender, ethnicity, sexuality, etc.) are significantly below those of another then there is prima facie evidence of discrimination – a clear cause for concern that should be examined. Such an approach is totally incompatible with hereditarian notions of 'intelligence' (as a genetically based and fixed capacity) and with Social Darwinist philosophy in general (Hawkins 1997). The focus on examination outcomes reflects their importance as perceived markers of 'success' and 'failure' within the education system. Education, in its wider sense, is about more than the acquisition of particular qualifications. Nevertheless, it is clearly the case that education is increasingly judged in relation to such narrow indicators and that young people themselves are considerably disadvantaged if they are denied equal opportunities to attain them.[4] It is for this reason that debates about education and equity frequently focus on patterns of experience and achievement in relation to public examinations.

The social construction of difference

We take the position that groups defined socially by class, gender, 'race', ethnicity and sexuality are inherently no less capable of educational participation and success. These groups are defined by social convention, not by inherent, fixed or 'natural' differences. In the case of gender, for example, although some sex differences have a biological character, their social significance and attendant consequences differ between societies and over time. Gendered differences are socially constructed, not naturally given (cf. Bradley 1992; Butler 1990; 1993; Irigaray 1977). Similarly, the idea of 'race' is often falsely assumed to relate to fixed and determining differences that separate different parts of the human species. In fact there are no meaningful and consistent biological characteristics sufficient to justify the term 'race' as applied to any subset of *Homo sapiens*. Those characteristics conventionally labelled as 'racial' phenomena (especially physical markers such as skin tone) are assigned different meanings in particular historical and social contexts (cf. Banton 1988; Demaine 1989; Mason 1995; van den Berghe 1988). Far from being a fixed and natural system of genetic difference, therefore, 'race' is a system of socially constructed and enforced categories that are constantly re-created and modified through human interaction. For this reason some critics prefer to use the term 'social race', to highlight the constructed nature of the categories (cf. Gillborn 1995).[5]

The processes by which these constructed differences come to be related to inequalities in experience and outcome are complex, varied and unstable. In relation to 'race', for example, *racism* can operate most clearly through the conscious assigning of different degrees of status to the supposedly separate groups identified in the current system of 'race' classification. This is an obvious and long-standing form of racism characterized by a belief, first, in the separate existence of discrete human races, and second, that those 'races' are hierarchically structured. It is an approach that is centuries old, has cost millions of lives and, as we note later, continues to be peddled as 'science' in some quarters. A less obvious form of racism, however, has been identified as operating through a discourse of 'culture' (rather than 'race') and 'difference' (rather than 'superiority'):

You do not need to think of yourself as superior – you do not even need to dislike or blame those who are so different from you – in order to say that the presence of these aliens constitutes a threat to our way of life.

(Barker 1981: 18)

This kind of perspective (variously known as the 'new racism' or 'cultural racism') has become an especially powerful force in contemporary politics and popular culture (cf. Ansell 1997; Barker 1981; Carrim 1995; Goldberg 1993; 1997; Modood 1996). Part of its power lies in the fact that the new racism need not even trade in 'race' categories.[6] The presence or absence of 'racial' terms, however, is not necessary to define a discourse as racist. After David Wellman (1977; 1993), we take the position that racism is best identified through its effects. Any set of practices or beliefs that systematically disadvantage members of one or more minority ethnic groups can be defined as racist. This approach allows social science finally to catch up to the pervasive and complex forms that racism can take:

Racism can mean culturally sanctioned beliefs which, regardless of the intentions involved, defend the advantages whites have because of the subordinated position of racial minorities . . . racism is much more subtle, elusive, and widespread than sociologists have acknowledged. Part of the reason they have been unable to see racism in this light is conceptual: They have not 'looked' for these expressions of it. The other part is methodological: Traditional instruments used by sociologists in large-scale surveys are not yet sensitive to these manifestations of racism.

(Wellman 1993: xi)

We adopt a similar approach as a means of identifying class bias and sexism as complex, sometimes 'hidden', often unintended features of human interaction and institutional procedures. Like David Wellman, we believe that quantitative approaches are not best suited to identifying and exploring inequalities such as racism. The wider patterns of inequality can be mapped and highlighted through survey research (see Chapter 2) but such approaches cannot reveal the processes that produce those patterns. It is for this reason that the present study relies primarily on qualitative research methods.

Researching reform

This study arose from a desire to explore the changing realities of secondary education at a time of rapid educational reform unlike anything since the post-war settlement. One of us began their research career in a comprehensive school in the 1980s (Gillborn 1987; 1990a) and, in part, this project was designed to repeat some of the key features of that work. More specifically, the research was proposed as a means of understanding recent changes to the examination system. A unified examination, the General Certificate of Secondary Education (GCSE), had replaced the previous dual system and a further development had seen the introduction of *tiering*, whereby pupils entered for the same examination would find themselves taking different examination papers from which they could achieve only a limited range of grades. This project was designed specifically to examine whether tiering had an impact upon equity.[7] Once the fieldwork was under way, however, it became increasingly difficult to view tiering separately from the range of other reforms, all of which seemed to be mutually reinforcing. These issues arose through our data collection and, as reflexive researchers, we chose to take advantage of the flexible nature of qualitative research which allows for modification of concerns and new research questions as part of the field-work enterprise itself (cf. Burgess 1984; Glaser and Strauss 1967; Hammersley and Atkinson 1995; Strauss 1987). In this way the scope of the project was widened to include a concern with how the reforms more broadly were being experienced (by teachers and pupils) and to examine how they affected issues of equity and achievement in school.

The project was designed to focus on three schools. Working in a single school would have allowed us to undertake a more intensive study, but we hoped to begin to assess the diversity of responses to education reform at the school level. In particular, we were aware of the new school types arising from the reforms, such as the introduction of grant-maintained (GM) status, and we wanted to include a school that had embraced these developments. We also sought to address some of the contextual factors that might influence the specific ways in which schools attempt to fulfil the demands placed upon them. We wished, for example, to include schools that catered for a range of pupils from minority ethnic groups and to look beyond London for at least one of our sites.

We successfully negotiated access to three schools, two in London and one in the Midlands. Unfortunately the latter withdrew from the project just as the fieldwork phase got under way. Relations with the school had been excellent and our initial data collection was already scheduled when, without warning, the local press ran a negative story about a piece of educational research conducted in the city (by a local university). The story raised tension among local schools and, at very short notice, our third school decided to withdraw from the project. We were then unable to find a suitable replacement and schedule fieldwork in time for a third school to be included as an equal part of the project. We decided to proceed with the two schools that remained and, in almost all respects, they continued to provide an excellent sample. Our main regret was that the third school had included a good proportion of pupils from various South Asian ethnic backgrounds, meaning that our analyses by ethnic origin would mostly be restricted to comparisons between Black (African Caribbean) pupils and their white peers.[8]

The two remaining schools were selected on the basis of certain differences and similarities. Both are situated in outer London boroughs, one in south-east London and one in south-west London. Both are coeducational and multi-ethnic. One is a comprehensive school with a strong reputation and a relatively good record of attainment in GCSE examinations; in contrast, the other is a grant-maintained school with a weaker examination record and variable reputation. We were interested in exploring what impact the relative 'success' of each school, in terms of GCSE outcomes, might have on organization, structure and practice in relation to selection and setting. We also hoped to explore how the move to GM status might have reflected, and/or enabled, differences in attitude to selection and attainment within the school. The schools were identified through existing contacts that we and colleagues had with local education authorities (LEAs) and other networks. We had not undertaken research previously in either of the schools and we were not familiar with the school leaders or staff.

Access to each school was negotiated with the headteacher. In both schools the headteacher then identified a deputy headteacher who would act as a key contact/informant and gatekeeper for our research. In the case of Taylor Comprehensive this was the deputy headteacher with designated respons-ibility for the curriculum. This deputy supported the research throughout but passed day-to-day matters concerning the project on to the relevant head of year. We were given open access to the school, its staff and pupils, and arrangements for field visits were made with individual teachers as appro-priate. In Clough GM the 'third' deputy headteacher, with designated re-sponsibility for careers education and guidance, took the lead in relation to the research. Access to the school, its staff and pupils was controlled by this deputy throughout the project. Contact with heads of year, faculty heads, other teaching staff and pupils themselves had continually to be negotiated through this single member of the school's senior management team (SMT). As such, our freedom of access to and movement around Clough GM was far less open than in the case of Taylor Comprehensive.

Our fieldwork was limited to a period of two academic years. Our concern with experience and achievement in GCSE courses prompted a particular interest in pupils in Key Stage 4 when (aged 14–16) they pursue examina-tion courses in a smaller range of subjects. We were also keen to examine how such courses had been selected via the options decisions in year 9 (when pupils are aged 13–14), a period when a great deal of organizational and academic preparation for Key Stage 4 is undertaken. In particular, we were interested in the impact that the options might have in terms of setting, selection and equity. It was decided, therefore, to focus on two year groups: first, year 9, when these preparations for Key Stage 4 are under way and when pupils and teachers are engaged in discussions about possible academic and other futures; and second, year 11, the final year of compuls-ory schooling, when pupils may have a clearer view of their likely attain-ments, and when the final GCSE examinations are taken.

The fieldwork for the study was undertaken over the course of six terms between autumn 1995 and summer 1997.[9] During the 1995/6 academic year the research focused on year 9. Fieldwork during the 1996/7 academic year was concerned with year 11. We spent approximately one day per week in each of the study schools over the two-year period. Additionally there were periods when the fieldworker would visit the same school more than once during the same week, usually when particular events had to be observed or interviewees seen.[10]

We wanted to build rapport with a range of pupils in both schools and, conscious of the need to avoid seeming to single out individuals for 'special attention', we decided to use existing tutorial groups as the basis for our pupil sample. Both schools identified themselves as having tutor groups that reflected the range of gender, ethnicity and 'ability' in the year group. At the beginning of the 1995/6 academic year the deputy headteacher in each school was asked to identify a single year 9 tutor group that would act as the focus for the study during the year. This was repeated the following year in relation to year 11. Members of these tutor groups were interviewed in self-selected friendship groups. Interviews with year 9 pupils explored their perceptions of the school and the options process as well as GCSEs and their expectations for the future. Interviews with year 11 pupils focused on their perceptions of the school, their reflections on the options process, their experience of GCSE courses and their expectations beyond the end of compulsory schooling.

Key members of staff were also interviewed. Form tutors and heads of year were interviewed concerning the organizational issues surrounding options and GCSEs and were also asked to reflect on the members of the selected tutor groups. Heads of faculty from across the school were interviewed concerning GCSE courses and their perceptions of the school and its pupils. The headteacher and deputy headteachers of each school were also interviewed. Key members of staff took part in successive interviews over the course of the study.

A selection of lessons was observed. The tiering of GCSE syllabuses and examinations was a central concern of the research, and so we decided to concentrate our time on work in two subjects – English and mathematics. These subjects were chosen due to their status as 'core' and, therefore, compulsory subjects in the National Curriculum. All pupils spent a standard period of time each week in these subject areas (this was not the case in science at the time the research commenced). In addition, we felt that mathematics and English departments may respond differently to tiering due to the long-standing practice of setting common in mathematics compared with the use of mixed-ability teaching often found in English departments. In each school a selection of year 9 and year 11 English and mathematics lessons were observed. Lessons for observation were selected to reflect a range of teacher experience and status and the 'ability' range of pupils as defined by the schools. Where departments organized teaching groups on the basis of 'ability' the sample also reflected the setting and selection practices in the department.

The level of access and participation at Taylor Comprehensive allowed us also to observe many assemblies, a number of parents' evenings and staff meetings during which options, GCSEs and other related issues were discussed. We also took the opportunity to spend time observing and talking to teachers and pupils informally during tutor group periods; personal, social and health education lessons (which played a key role in the options process and preparations for GCSEs); between lessons; and during breaktimes. On the whole, such access was less easy in Clough GM because of the rather more formal gatekeeping role that the member of SMT maintained throughout the project.

Both Taylor and Clough provided a great deal of documentary information concerning the school, its organization and structure, policy and curriculum. They both gave a substantial body of statistical data, drawn from the schools' own databases, concerning pupils' demographic profiles, attainment at various stages during schooling, set and group placements, and 'predicted' and actual outcomes for GCSE examinations.

Our fieldwork and analysis have been led by an appreciation of Foucauldian notions of discourse, disciplinary power and its techniques. We have not sought to draw out 'truths' but have been concerned to understand the nature of those discourses that are mobilized inside schools in relation to equity, inequality and education reform. We have also drawn on Stephen Ball's understanding of the policy cycle in making sense of the relationship between policy making at the macro and micro level and the day-to-day practices that this both draws upon and stimulates inside the school. However, this study is not intended to represent either a dedicated Foucauldian analysis or a study of the policy cycle itself. Like Ball we want to pursue a form of 'applied sociology' (Ball 1994) that uses a range of methodological and theoretical tools as a means of exploring the social construction of educational inequality. We draw on elements of Foucault's analysis, therefore, but want to remain accessible to a practitioner audience and free to apply other approaches without being locked into a particular and rigid Foucauldian approach (cf. Gillborn 1995; Gore 1993). Our ongoing analysis and research has been responsive to those themes that have emerged during the course of the study and theorizing has, to this extent, been 'grounded' in our data. By the end of our fieldwork we were confident that we had reached a point of theoretical saturation in relation to those findings detailed in the chapters that follow. Before we outline the content of the book, however, it is useful to say a little more about each of the schools that provide the context for the study.

Taylor Comprehensive School

Taylor is a coeducational, multi-ethnic comprehensive school situated in an outer London borough. The school has a seven-form entry and enjoys a consistently full roll. The school also has a popular sixth form, to which around 80 per cent of the school's leavers return following their compulsory schooling. The sixth form also recruits students from other local schools, including a number from the independent sector.

At the time that the research began the headteacher had been in post for a number of years, having been promoted through the management structure of the school. He had been active in the teachers' union movement and left-wing politics. The staff team was well established, staff turnover was low and teaching posts in the school were said to be sought after by teachers in the borough. Part-way through the research period the headteacher retired. The outgoing headteacher had enjoyed the support of teaching staff, and it was commented by senior staff that he would be 'a hard act to follow'. A new headteacher was recruited from outside the school but the change in leadership had only limited impact on school organization, structure and policy. A key policy that was retained by the incoming headteacher, for example, was a long-standing commitment to maintaining 'mixed-ability' teaching throughout the school.

The school's pupil population is about equally balanced between the sexes. The majority of pupils in the school are white (around 75 per cent). The other main ethnic groups are African Caribbean (10 per cent), South Asian (2 per cent) and Chinese (around 3 per cent). English is an additional language for almost 9 per cent of pupils. The school serves both working-class and middle-class communities. Around one-third of pupils are in receipt of free school meals (a crude proxy for poverty) but the school also attracts a significant number of pupils from middle-class professional families. A number of school staff report that Taylor is known locally as 'the teachers' school' due to the number of pupils attending whose parents are teachers. The school has also been described by staff as 'truly comprehensive' – a statement that, as we will see, relates both to its composition and ethos.

Attainment in the school is relatively high in relation to most external indicators. The school exceeds the national average level of attainment at GCSE and has seen year-on-year improvements in exam performance. In the 1996/7 academic year more than half (around 55 per cent) of year 11 pupils who entered for GCSE examinations attained the benchmark of five or more 'higher-grade' passes (at grades A*-to-C).[11] The school is ranked highly in the local 'league table' of schools. A few single-sex, voluntary-aided schools outperform Taylor, but the school is consistently ranked as the highest attaining coeducational LEA-maintained school in the borough.

Clough Grant Maintained School

Clough GM is a coeducational, grant-maintained school situated in an outer London borough.[12] The school has an eight-form entry but is consistently under-subscribed. Clough does not have a sixth form. The school was a comprehensive maintained by the LEA before becoming grant-maintained. As a comprehensive Clough had a poor reputation locally. Later in this book we discuss the school's move to GM status in more detail, but it is clear that a major concern was to increase the school's financial resources, raise its profile and thereby attract greater numbers of pupils.[13]

When our research began, the headteacher had recently been promoted from his previous position as deputy headteacher in the school. On his appointment the headteacher introduced a number of new policies and practices that focused on raising levels of attainment in GCSE. Central to these moves was the introduction of selection by 'ability' for a proportion of admissions and a move to setting by 'ability' across the school. While opinion among the teaching staff was divided in relation to these changes, they had the full support of senior managers in the school (see Chapter 3).

Clough's pupil population is unevenly distributed by gender, with boys accounting for approximately 60 per cent of pupils. This is reported to be the result of the school's poor reputation, coupled with its proximity to two single-sex girls' schools. The majority of pupils are white (around 57 per cent). The other major ethnic groups in the school are African Caribbean (16 per cent) and South Asian pupils (20 per cent). The school population is described by teachers as overwhelmingly working-class, and it is reported that many of the current pupils have parents who attended the school themselves. Just under a third of pupils are in receipt of free school meals. In recent years the profile of the communities served by the school has altered somewhat, with the arrival of a number of refugee communities in the area. This has increased the proportion of pupils for whom English is an additional language. Unlike Taylor, the school reports that it does not have a 'comprehensive' intake: as we detail in Chapter 3, many teachers believe that the school has a disproportionate number of pupils of below average 'ability'. Its relatively low levels of GCSE attainment are seen by senior managers as the key difficulty faced by the school. Clough GM is below the national average level of attainment in GCSE, and the new headteacher and board of governors have set targets for year-on-year improvement. In the 1996/7 academic year just under one-third of year 11 pupils who entered for GCSE examinations attained the benchmark of five or more passes at grades A*-to-C. The school is ranked relatively poorly in the 'league table' of local borough schools.

An outline of the book

The changes that are occurring in British secondary schools cannot be understood in isolation from the numerous reforms that have been pursued by successive governments. Chapter 2, therefore, describes the wider context for the study by reviewing the principal education reforms of the late 1980s and 1990s. These reforms include the introduction of a statutory National Curriculum, an enforced system of testing at particular 'key stages', increased inspection regimes and the publication of 'performance' data on every school in England and Wales. The reforms constitute a web of interconnecting demands and constraints within which schools are subject to public surveillance of a crude and highly disciplinary nature: it is these reforms that shape the rationing of education detailed in subsequent chapters. We argue that despite superficial changes in the language of education policy (dropping 'market' ideology and espousing 'inclusivity' and social justice), in almost every major respect Tony Blair's 'New Labour' administration has embraced, and even extended, the same package of reforms pursued by previous Conservative governments. In particular, education policy is distorted by an obsessive concern with a narrow range of elite, measurable 'standards' as described in the published performance tables (popularly known as 'league tables'). The reforms have been associated with a pattern of year-on-year increases in the proportion of pupils attaining the 'benchmark' level of five or more 'higher grade' GCSE passes. At the same time, however, many areas of inequality have worsened. The chapter includes the first published account of recently analysed statistics that vividly demonstrate the growing inequalities of achievement between different groups of pupils. Despite the public concern over 'boys' under-achievement', the data show conclusively that the most pronounced inequalities relate to differences in ethnic origin and social class. The rest of the book is concerned with how these inequalities are generated, institutionalized and extended at the school level.

Chapter 3 begins our detailed analysis of life in the two case-study schools. Both are caught within the interlocking demands of the various reforms and the need continually to raise their performance in the published 'league tables'. This is what we term the *A-to-C economy*; a situation where almost every aspect of school life is re-evaluated for its possible contribution to the headline statistic of the proportion of pupils attaining at least five higher-grade GCSE passes (A*-to-C). Clough GM sees the increased use of selection by 'ability' as a key strategy in its attempts to rise up the 'league table'. We show that 'ability' is assumed as a fixed, generalized and measurable potential. At school, just as in national policy, there is an assumption that some pupils have 'more' ability and learn faster than their peers. This assumption is deeply implicated in the institutionalization of inequality by 'race' and class. In Clough, for example, the attempt to raise the 'ability' profile of the school's intake is seen as synonymous with increasing the number of pupils from middle-class backgrounds. The school collects data on every pupil in an attempt to identify their 'ability'. One of the most important sources is described by a senior teacher as 'an IQ test' based on an instrument and analysis that the school buys in from an outside testing organization. We examine the nature and consequences of such a test and raise doubts about its usefulness and equity in multi-ethnic contexts. We argue that the use of such tests may systematically disadvantage children from particular minority ethnic backgrounds.

Chapter 4 builds upon the analysis of 'ability' and selective assumptions in Clough GM by examining how different pupil-grouping strategies are being adopted. The school increasingly separates pupils according to official judge-ments of their 'ability'. This is seen in the use of 'setting' in some subject areas and the introduction of so-called 'fast' groups. In key respects this system remakes the kind of differentiation seen in 'streamed' environments common before the introduction of comprehensive education in the 1960s and 1970s. In Clough the system results in 'left-over' mixed-ability groups for which teachers have lower expectations. Additionally, the school inter-prets different forms of pupil *need* as forms of pupil *deficit*: pupils for whom English is an additional language or who have been statemented as having special educational needs are disproportionately placed in particular groups and viewed as unlikely to achieve academically. From the moment they enter the school, therefore, the pupils face a range of assumptions that begin to shape their markedly different educational careers. These differences be-come apparent to many pupils during the subject options process in year 9. Although it is presented as a point of 'choice' and active decision making, the options process provides a point of selection where the school seeks to engineer different choice patterns according to assumed 'ability'. Through-out this period pupils are repeatedly reminded of the importance of GCSE examination success, always within the particular demands of the A-to-C economy.

Chapter 5 considers the further selection and separation that occurs in the upper school (Key Stage 4) when pupils are aged 14–16. Drawing on data from both our case-study schools we show how setting by 'ability' is being increasingly adopted at this point, even in Taylor Comprehensive where it is opposed in principle by the school's overriding ethos. We describe the diffi-cult and sometimes disturbing decisions that teachers are asked to make regarding the 'appropriate' place for particular pupils. The demands of GCSE tiers are unfamiliar to many teachers, who experience them as a point of danger and uncertainty – when they must balance the perceived needs of their pupils, their subject department and the school itself. Despite the pro-nounced differences in character between our case-study schools, decisions about GCSE tiering in both seem to operate further to institutionalize inequalities of opportunity. Black pupils and their peers in receipt of free school meals are especially disadvantaged by the system. Indeed, in some respects GCSE tiering seems to have introduced a form of examination differentiation that is more regressive and less open to pupil/parent resist-ance than the heavily criticized dual examination system that the GCSE replaced in the late 1980s.

In Chapter 6 we consider the various strategies that our schools adopt in a final push towards maximizing performance in terms of the A-to-C economy. In particular, both schools seek to change predicted D grades into actual C grades. It is here that the processes of educational rationing become most explicit. We show the importance of three interrelated elements in the discourse: first, the underlying view of 'ability' as a fixed, generalized and measurable potential; second, the schools' production of predicted grades;

and finally, the view of 'under-achievement' that is mobilized to identify pupils who are deemed 'suitable for treatment' in a range of special initiatives. In this way the schools are adopting a form of *educational triage*, a means of rationing support so that some pupils are targeted for additional teacher time and energy while others are seen as inevitable casualties of the battle to improve 'standards' in the 'league tables'. The rationing decisions are based on the particular (crude and divisive) view of 'ability' already identified as a fundamental characteristic of contemporary education policy and practice. In accordance with this view, it is possible for two pupils to be predicted to obtain the same results but for one to be seen as 'under-achieving' (and therefore a suitable case for extra help) while the other is thought to be attaining at a level appropriate to their perceived 'ability' (or lack of it). We examine how the rationing process is operationalized and reveal that, once again, Black pupils and those in receipt of free school meals are disproportionately likely to be seen as without hope. The range of special initiatives includes one-to-one mentoring and, in Clough GM, a pupil league table that translates the surveillant and disciplinary technology of the school performance tables into an individualized policy of naming and shaming. Despite the effort to transform D grades into C grades, however, the schools' results suggest that these initiatives often function as elaborate insurance policies that provide a second chance for pupils already predicted to achieve success.

The processes of selection, labelling, differentiation and educational rationing position pupils as the subject of multiple discourses. These processes are managed by teachers who make decisions about pupils but rarely involve the young people themselves in any meaningful way. In Chapter 7 we pull together the pupils' own views of their experiences. In some ways pupils experience and perceive the processes differently depending on their place within them; those in the highest teaching groups who are entered for Higher-Tier exams, for example, often display the most detailed understanding of selection in the schools. As they move into their final year of compulsory schooling, however, many pupils become increasingly clear about the selective and often unfair nature of their experiences. Pupils identify systematic differences in treatment according to 'ability' and 'behaviour', for example, and seem often to relate these issues to matters of social class. Pupils also note the existence of racism as a pervasive, though sometimes hidden, aspect of school life.

In our final chapter we draw together the main strands of the study. We conclude our discussion of triage by showing how the final statistics of GCSE achievement reflect the racist and class-biased nature of the rationing of education that has effectively characterized the pupils' experiences throughout their time in Clough GM and Taylor Comprehensive. This is not to say, however, that there are no meaningful differences between the schools. In certain respects, for example, our data suggest that (contrary to popular expectations) the more selective environments have been the most restrictive of achievement. This is further evidence of the need to resist the increasingly closed and authoritarian nature of contemporary education reform (at both the national and school level). We argue that the use of setting, the interpretation of 'ability' tests, and the introduction and extension of GCSE tiering, each operate to further institutionalize and extend inequalities of opportunity, especially those associated with ethnic origin and social class.

The view of 'ability' that currently dominates policy and practice is especially dangerous. The assumption that 'ability' is a fixed, generalized and measurable potential paves the way for the operationalization of deeply racist and class-biased stereotypes. Without debate, and sometimes without realizing, this approach takes for granted exactly the same position that figures in the work of writers determined to rehabilitate crude hereditarian notions of intelligence which present patterns of educational and social inequality as 'natural' and fair (cf. Herrnstein and Murray 1994). We refer to this development as *the new IQism* – an approach that affirms traditional notions of IQ, without conscious deliberation of the consequences, and even masquerades as part of an inclusive project concerned with social justice and equity.

Finally, we reflect on some of the new forms of racist discourse prominent in contemporary policy and practice, a discourse that adopts a blinkered perspective whereby 'race' inequality is reduced to the status of individual differences. This points to the need dramatically to reimagine the nature and goals of education. The terms of debate in Britain have become increasingly closed and determinist. If policy makers and practitioners are genuinely concerned with issues of social justice they must refuse the demands of the A-to-C economy and rethink key parts of the reforms (such as school 'league tables') that are antithetical to equity in education.

2

Reforming education

policy and practice[1]

Labour moves the GCSE goalposts
(Times Educational Supplement headline, 23 October 1998: 1)

Boards ditched for the sake of ranking
(Times Educational Supplement, 8 March 1996: 11)

Attention now focuses more than ever before on pupils' performance in public examinations at the end of their compulsory schooling. These two headlines, from the UK's largest-circulation newspaper for teachers, capture something of the obsessive concern with examination grades that has developed over recent years as a direct result of successive education reforms. The former refers to a suggestion that a new national target was to be announced requiring that 95 per cent of 16-year-olds should attain at least one pass grade (of G or above) in GCSE exams by the year 2002. In 1998 this minimal level of certification was achieved or exceeded by 92 per cent of 16-year-olds (Cassidy 1998a: 1), making a rise of an additional three percentage points over four years appear relatively modest. That such a target should make headline news on the front page of the paper, however, signals the significance attached to *any* target for pupils at the lower end of the achievement scale. The dominant policy concern, over the previous decade and still continuing under a Labour administration, has been with the *top* end; those achieving at least *five* higher-grade passes. As we show in this chapter, this concern has shaped numerous policy initiatives that have led schools to prioritize this measure above all others. Indeed, the second headline at the head of this chapter refers to an earlier story, in the same publication, that revealed the lengths to which some would go in maximizing their performance against this higher-grade 'benchmark'. In this case several subject departments in a school are said to have changed to new examining boards precisely because they judge them to offer a better chance of reaching the all-important grade C or above. The school's 'director of studies' is quoted as saying: 'Results are the be-all-and-end-all . . . if we can play the system and it helps our children, then we will do it'. This statement offers a clue to a number of ideas that reoccur throughout our study, not least the overwhelming concern felt by schools about being subject to external evaluation on the basis of exam results. Also note the elision involved in asserting that something which benefits the school automatically benefits its pupils: our data show this to be a dangerous fallacy.

Throughout this book we use detailed interview and observational data to explore the consequences of education reform at the school level. Our conclusion is that almost every aspect of the schools' activities (pedagogy, organization, the academic and pastoral) have been interrogated for ways they might enhance performance in relation to the benchmark of five higher grades – what we call the 'A-to-C economy' (see Chapter 3). Before we examine the detail of our empirical data, however, it is necessary to set the broader context for the study. In subsequent sections of this chapter we explore how the reform of compulsory education has been associated with two related trends: a raising of overall levels of achievement, but a growing inequality of achievement between particular groups based on gender, ethnic origin and social class background. We begin by outlining the education reforms that have shaped the last decade of policy, first under successive Conservative governments, and more recently under the self-styled 'New Labour' government led by Tony Blair.

Education reform

To those who say where is Labour's passion for social justice,
I say education is social justice. Education is liberty. Education
is opportunity.
> (Tony Blair, speaking shortly before the 1997
> general election that returned him as leader
> of the first Labour government for 18 years)[2]

Performance tables help focus debate on standards. Parents need
the tables to inform their decisions about their children's future;
local education authorities and schools, to focus their attention
on areas where action is needed.
> (Estelle Morris, Labour Education Minister,
> speaking eight weeks after the general election)

The British educational system is currently dominated by the rhetoric of 'standards'. Originally the preserve of the New Right and successive Conservative governments, the term has been colonized by the restyled centrist 'New' Labour Party. Speaking as the first Labour Education Secretary for almost two decades, for example, David Blunkett was quick to proclaim that 'Standards not structures are now the prime concern' (Blunkett 1997), a message he has often repeated since (Blunkett 1998). In understanding the context for contemporary education reform it is worth considering this notion a little further: the government's confidence in the relative unimportance of structures suggests an acceptance of a paradigm that views communities, schools, teachers and pupils as participants in a common enterprise in which all have the opportunity to succeed. It is true that within its first year in power New Labour reasserted a concern with 'equal opportunities' and even created a separate policy unit to address 'social exclusion'. Nevertheless, as we detail later in this chapter, these developments do *not* herald a radical new policy perspective and, in practice, there continue to be strong continuities between the restorationist project of the Conservatives (under Margaret Thatcher and John Major) and the 'New Britain' proclaimed by Tony Blair.

In its election manifesto, and in subsequent policy pronouncements, much has been made of Labour's 'zero tolerance of underperformance' (Labour Party 1997: 7). This is presented publicly as having high expectations for all and as a bold refusal to write people off simply because of their social circumstances. The rhetoric sounds progressive, but in practice the result has been to construct a tyranny of standards: all schools must strive continually for more and more success; judged by traditional, biased and elitist criteria, where those who fail to measure up must look to themselves for the cause. As we will show, despite the change from Conservative to Labour administrations, and some superficial changes in policy, the overall shape and drive of education reform has remained largely consistent. The annually published school performance tables, for example, continue to be assigned a special place in education policy, as both a means to, and an index of, raising standards. And yet, behind New Labour's talk of social justice and inclusivity lies a reality of increasing inequality and social exclusion, where Conservative reforms are not only retained, but given a sharper (even more disciplinary) edge.[3] Before we consider further the particular policy shifts promoted by the Labour government, therefore, it is useful to map briefly the principal reforms enforced by successive Conservative administrations. There is neither space nor need to explore each in detail here, but some awareness of the range and interlocking nature of the reforms is essential to an understanding of the situation facing schools, teachers and their pupils.

Conservative reforms of compulsory schooling

During 18 years of Conservative government the British education system underwent extensive and multiple reforms that changed the structure, funding and content of public education. Central to these changes has been the imposition of a market model, in which schools are framed as providers which must compete (against other schools) for pupils. The rationale for these changes was often made in relation to a market-led assumption of demand and supply relationships, where demand for high-quality education (linked to parental choice and school autonomy) would necessarily lead to an improvement in the education provided by schools (which would other-wise face closure because 'consumers' would go elsewhere). There are numer-ous ways, however, in which the education system does not conform to the market model, not least the fact that education is compulsory and that the state continues to act as a major provider and regulator. Consequently, some writers have adopted the term 'quasi-market' as a more accurate description of the emerging situation. These developments have not been limited to Britain, but are also broadly evident in parts of Europe, the United States and New Zealand (cf. Levačić 1995; Whitty 1997a; Whitty *et al.* 1998). In Britain this (quasi-)marketization of the education system has been achieved through a series of related measures, of which the following are among the most important.

Devolved funding
One of the many landmark changes made as part of the Education Reform Act (1988) was the introduction of so-called 'local management of schools' (LMS), which removed the bulk of schools' budgets from the control of LEAs. These devolved budgets are calculated according to a governmentally approved common funding formula (based mostly on the number of pupils on the school roll). The more pupils a school has, therefore, the greater its budget. In practice, however, there is evidence that schools do not simply seek to maximize total numbers, but are increasingly wary of pupils whose needs might make unusual or 'excessive' demands on school budgets – such as those with special learning needs, minority pupils for whom English is an additional language, and homeless pupils whose parent(s)/carer(s) have no stable shelter (Bowe *et al.* 1992; Power *et al.* 1995; Troyna 1995a).

Parental choice
Within the education market place, policy adopts a view of parents as con-sumers who are free to choose between schools. Both major political parties now enshrine 'choice' as a key part of their rhetoric. In reality, however, parents have a right to express their *preference* for a certain school but have no guarantee of access. There is strong evidence to suggest that local choice markets operate in ways that reflect and reinforce existing social class and ethnic divisions. Parents/carers do not have access to the same networks of information, nor do they enjoy certain material conditions, such as transport and other practical provisions, that can render 'choice' a foregone conclusion (cf. Ball *et al.* 1998; Gewirtz *et al.* 1995; Reay and Ball 1997; Vincent 1996).

Diversity and competition
The market model requires that consumers have a choice between different products: not only between different state-funded comprehensive schools, but also between privately funded schools and new types of school. Con-sequently, again as part of the 1988 Reform Act, new types of state funding were introduced, presented explicitly as a means of promoting diversity of

provision and expanding choice by challenging (undermining) local compre-hensive provision. For example, city technology colleges (CTCs) and grant-maintained (GM) schools have been established to operate independently of the local state. CTCs and GM schools have differing histories and ideologies (cf. Power *et al.* 1994; Walford and Miller 1991; Whitty *et al.* 1993) but both operate independently of LEAs, typically enjoy disproportionately high levels of resourcing and, in the final stage of Conservative administration, were promised greater freedom to select pupils by ability at the point of entry (Department for Education and Employment (DfEE) 1996). Although the Labour government is opposed, in principle, to selection at the point of entry, it has refused to remove such powers where already granted. Rather, a ballot of local parents is envisaged before selection at entry can be removed.

Curricular control

One of the central components of the 1988 Reform Act was to create the framework for a statutory 'National Curriculum' that all state schools must teach. The nature and content of the National Curriculum are centrally controlled, while practice at the school level is audited through inspections, carried out by the Office for Standards in Education (Ofsted), and the use of standardized tests (known as standard assessment tasks, or SATs) for pupils at the end of designated 'key stages' in their schooling (at ages 7, 11, and 14).[4] Both the content and scale of the National Curriculum have already undergone review and revision. Most significantly, the statutory element was 'slimmed down' in the mid-1990s, but still dictates approximately 80 per cent of timetable allocation in secondary schools (Dearing 1994). Addi-tionally, the architect of the changes personally recommended that 'the bulk of the time released' by the move should be used for additional work in 'the basics' already central to the statutory element (Dearing 1994: 7).

The operation of the National Curriculum, and recommendations con-cerning its future content, are overseen by the Qualifications and Curric-ulum Authority (QCA). Its head, Dr Nicholas Tate, is a leading advocate of the use of the curriculum to foster a 'common culture' (Tate 1996a; 1996b). Tate's curricular prescriptions have been criticized for embodying a deeply ideological and partial view of Britain as a largely homogeneous Christian nation with a proud civilizing history based on its colonial exploits (Gillborn 1997a; Phillips 1996). Although the statutory curricular elements allow some space for teachers to introduce their own material (including anti-racist and anti-sexist studies, should they wish), the National Curriculum has been attacked for a general failure to engage with issues of cultural diversity and social inequality (cf. Runnymede Trust 1993).

Standards

As we have noted, the call to 'raise standards' has been adopted by both main political parties. We comment on the discursive operation of this term in more detail later in this chapter. For the moment it is sufficient to note that, in practice, policy makers tend overwhelmingly to equate 'standards' with measurable outcomes in externally examined tests, especially SATs, at ages 7, 11 and 14, and the GCSE for 16-year-olds. Pupils can be entered for GCSEs in numerous separate subjects: their results act as a major selection device in their attempts to enter the labour market and/or further and higher education. Perhaps most importantly, however, aggregate measures of GCSE performance (for every school and LEA) are published nationally and used widely to infer the *quality* of education provided in a school and/or LEA. These 'performance tables' are presented officially as a means of improving consumers' knowledge of the service on offer in local schools: Gillian Shephard, the last Conservative Secretary of State for Education, described them as shining 'a bright light into every classroom in the land' and asserted a bold and simple link with the standards agenda:

> The remarkable success of five years of secondary school performance tables has confirmed what we always knew to be true – the publication of tables drives up standards. They give parents clear information about schools which are doing well and those which are doing badly. They make schools and local authorities accountable for what they are doing.
> (Quoted in the *Times Educational Supplement*, 14 March 1997: 8)

This statement is indicative of several important elements in the package of reforms endured by schools during the late 1980s and throughout the 1990s. First, there is a breathtaking certainty about politicians' belief in their programmes. Many of the reforms were enforced nationally with only the briefest of consultations and no meaningful trials, pushed through simply because of 'what we always knew to be true'. Second, the nature of the link between 'standards' and the performance tables is asserted in a particular way; it is an enforcing, top-down emphasis in which central government sees itself in opposition to the 'producer interests' of schools and academics who have supposedly depressed standards for so long. Hence, 'the publication of tables drives up standards' – it is almost as though the mechanisms are now beyond the control of schools and teachers. Finally, the process by which these changes occur is specified as concerning *accountability*. In fact, as will become clear throughout this study, perhaps the most important function of school performance tables has been to increase to unprecedented levels the intensity of surveillance that schools, headteachers and individual teachers experience. Policy discourse presents the performance tables as an exercise in 'information' and 'accountability'; for many working in schools, however, *surveillance* and *control* are more adequate descriptors.

Accountability: surveillance and control
According to the market model, the rational consumer, who chooses between schools competing in the market place, must be aided by information on the relative quality of the products available. Since 1992 Conservative administrations have used this as the rationale for the annual publication of

'performance tables' listing various 'measures' individually for all secondary schools in England. The culture of targets and tables was extended further in 1997 when tables were published for the first time detailing results for 11-year-olds in primary schools; this was described by the then Secretary of State for Education as 'the biggest public information campaign since the Second World War' (DfEE 1997a).

The measures for secondary schools include the percentage of final-year pupils entered for GCSEs and various indications of their exam outcomes. No attempt is made to allow for differences in schools' social compositions or levels of resourcing: state-funded comprehensives (working with diverse communities and meeting a range of special educational needs) are listed alongside private, elite institutions that select all or part of their pupil body according to previous test results. Consequently, the long-established association between socio-economic status and educational attainment is free to distort the figures without control.

Since their inception the performance tables have been commonly referred to as 'league tables'. This betrays their main purpose and function. According to the rhetoric of the market place, the tables are meant to provide 'objective' indicators of quality so that consumers can discriminate between competing institutions. In practice, they provide crude and misleading data as the basis for the hierarchical ranking of individual schools and LEAs nationwide. The dominant 'benchmark' is the proportion of pupils attaining GCSE higher-grade passes (grades A*, A, B and C) in at least five separate subjects – historically this level was once significant as a cut-off point for entry to the professions and higher education. Each year the government has added new indicators to the lists, but the most frequently cited measure (by the press, politicians and practitioners alike) is the proportion of pupils reaching the 'five A-to-C' barrier (see, for example, Figure 2.1).[5] Note, in particular, that schools are arranged in league order, according to the proportion of pupils who achieved at least five higher-grade GCSE passes. Note also that the top three places are taken by independent (private) schools that operate a selective admissions policy. The bottom four places are taken by comprehensive schools, funded by the local state, and practising no form of selection on admission.

A measure of the significance accorded to the performance table data is the annual ranking of 'best' and 'worst' schools, again produced on a national basis by most daily newspapers. In Figure 2.2, for example, note that the dominant criterion is again the proportion of pupils attaining at least five higher-grade passes.

New Labour and the Conservative reforms

The Labour administration, elected in May 1997, has been quick to continue the recent history of placing education at the centre of government policy initiatives. Just 67 days after its election, the new government's first White Paper (a detailed statement of policy intent) took education as its theme and

Figure 2.1 Secondary school league table for a London borough

School	6th form			Pupils aged 15	GCSE				
	2+ A-level entries	A level points	Truancy		% at least one pass	('94)	% 5 or more A–C passes or equivalent GNVQ ('95)	('96)	'97
Godolphin and Latymer School — Ind sel girls 10–19	97	27.4	&	104	100	(97)	(98)	(100)	99
Latymer Upper School — Ind sel boys 7–19	124	24.0	&	140	100	(94)	(100)	(99)	99
St Paul's Girls' School — Ind sel girls 10–19	92	27.9	0.0	81	100	(99)	(100)	(100)	99
Lady Margaret School — VA comp girls 11–18	44	18.5	0.1	66	100	(69)	(83)	(90)	79
London Oratory School — GM comp boys 7–18	137	20.6	&	182	100	(54)	(62)	(70)	77
Sacred Heart High School — VA comp girls 11–16	–	–	0.5	114	100	(60)	(47)	(61)	76
Burlington Danes CofE School — VA comp mxd 11–18	13	11.8	3.0	167	91	(30)	(28)	(24)	33
Ravenscourt Theatre School — Ind sel mxd 4–16	–	–	0.4	12	100	(0)	(20)	(0)	33
Fulham Cross Secondary School — C comp girls 11–18	15	14.6	2.1	111	91	(31)	(30)	(26)	25
Phoenix High School — C comp mxd 11–18	9	9.6	7.1	131	86	(11)	(5)	(14)	16
Henry Compton School — C comp boys 11–18	3	5.3	6.9	96	81	(11)	(7)	(11)	14
Hurlingham and Chelsea School — C comp mxd 11–18	10	14.9	3.5	106	93	(13)	(9)	(9)	11
LEA averages		18.4	2.7		91.9	31.9	31.8	35.3	40.1

Source: Schools Report, *The Times*, 18 November 1997.

Figure 2.2   National 'best' and 'worst' league tables for secondary schools

GCSE: top comprehensives	Percentage of pupils passing five GCSEs at A*–C
Old Swinford Hospital, Stourbridge	98
Watford Grammar School for Girls, Watford	93
Coopers' Co. and Coborn School, Upminster	92
Hertfordshire and Essex High School, Bishop's Stortford	90
Coloma Convent Girls' School, Croydon	89
Emmanuel City Technology College, Gateshead	89
Watford Grammar School for Boys, Watford	89
Sexey's School, Bruton, Somerset	88
St Albans Girls' School, St Albans	88
Queen Elizabeth Grammar School, Penrith	87
Brentwood Ursuline Convent High School, Brentwood	86
Dame Alice Owens School, Potters Bar	86
King's School, Peterborough	85
Cardinal Vaughan Memorial School, Kensington	84
Brooke Weston CTC, Corby	83
Thomas Telford School, Telford	83
Arden School, Solihull	82
Holt School, Wokingham	82
St George's School, Harpenden	81
Bishop Luffa CofE School, Chichester	80
Ecclesbourne School, Belper	80
Hutton Grammar School, Preston	80
Presdales School, Ware, Herts	80
Ranelagh School, Bracknell, Berks	80
Silverdale School, Sheffield	80
St Augustine RC (GM) Comp. School, Trowbridge	80
Bullers Wood School, Chislehurst	79
Haybridge High School, Stourbridge	79
Lady Margaret School, London	79
Langley Park School for Girls, Beckenham	79
Sacred Heart of Mary Girls' School, Upminster	79
St Aidan's CofE High School, Harrogate	79
Loreto College, St Albans	78
Thornden School, Eastleigh	78
Dixons City Technology College, Bradford	77
Harrogate Grammar School, Harrogate	77
London Oratory School, London	77
Parmiter's School, Watford	77
Wellsway School, Bristol	77
Wymondham College (GM), Wymondham	77

GCSE: highest failure rate	Percentage of pupils with no GCSEs at any grade
Blakelaw Sch, Newcastle upon Tyne	42
Windsor HS, Salford	41
Copperfields College, Leeds	39
West Gate Community College, Newcastle upon Tyne	38
Eston Park Sch, Middlesbrough	37
Deansfield HS, Wolverhampton	36

Merrywood Sch, Bristol	36
Ashmead Sch, Reading	35
Ducie HS, Manchester	34
Shorefields Community Sch, Liverpool	34
Edward Sheerien Sch, Barnsley	33
Middleton Park HS, Leeds	33
Ridings Sch, Halifax	32
Forest Comprehensive Sch, Nottingham	31
Amy Johnson Sch, Hull	29
Kingsmeadow Sch, Gateshead	29
Mary Linwood Sch, Leicester	29
Primrose HS, Leeds	29
St Alban's CofE Sch, Birmingham	29
Beanfield Sch, Corby	28
College HS, Birmingham	28
Croxteth Community Comprehensive Sch, Liverpool	28
Kaskenmoor Sch, Oldham	28
Moreton Community Sch, Wolverhampton	28
St Chad's Sch, Tilbury, Essex	28
William Crane Comprehensive Sch, Nottingham	28

GCSE: bottom of the league	Percentage of pupils passing five or more GCSEs at A*–C
Ramsgate Sch, Ramsgate, Kent	1
Campion Boys' RC Comprehensive Sch, Liverpool	2
High View Sch and Technology Centre, Derby	2
Our Lady of Fatima HS, Liverpool	2
William Crane Comprehensive Sch, Nottingham	2
Copperfields College, Leeds	3
Handsworth Wood Boys' Sch, Birmingham	3
Amy Johnson Sch, Hull	4
Pen Park Sch, Bristol	4
Skerton HS, Lancaster	4
Aston Manor Sch, Birmingham	5
Battersea Technology College, London, Wandsworth, London	5
Frankley Community HS, Birmingham	5
Gillingham College, Gillingham, Kent	5
Holmesdale Community Sch, Snodland, Kent	5
Parkside Sch, Plymouth	5
Perronet Thompson Sch, Hull	5
Ashmead Sch, Reading	6
Bowling Community College, Bradford	6
Dartford West Boys' Sch, Dartford, Kent	6
Haven HS, Boston, Lincs	6
Henry Mellish Sch, Nottingham	6
Middleton Park HS, Leeds	6
Moston Brook HS, Manchester	6
Ridings Sch, Halifax	6
Spurley Hey HS, Manchester	6
St Alban's CofE Sch, Birmingham	6

Source: Schools Report, *The Times*, 18 November 1997.

proclaimed a commitment to *Excellence in Schools* (DfEE 1997b). The title captures something of the current nature of Labour education policy, with the unashamed concern for 'excellence' echoing the popular authoritarianism of Thatcherite politics.

The most immediate sign of change was the new government's rejection of the market as an effective and just means of allocating opportunity and rewards. Unlike its Conservative predecessors in power, New Labour does not parade the market as the natural and best solution to every social problem. In stark contrast, there is a readiness to accept that inequality is a real and important aspect of contemporary Britain: witness, for example, the opening sentence of the White Paper, which proclaimed 'the Government's core commitment to equality of opportunity and high standards for all' (DfEE 1997b: 3). Modest though this is, there is a clear implication not only that *in*equality of opportunity exists but also that its elimination is a legitimate policy objective: this marks a clear contrast with the 'equiphobia' (Myers 1990, cited in Troyna 1993: 45) of Conservative administrations that deliberately and explicitly sought to equate 'equality' with uniformity and mediocrity (cf. Gillborn 1995: 32). Unfortunately, despite these superficial changes, little of substance has changed.

Labour and the school performance tables

Labour's acknowledgement of social inequality, unless backed by far-reaching changes in policy analysis and action, is wholly inadequate as a response to the succession of Conservative reforms. Labour does not see 'the market' as a panacea and yet it has embraced almost all the reforms that were enacted to establish an educational market. Beneath the rhetoric of inclusion and 'high standards for all', Labour has continued the pressure on education to meet a succession of externally determined and assessed 'standards' benchmarks. The obsession with 'market forces' is virtually the only significant casualty in the discourse established by the Conservatives and repeated by Labour. After more than a year of 'naming and shaming' individual schools, the government eventually pulled back from further deliberate humiliation of named institutions (*Times Educational Supplement*, 2 October 1998: 1). Nevertheless, 'choice', 'diversity' and, above all, 'standards' continue to be the watchwords of British education policy.[6] More worrying still, not only have the key words remained, but so too have the very mechanisms and structures that gave them such retrogressive force under Conservative governments. As we have noted, for example, 'standards' have increasingly been judged in relation to the school and LEA performance statistics enshrined in the annually published 'league tables'. Labour has not only retained the tables, and every 'measure' within them, but also added its own new elements:

> This year secondary tables will include for the first time measures of how schools have improved. They will show the proportion of pupils

who, on reaching school leaving age, achieved at least five higher-grade GCSEs in the last four years. This school improvement index will be presented in easy-to-understand bar charts so parents can see how well a school is improving – or whether its results have been falling back.

(Estelle Morris, Labour Education Minister, 25 June 1997)

In this way, Labour's version of the school league tables valorizes still further the traditional (and somewhat exclusive) 'benchmark' criteria of five or more higher-grade GCSE passes (which has only ever been attained by a minority of the age group).[7] Worse still, the so-called 'school improvement index', by focusing on each school's recent record, finally enshrines overtly what has previously been implicit – that no matter how well a school 'performs', the 'league tables' (in tandem with the other reforms) require continual gains year after year. In this context schools are in competition not only with each other but also with themselves.

Labour and equality of opportunity

As we have noted, the first sentence of Labour's first White Paper reasserted equality of opportunity as a policy concern. This is in contrast to the Conservative's refusal to accept social conditions as a key factor in school performance and has been heralded as an important step forward. However, on closer inspection, and with the passing of time, it is clear that Labour's understanding of equality of opportunity remains at a relatively superficial level. In the previous chapter we outlined several different understandings of the term; to date Labour's education reforms have engaged only with the first of those understandings, concerned with formal equality of access and provision.

In order to see how this is reflected in policy it is useful to take the example of 'race' and ethnic inequalities. In a further break with Conservative precedents, which had removed 'race' from the education agenda (Gillborn 1995; Troyna 1993), the 1997 White Paper included several discrete references to inequalities of experience and outcome by ethnicity. The main body of the document carried a section entitled 'Ethnic minority pupils' that referred, among other things, to inequalities in achievement and offered modest commitments to consult on ethnic monitoring and 'best practice' in multi-ethnic schools (DfEE 1997b: 34–5). In the document's appendix a further paragraph, paraphrasing a review of research published by Ofsted (Gillborn and Gipps 1996), offered a little more detail on current inequalities of attainment (DfEE 1997b: 81). In a document of more than 80 pages, the provision of three paragraphs is, at best, a small beginning. In fact, *Excellence in Schools* set a pattern that was repeated later by another flagship policy document, the first report of the new Social Exclusion Unit (SEU) which, once again, took education as its first theme.

Like the education White Paper, the SEU's first report, on truancy and school exclusion,[8] included a discrete section acknowledging ethnic inequalities and sketching current research evidence on the issue. The SEU report draws attention to the massive over-representation of Black pupils among those expelled from school[9] and, citing an Ofsted special inspection (Ofsted 1996), acknowledges the different profile of excluded Black young people – often judged of 'higher ability' and less likely to have suffered 'deep-seated trauma' at home than white excludees (SEU 1998: 11). Additionally, a wider review of academic research (Gillborn and Gipps 1996) is cited, including the view that white teachers might actively be involved in producing the inequalities via a range of differential expectations and responses to pupil behaviour.

The first education White Paper, *Excellence in Schools*, and the first report of the Social Exclusion Unit, therefore, share important characteristics: significantly, both break with the aggressively 'colour-blind' stance of Conservative policy. The documents openly acknowledge 'race' inequalities; detail the extent of 'race' inequality; and cite research that suggests an active role for schools and teachers in creating and/or amplifying inequality.

However, the two reports also share less fortunate characteristics: in particular, both treat 'race' and ethnicity as an 'add-on' of marginal importance to the central issues. The consideration of ethnic inequalities remains separate to the rest of the discussion and does not impinge on the arguments feeding into the wider formulation of policy. Consequently, an understanding of racism and 'race' inequality remains completely absent from how the principal policy issues are conceived. Hence, policy continues to pursue colour-blind targets. This threatens far-reaching consequences. First, despite the superficial acknowledgement of existing 'race' inequality, the policies actually fail specifically to address that inequality. Second, because policies frequently have racialized effects, despite colour-blind language, this failure to address ethnicity means that the existing 'race' inequalities are actually likely to increase. Let us explain by taking the example of Labour's support for grouping pupils by 'ability'. *Excellence in Schools* argues the need to extend the use of selection within schools:

> The demands for equality and increased opportunity in the 1950s and 1960s led to the introduction of comprehensive schools. All-in secondary schooling rightly became the normal pattern, but the search for equality of opportunity in some cases became a tendency to uniformity. *The idea that all children had the same rights to develop their abilities led too easily to the doctrine that all had the same ability.* The pursuit of excellence was too often equated with elitism.
>
> (DfEE 1997b: 11; emphasis added)

Labour has been keen to dismiss as dogma any attempt to reject the common-sense notion that children differ in their 'ability' and therefore should be taught separately. This position was articulated in speeches leading up to the general election and in the Party's election manifesto:

We favour all-in schooling which identifies the distinct abilities of individual pupils and organises them in classes to maximise their progress in individual subjects.

(Labour Party Manifesto 1997: 3–4)

We must modernise comprehensive schools. *Children are not all of the same ability, nor do they learn at the same speed*. That means 'setting' children in classes to maximise progress, for the benefit of high fliers and slower learners alike.

(Labour Party Manifesto 1997: 7; emphasis added)

These proposals, to extend selection within schools by the widespread adoption of 'setting by ability', completely ignore previous research (in Britain and the USA) that reveals such selection as disadvantaging working-class and ethnic minority pupils (for summaries of the relevant literature, see Gillborn and Gipps 1996; Hallam and Toutounji 1996; Hatcher 1997; Slavin 1996; Sukhnandan and Lee 1998). The present study will provide further evidence to suggest that exactly these processes are being recreated on a daily basis as schools struggle to meet the needs of the performance tables. At this point in our analysis, however, it is important simply to note that the warning bells should already have been heard even as the policies were being drafted. Decades of research have shown that a pupil's chances of being failed by tests of 'ability' vary according to ethnic origin. An individual's position, of course, is not predetermined, but the overall differences in group position could not be clearer. Selection by 'ability' unfairly disadvantages ethnic minority pupils. The colour-blind nature of specific policy proposals belies the racialized reality of life in contemporary Britain and, therefore, threatens racist consequences. That is, people's experiences of success and failure are not independent of ethnic origin; the demographics of educational attainment and economic success display clear and consistent patterns in relation to ethnic origin – the patterns are racialized (more on this below). By failing to take these realities into account policy will at best miss the opportunity to close existing ethnic inequalities, and at worse it will strengthen processes that further entrench ethnic inequality – that is, its consequences will be racist. We develop these points further during this study. For the moment it is sufficient to note that although 'race' and ethnic inequalities are cited in policy texts, an awareness of the issues has not informed policy on the performance tables, on within-school selection, or on attempts to reduce the number of permanent and fixed-term exclusions (expulsions and suspensions) from school.[10]

Labour's opposition to selection on entry demonstrates a concern with formal access and participation. However, none of the more critical or robust interpretations of equal opportunity are satisfied by their support for selection *within* schools or their failure to act decisively on the racialized pattern of exclusion, success and failure.

Labour and assumptions of community deficit

In a perceptive and damning critique of Conservative policies on home–school relationships, parenting and 'consumer choice' in education, Carol Vincent and Sally Tomlinson (1997) build upon a Foucauldian analysis to explore 'the swarming of disciplinary mechanisms' in this field. They argue that despite the rhetoric of 'partnerships', 'choice' and parental agency, too often such initiatives embody a deficit perspective that positions certain pupils, their parents and communities as problems that must be addressed. Working-class and minority ethnic communities are especially likely to be viewed in this way. Such perspectives are a form of what Michael Apple and Christopher Zenk (1996: 69) call 'a *pathological* analysis' that identifies the reasons for failure as residing within the victims themselves. In this way, those who bear the brunt of multiple economic, social and historic structures of inequality are identified as the *cause* of their situation, rather than agents caught within a particular nexus of oppressive relations. These discourses are subtle and extensive, they find expression in the policies and practices of many different agencies working at the interface of state–community relations. In education the language is frequently welcoming, even egalitarian, but the consequences are a construction of working-class and minority parents and communities as pathological and deficient – as a drag on the achievements and aspirations of their children. The proffered solution is to get them to be more like the (white) middle-class model of the ideal parent enshrined in policy folklore. Labour have tended to adopt exactly this approach in their presentation of 'disadvantage'.

Parental support

Learning together

1 Parents are a child's first and enduring teachers. They play a crucial role in helping their children learn. Family learning is a powerful tool for reaching some of the most disadvantaged in our society. It has the potential to reinforce the role of the family and change attitudes to education, helping build strong local communities and widening participation in learning . . .

(DfEE 1997b: 53)

So begins the sixth chapter of Labour's first White Paper, entitled 'Helping pupils achieve'. It is significant that the section of the document that expressly addresses means of raising achievements should begin with a reference to parents rather than schools, teachers, examiners or any of the other agencies involved. Furthermore, the reference hints at some of the major strands in contemporary discourses of parental and community deficit: it assumes the need 'to reinforce the role of the family' and 'change attitudes to education'. We are not told who these people are but the idea that they need 'reaching' symbolizes the sense of families, even whole communities ('some of the most disadvantaged in our society') somehow adrift from normal (white middle-class) aspirations and attitudes. Such perspectives saturate the White Paper.

In discussing the establishment of Education Action Zones, for example, the White Paper ascribes a special responsibility to parents and communities:

> We want to develop new and imaginative ways of helping schools to achieve our overall objectives. That will require effort from all concerned, and *particularly parents and the local community*. The initiative will only succeed on the basis of active partnerships . . .
>
> (DfEE 1997b: 39; emphasis added)

'Active partnerships' like these seem shaped by powerful, though usually hidden, rules. When such initiatives are examined in detail there is a mismatch between the openness and inclusivity of the language and the realities of policies that reveal 'an implicit marginalising and controlling of parents . . . Parents are audience, volunteers, supporters-from-a-distance; the roles are passive and narrowly defined' (Vincent and Tomlinson 1997: 366). Indeed, the detail of the White Paper provides numerous other examples, such as 'family learning', where parental deficits are viewed as a major cause of pupil failure (see Gillborn 1998a). Repeatedly parents and local communities are positioned as a major deficit in their children's education. Our point here is not to question the value of 'family learning' and adult education *per se* (undoubtedly, some adults can reap enormous rewards by gaining the skills and qualifications originally denied them by their childhood education): our concern is to challenge the idea that children cannot learn without equivalent parental knowledge and understanding. The success of bilingual learners, for example, clearly demonstrates that where parents cannot read or write fluently this does *not* represent a fundamental barrier to their children's progress (see Gillborn and Gipps 1996). Second, like Apple and Zenk (1996: 69), we want to argue the need 'to locate these issues in a more critical appraisal of their larger political and economic contexts'. We need to refuse the logic of contemporary policies that construct parents and communities as the key reason why certain pupils (mostly working-class and/or from minority ethnic groups) are failed by state education systems: such policies frequently remove the school (its teachers, curricula and structures) from critical gaze, and almost always negate any genuine consideration of wider structural constraints. As our study will demonstrate, schools are far from autonomous in their actions but neither are they neutral institutions where predetermined inequalities are unproblematically realized – they are active in the creation and re-creation of inequality.

Labour and school change

We want to conclude our consideration of Labour and contemporary education policy by commenting on official understandings of how schools change. It is possible to discern an approach that is highly technicist, sociologically naive and, in its consequences, deeply regressive. One of Labour's first innovations in government was to establish within the DfEE a unit that would play a vital role in developing and implementing its policy: the *Standards and*

Effectiveness Unit. The title is significant: the inevitable repetition of 'stand-ards' further evidences the continuity with Conservative discourse, but the second part of the couplet is equally important. The unit's head, Professor Michael Barber, is a leading writer on school effectiveness and improve-ment, a prominent and growing school of work that has attracted consider-able controversy (cf. Hatcher 1998). In particular, sociological critics have attacked the naive basis of many studies that seek to identify (recipe-style) the elements that predispose a school towards being more or less 'effective'. School effectiveness research is built on the assumption that it is possible, statistically, to reveal the 'value added' by an institution by controlling for differences in pupil population, resourcing and so on. In response, it has been argued that such work sanitizes racism, sexism, poverty and disablist practices by regarding them as '"noise" – as "outside" background factors' that can be isolated statistically and then 'stripped away so that the researcher can concentrate on the important domain of school factors' (Angus 1993: 341). Some research under the school effectiveness banner does not fall easily into such criticism; there are cases of complex and important issues being addressed in balanced and critical ways that openly acknowledge con-tinuing uncertainties and dilemmas (cf. Mortimore & Whitty 1997; Sammons 1995; Thomas *et al.* 1997). There is a good deal of work, however, that assumes a most simplistic view of the mechanisms by which schools change and the ways that social inequality might be implicated. Barber's confidence in the universal applicability of school effectiveness work, for example, sug-gests an almost complete failure to engage with issues of class, gender, ethni-city and disability. As Angus feared, such issues have indeed been controlled out of this perspective. The following quotation, for example, is taken from an article entitled 'Why simply tackling poverty is not enough':

> 20 years' worth of research evidence . . . shows incontrovertibly that while, of course, social factors are important, school can and does make a difference. . . . Not only have they [school effectiveness researchers] demonstrated how much difference school makes (enough, in some cases, to be the deciding factor in relation to success and failure in future life) but also what the characteristics of the more successful schools are . . .
>
> The challenge for education policy is clear. Now we know what makes a good school, a good department and a good teacher, how do we create the conditions which will make it happen in every school and classroom in the country?
>
> (Barber 1997: 17)

The aim is worthy, but such an unreflective and uncritical reading of the current literature is clearly implicated in a line of analysis that pays lip-service to 'social factors', then proceeds to behave as if such things are really little more than excuses for incompetence (by schools/teachers), lack of effort (by pupils) and/or bad parenting (by carers and communities). Such perspect-ives come to embody the powerful deficit perspectives already noted earlier.

Despite a change in government, therefore, the overall shape of British education reform remains much the same. A constellation of separate, but related, measures has produced a particular and negative situation where the drive to 'raise standards' has set up a series of interlocking constraints acting upon schools, teachers and pupils. In the remainder of this book we explore some of the school-based processes through which these developments are experienced and mediated, resulting frequently in the rearticulation of all-too-familiar patterns of differential participation and achievement. In the next section of this chapter we outline evidence of the growing inequalities that are associated with the policies we have considered here. These data present the wider context within which our school-based study is located.

The consequences of reform: 'raising standards' and deepening inequality

In many areas of social policy the 1980s and 1990s were characterized by growing economic and social polarization. Despite the rhetoric of citizens' charters (under the Conservatives) and social inclusion (under Labour) the period saw a widening of the substantive gaps between the 'haves' and 'have-nots'. If we take something as basic (and undeniably significant) as mortality rates, for example, in the 1990s the gap between the highest and lowest deciles of the population was actually greater than in the 1950s (Curtis 1998).[11] A similar trend can be seen in the economy, with the poorest households receiving an even smaller proportion of disposable income between 1980 and 1990.[12] These patterns arise from policies that in practice favour those in the strongest positions and give little or no attention to those denied an equal share in any improvements that accrue from change over time. In education also, these 'countervailing trends' of 'improvement and polarisation' (Budge 1995) are evident.

As we have shown above, throughout the late 1980s and 1990s the proportion of pupils attaining five or more higher-grade passes in GCSE examinations at the end of their compulsory schooling became established as *the* key performance indicator in education reform. As Figure 2.3 illustrates, the reforms have been associated with a clear improvement in relation to this 'benchmark'. Between 1988 and 1998 the proportion of 16-year-olds attaining at least five higher-grade GCSE passes rose from around 30 per cent to just over 46 per cent. It is not possible to ascribe this pattern of improvement to the education reforms alone, although it is difficult to make a credible argument against their direct and powerful impact. Our own data (presented in the rest of this book) document just how significant the five A*-to-C benchmark has become as a part of school life. The headline figure of year-on-year improvements, however, does not tell the whole story. At the same time that the official school performance tables trumpet continually 'rising standards' there have been growing signs of marked (and

Figure 2.3 Pupils attaining five or more higher-grade GCSE passes, England, 1988–98

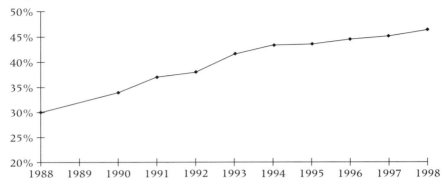

Source: adapted from data published in Payne (1995) and the Department for Education and Employment.

increasing) inequalities between different parts of the education system and between different pupil groups within it.

In a review article focusing on examination performance between 1992 and 1995, for example, Geraldine Hackett (1995) noted that in a significant number of LEAs an increase in the proportion of pupils gaining five or more higher-grade passes had been accompanied by an increase in the proportion ending their compulsory schooling with *no* pass grades (at any level).[13] Similarly, there are signs that pupils in the lowest-achieving part of the performance spectrum have shared least in the overall increases (Doe 1995). Also, official data indicate that the gap has increased between schools performing around the top and bottom quartile points.[14] Reviews of existing research, undertaken by independent academics for Ofsted, raised similar concerns in relation to inequalities based on gender and ethnic origin (Arnot *et al.* 1998; Gillborn and Gipps 1996). In the following sections we consider the evidence in relation to these issues and the related question of social class inequalities.

Gender and achievement

The supposed 'under-achievement' of boys (in comparison to girls) caused considerable public and scholarly comment during the late 1990s. Although data were already in existence showing a narrowing (and in some cases a reversal) of the traditionally anticipated gender gap (of girls lagging behind boys), the public debate began in earnest following an intervention by Her Majesty's Chief Inspector of Schools, Chris Woodhead. Writing in *The Times* newspaper, Woodhead announced that 'The failure of boys, and in particular white working-class boys, is one of the most disturbing problems we face within the whole education system' (Woodhead 1996: 18). *The Times* made the story its front-page lead that day and the issue was picked up subsequently by several other dailies including its more populist 'sister' publication:

Anti-school bias 'blights boys for life': white dropouts in cycle of failure
(The Times, 6 March 1996: 1)

Great white dopes: working-class white boys are the big failures in Britain's schools
(The Sun, 7 March 1996: 2)

This story was enthusiastically repeated throughout the media, on TV, radio and in various popular publications. The educational press began running a succession of pieces trying to identify what was going wrong with boys' education. Covering everything from 'curriculum oestrogen' (Pyke 1996) to asserted sex differences in neurological and physiological maturation (Hugill 1998), the story refused to go away. More balanced critiques slowly emerged – for example, emphasizing that by no means all boys fail; that their failure is closely related to other issues (not least social class); and that the moral panic building around the issue frequently adopts a sexist tone that projects the problem as located in women teachers and/or girl pupils, who are assumed to be denying boys a fair chance (cf. Epstein *et al.* 1998a; 1998b; Murphy and Elwood 1998). Reviewing the academic evidence, Madeleine Arnot *et al.* (1998: 11) concluded that in many respects the gap had indeed widened significantly during the 1990s:

The gender gap in performance in relation to the five or more A*–C passes hurdle emerged at the end of the 1980s; within four years the position had changed from one of rough equality between the sexes to clear disparity.

The growing gender gap can be seen clearly in Figure 2.4. Nevertheless, Arnot *et al.* (1998: 4–14) were careful to emphasize that girls did not universally outperform boys and that different patterns pertained at different age points and in particular curriculum areas. Interestingly, throughout the debates, the racialized nature of Woodhead's original intervention has gone largely unremarked and unchallenged. As the headlines quoted above clearly demonstrate, the issue was phrased as not simply about boys, but about *working-class white* boys. In the rest of this section we examine the evidence on 'race' and class inequalities more closely.

'Race', ethnicity and achievement

The relative 'under-achievement' of ethnic minority pupils has been a major issue in British educational research for several decades. A committee of inquiry reported on the issue twice during the 1980s (Rampton 1981; Swann 1985) and several large-scale surveys have also documented the unequal performance of pupils from different ethnic backgrounds (for a review, see Drew and Gray 1991). With the succession of education reforms in the late

Figure 2.4   Pupils attaining five or more higher-grade GCSE passes, by gender, 1988–93

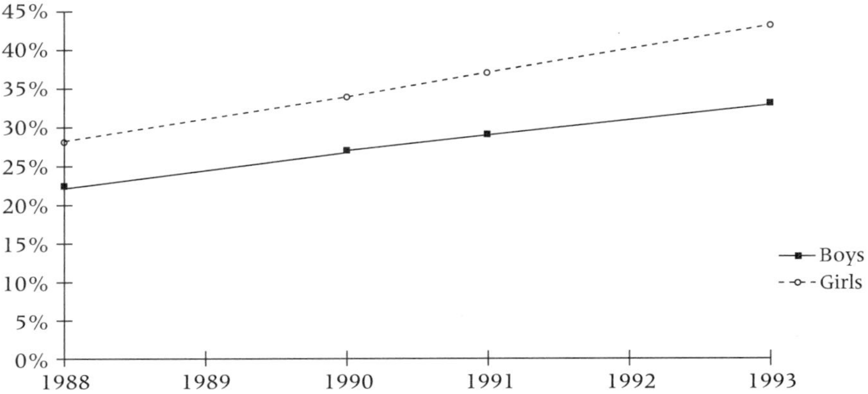

Source: Demack *et al.* (1998).

1980s and 1990s, however, came a shift in policy discourse and the related agendas of educational researchers. The 1988 Education Reform Act set a 'colour-blind' precedent that was followed by all subsequent Conservative reforms. Issues of 'race' and cultural diversity were effectively removed from the educational agenda (cf. Gillborn 1995; Troyna 1993). Educational research continued to examine 'race' and racism in schools, but much less attention was paid to the overall patterns of achievement. Rather, attention focused more often on small-scale qualitative studies (e.g. Connolly 1995; 1998; Foster 1990; Gillborn 1990a; Mac an Ghaill 1988; Mirza 1992; Nehaul 1996; Sewell 1997; Troyna and Hatcher 1992; Wright 1986; 1992). These studies revealed a good deal about the racialized processes of life in multi-ethnic schools, but the absence of broadly based statistical work was significant. This meant that when Woodhead's original statement was made, concerning what *The Sun* described as 'Great white dopes' (see above), there was not in the public domain any clear statistical work by which to judge his assertions. It was some time *after* Woodhead's statement that a review of relevant research was published, including findings that questioned the certainty of his generalizations. For example, Woodhead's article in *The Times* made some rather specific claims:

> Research shows that white working-class boys are the least likely to participate in full-time education after the age of 16, and that white boys are the most likely to be completely unqualified on leaving compulsory education.
>
> (Woodhead 1996: 18)

Additionally, he was quoted as stating that 'children from almost all ethnic minorities are achieving better examination results than white boys from poor inner city areas' (*The Times*, 6 March 1996: 1). The same article drew on Ofsted inspection data to claim that 'white teenagers' were 'lagging behind all but their Afro-Caribbean counterparts'. In fact, a review of research on ethnicity and achievement (funded by Ofsted but not public at the time of Woodhead's statement) included data that contradicted this view, showing that the gap between white and minority groups was actually *growing* in some areas.

Conducting a review of a decade's research on the achievements of ethnic minority pupils, Gillborn and Gipps could not draw on national statistics (at that time the DfEE did not monitor achievement by ethnicity).[15] An analysis of locally based statistics, however, indicated that in several LEAs the ethnic group that had historically achieved at the highest level (usually, but not always, the white group) had enjoyed a greater improvement in performance than their peers of other ethnic backgrounds. Because of variation in the ethnic categories used, and the size of local populations, only tentative conclusions could be drawn concerning general patterns of achievement. This was especially so in relation to different South Asian communities, where the blanket category 'Asian' is now seen as unhelpful but where more specific data were often lacking (cf. Gillborn and Gipps 1996: 18–30; Modood 1992, 1996). The situation was somewhat clearer for African Caribbean pupils. In many cases the groups performing best and worst were white pupils and their Black (African Caribbean) peers, respectively. In Birmingham in 1995, for example, twice the proportion of white pupils achieved five higher-grade passes compared with their African Caribbean peers (Gillborn and Gipps 1996: 33). Overall the data were significant enough to support the conclusion that 'African Caribbean pupils have not shared equally in the increasing rates of educational achievement . . . In some areas there is a growing gap between the achievements of African Caribbean pupils and their peers' (Gillborn and Gipps 1996: 2). Gillborn and Gipps cite additional data from Birmingham that question Woodhead's view that only Black (African Caribbean) pupils fair worse in inner cities than whites. Since the data refer to a single LEA they are not conclusive, but the significance of Birmingham is that it has the largest population of ethnic minority pupils in Britain. Here the data show that of the various minority groups identified by LEA statisticians, only 'Indian' pupils have less chance of leaving compulsory education completely without qualifications. On several measures white pupils in Birmingham fair *better* than their peers of African Caribbean, Pakistani and Bangladeshi ethnic backgrounds: in contradiction to Woodhead's analysis, whites were *more* likely to achieve five higher-grade passes and *less* likely to achieve no graded results (Gillborn and Gipps 1996: 33). Subsequently, this analysis has been supported by more broadly based statistics from the Youth Cohort Study (YCS) of England and Wales.

Newly analysed findings from the YCS confirm both the trends discussed above; there are growing gaps by gender and ethnicity. The strength of the YCS is that it draws on a large and nationally representative sample of

Figure 2.5   Pupils attaining five or more higher-grade GCSE passes, by ethnic origin, both sexes, 1988–93

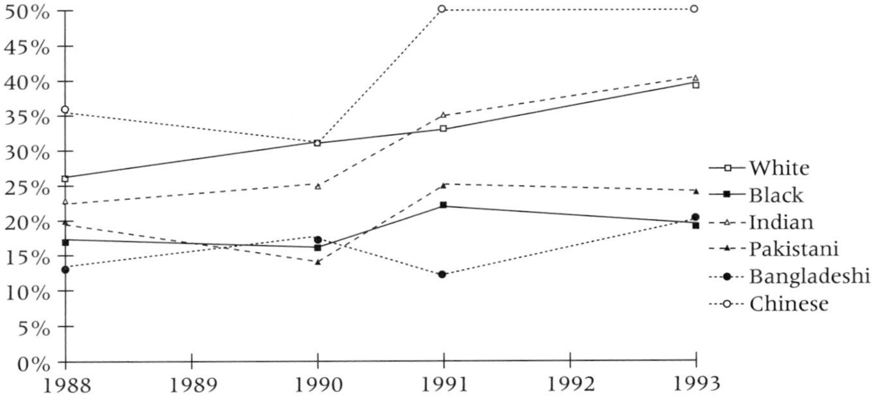

Source: Demack *et al.* (1998).

young people: around 13,000 in each biannual cohort. The findings, presented publicly for the first time at the British Educational Research Association annual meeting in 1998, not only confirm the patterns suggested in previous work, but also offer a more detailed picture of how different ethnic groups have shared unequally in the changing rates of attainment during the late 1980s and 1990s.[16]

The YCS data paint a clear picture of growing inequalities of achievement between the white group and pupils from several minority ethnic backgrounds. Only two of the different ethnic categories covered in the study enjoyed a year-on-year improvement: the white and Indian groups. The consequence is a growing gap between the majority white group and pupils classified as 'Black', 'Pakistani' and 'Bangladeshi' (see Figure 2.5). More recent YCS data are also available for the white and 'Black' groups and charting this separately reveals even more clearly the growing inequality of achievement by ethnicity (see Figure 2.6).[17] By charting the so-called 'Black–white gap' from the earliest YCS breakdown by ethnicity (for 1985) to the most recent (for 1996) we can see that although more Black pupils than ever before now reach the hurdle of five or more higher-grade passes, their share in the overall improvement has not matched that of their white peers. The result is that in a little over a decade the 'Black–white gap' has actually increased by half.[18]

Social class and achievement

During the years of Conservative government the issue of social class inequality (like 'race' and ethnicity) was systematically removed from the political

Figure 2.6   The Black–white gap: pupils attaining five or more higher-grade GCSE passes, by ethnic origin, both sexes, 1985–96

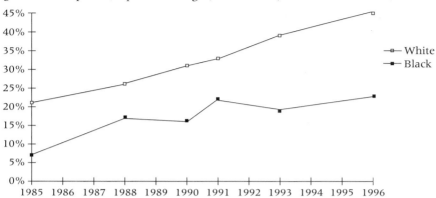

Source: adapted from YCS data published previously in CRE (1998: 2), Drew (1995: 76) and Demack *et al.* (1998).

agenda. Margaret Thatcher's (in)famous statement that there is 'no such thing as society' perfectly encapsulated an ideological drive that reduced everything to individualized relationships between providers and consumers, and understood inequality variously as a sign of personal/community deficit or part of the necessary spur to achievement in a meritocracy:

> There are individual men and women, and there are families. And no government can do anything except through people, and people must look to themselves first . . . If irresponsible behaviour does not involve penalty of some kind, irresponsibility will for a large number of people become the norm. More important still, the attitudes may be passed on to their children, setting them off in the wrong direction.
>
> (Thatcher 1993: 626–7)

It is hardly surprisingly, in this context of punitive social policy, that (as we noted earlier) social class inequalities in income, health and other major indicators were seen to rise under Thatcherism. Data from the YCS confirm that during the late 1980s and early 1990s, at precisely the point when overall educational achievements were rising sharply, the inequalities of achievement (the 'gaps') between social classes also increased. It should also be noted that these inequalities are greater than those noted by gender and ethnic origin. As can be seen in Figure 2.7, almost without exception, between 1988 and 1993 the gaps between the social classes grew in relation to the proportion of pupils attaining five or more higher-grade passes. It is also interesting to note the size of the differences between, and within, the manual and non-manual groups. There is a significant gap not only between manual and non-manual occupations in general, but also between the different

Figure 2.7   Pupils attaining five or more higher-grade GCSE passes, by social class, both sexes, 1988–93

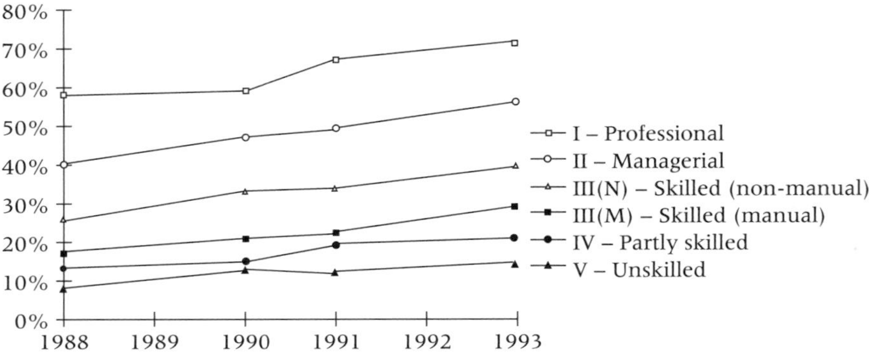

Source: Demack *et al.* (1998).

categories of non-manual occupations.[19] It is clear that social class remains a hugely important factor associated with significant and increasing inequalities of achievement.

Conclusions

After long periods as a poor relation to other areas of social policy, during the 1980s and 1990s the education system became a central arena for political policy making in Britain. Successive Conservative governments assigned a central role to education as part of their wider project of cultural restoration-ism. The battle over 'British values' and the rejection of 'progressive' methods was signalled in a series of reforms that introduced a statutory curriculum, required formal testing at specified key stages, changed the balance of resourc-ing, and even introduced new types of school to the compulsory system. Amid all these changes the mantra of 'raising standards' was chanted loud and clear. The election of a Labour government, after 18 years of Conservative rule, has done little to blunt the regressive and iniquitous edge of the reforms. Although 'social justice' and 'inclusion' have been added to the lexicon of public policy, in education the vast majority of Conservative reforms remain in place. New Labour has taken up the 'standards' rhetoric and failed decisively to act against the significant and growing inequalities that now characterize the system.

The reshaping of education in Britain has placed an unprecedented focus on pupils' results in external examinations. Perhaps not surprisingly, the period witnessed a year-on-year improvement in the headline 'benchmark' figure of the proportion of pupils attaining five or more higher-grade passes in GCSE exams. At the same time, however, relative inequalities of achieve-ment actually worsened, showing increasing gaps between pupils based on gender, ethnic origin and social class. It is against this background of unprecedented external surveillance and disciplinary control, alongside widening inequalities, that the present study was undertaken. Our aim, in the following chapters, is to explore the dynamics of reform through detailed material on life in two London secondary schools. Our analysis of Taylor Comprehensive and Clough GM shows how the reforms of the British education system have been experienced, mediated and remade at the school and classroom level. At every turn there is scope for a worsening of social inequality. As our data testify, despite the best intentions of some teachers, and the struggles, effort and resistance of many pupils, the reforms seem relentlessly to embody an increasingly divisive and exclusionary notion of education.

3

Ability and economy

defining 'ability' in the A-to-C economy

In the previous chapter we documented some of the major education reforms of the 1980s and 1990s, arguing that they have constructed a system where the level of surveillance and the disciplining of schools exceeds anything previously possible in modern Britain. In this chapter we begin our detailed examination of how these policies have translated into changed practice at the level of the secondary school. In particular, we explore how the demand to 'raise standards' has been experienced and responded to in our two case-study schools, Clough Grant Maintained and Taylor Comprehensive, both coeducational schools serving multi-ethnic pupil populations in London. This approach allows us to examine how staff perceive the demands upon them and highlights the ways in which competing and contradictory perspectives, and subsequent responses, are negotiated, glossed over, or left in contradiction. What emerges is a picture of schools operating in responsive mode, desperately suturing together a range of practices in an attempt to 'succeed' within parameters laid down by government. Furthermore, we begin to identify which sectors of the school population are reaping the benefits of this drive for 'success' and which are being 'deselected'.

The key issues that we focus upon are present in both our case-study schools. In order to avoid unnecessary repetition, however, and to do justice to the multiple and interlocking processes at work in the schools, in this and the following chapter we have chosen to focus mainly upon only one of the schools. Later on, as we consider the range of practices in years 10 and 11, and especially the schools' new initiatives to raise achievement among targeted pupils, we focus equally on both institutions. Initially, however, we concentrate on our grant-maintained school, Clough, where debates about the pros and cons of selection have been prominent in recent staff discussions. We begin by outlining our notion of the 'A-to-C economy', which provides the wider context for life in both case-study schools.

The A-to-C economy

A school now lives or dies on its results.
(Pastoral head of year, Taylor Comprehensive)

the staff here now are under pressure to get As-to-Cs. I mean considerable pressure like, you know, that's never existed before.
(Head of department with more than 15 years' teaching experience, Clough GM)

We have already shown, in the previous chapter, how higher-grade GCSE passes have become the dominant criterion for measuring success or failure in the British educational system. Our argument is that these developments have created an *A-to-C economy* in schools where 'the bottom line' is judged in relation to how many higher-grade passes are achieved and, more specifically, what proportion of pupils meet the benchmark level of at least *five* such passes.[1] The economic metaphor is especially fitting: it encapsulates how participants, both teachers and pupils, experience the current situation (as competition); how they talk about it (where grades are the 'currency' of education); and how high are the stakes (survival for the school, and access to education and labour markets for young people). The notion of an A-to-C *economy* also captures something of the depersonalized nature of the processes within which teachers and pupils feel caught. There is a very real sense in which participants on both sides of the school desk feel trapped within a system where the rules are made by others and where external forces, much bigger than any individual school, teacher or pupil, are setting the pace that all must follow.

In both our case-study schools the A-to-C economy has been largely accepted as a fact of life (though not necessarily welcomed) by most members of staff. In particular, the headteachers and other members of the schools' SMTs have played a crucial role in translating the national reforms into a particular agenda for their institution. In Taylor Comprehensive, for example, in an internally circulated memorandum to staff the Headteacher identifies the school's main task as follows:

[to] prepare pupils for the demands of the GCSE. All else at KS4 [Key Stage 4] is subordinate to this supreme and unavoidable constraint.

The identification of the GCSE as a 'constraint' might be taken to suggest that the headteacher does not wholly subscribe to its 'supremacy'. However, its presentation as 'unavoidable' confirms the status accorded GCSE grades and, in the headteacher's eyes, this criterion is so powerful that pupils' interests are now synonymous with the terms of the A-to-C economy:

the best thing that we can do for our pupils is to strive to get the greatest possible proportion achieving that five high-grade benchmark.

The headteacher in Clough GM adopts the same position. He is certain that higher-grade passes are the only hard currency in this economy:

> we do emphasize the fact that if at all possible you should attempt to achieve a grade C. (. . .) I mean not necessarily because of league tables but because the *fact* of the matter is that Cs and above have some currency in the world out there, whereas Ds and below are still viewed by most people as failures. (. . .) the *hard facts* are that Cs are worth very much more than anything below a C.

GCSE grades A*-to-C have become *the* dominant concern for our case-study schools – this is the A-to-C economy. Before examining the consequences of this for selection in the schools, however, it should be emphasized that there is not a uniform acceptance of the terms of the A-to-C economy among *all* teachers. Even within the SMTs there is some dissension. This is most pronounced in Taylor, where the deputy headteacher responsible for pastoral care (that is, the social, as opposed to academic, aspect of education), is critical of what she sees as a narrow definition of success that is both exclusionary and potentially damaging:

> Success for some children can look to other people as minimal but everyone achieves success at different levels. So we don't emphasize or try to say – and it makes me so cross when I do hear people saying it – the emphasis on A-to-C. I mean, I'm not on to mine with the emphasis on getting GCSE A-to-C. But let's face it, there are a lot of children – and we are a fully comprehensive school – who work their hearts out and just will never reach a C. But for them an F is an achievement, an E is an achievement, for some a G is an achievement. So there's this risk of – because of the whole publicity as well surrounding the five A-to-Cs – the importance of five A-to-Cs. It's keeping the balance right along the way, that keeping people's self-esteem and self-concept, it's important to keep those high.

It is interesting to note that this broader definition of success (extended to include GCSE grades D-to-G) is coupled with a concern for pupils' 'self-esteem and self-concept': concerns that we might expect to be expressed by the SMT representative with responsibility for pastoral care. However, this dissent from what is often portrayed as a 'realist' or 'pragmatist' acceptance of the A-to-C economy is not an indication of similar resistance among all teachers with pastoral responsibilities. Whereas this teacher proclaims that she is 'not on to mine with the emphasis on getting GCSE A-to-C', most pastoral colleagues (in either school) adopt a position that higher grades *are* a dominant concern for the school and its pupils alike. They do not always approve of this, but the large majority have accepted the situation as something they *have* to work to. Even members of staff with significant pastoral responsibilities (such as heads of year charged with overseeing pastoral development for entire year groups) seem generally to accede to the terms and consequences of the A-to-C economy:

> The most important one [of all published data] is the number of kids getting five A-to-Cs (. . .) So a school has to be seen to have above the national average in those areas.
>
> (Head of year 9, Taylor Comprehensive)

> if you don't get A-to-Cs you're not seen as being successful. I think it's coming from Ofsted, it's coming from society, it's coming from government because they obviously know, publishing all these things that tell you how many, I mean all this is a focus on getting A-to-Cs. And it's all A-to-Cs, it doesn't matter if you get a D and you really progressed from, you know, it's not recognized in any way, shape or form that that's a success, that's not seen, it's all A-to-Cs.
>
> (Head of year 11, Clough GM)

In this and successive chapters we examine how the terms and conditions of the A-to-C economy influence the nature and scope of selection within the case-study schools. As already explained, we will mainly focus on Clough GM as a vehicle for examining these processes in the first years of secondary schooling (when pupils are aged 11–13). Before considering the precise mechanisms that have been adopted, however, it is useful to begin by examining the school's view of itself and, most importantly, the dominant discourses concerning 'ability' in the school.

Defining 'ability' and intake

It is commonly recognized that, despite their label, few British secondary schools are genuinely 'comprehensive' in relation to the social and academic character of their pupil populations (cf. Newsam 1996; Woods 1983). Before its abolition by a Thatcher government in 1990, however, the Inner London Education Authority (ILEA) attempted to judge the spread of 'ability' in its schools. Towards the end of their primary schooling all children in London were assessed using one or more standard instruments, most notably verbal reasoning tests and the London Reading Test (LRT). On the basis of test performance, individual pupils were allocated to one of three 'bands'. Bands 1 and 3 were the highest- and lowest-attaining pupils respectively, accounting for the upper and lower quartile. The middle 50 per cent were classified into band 2 (cf. Drew 1995; Gipps and Murphy 1994: 234–5). The majority of London boroughs have dropped the formal use of these bands as a means of determining 'quotas' for individual schools (Burstall 1996). Nevertheless, the significance of band allocations continues in a modified form. In particular, the distribution of band 1, 2 and 3 pupils is still seen by some educators as an indication of the nature of school intakes: many London teachers assume that a 'truly' comprehensive school will have an intake spread appropriately between bands according to the 25:50:25 ratio of the original model. Although ILEA no longer exists, in many parts of London the London Reading Test in particular remains an important authority-wide assessment at the end of pupils' primary schooling (the transition from Key Stage 2 to Key Stage 3). It is in relation to this history, and definition of the 'normal' distribution of attainments, that Clough characterizes itself as unlike most comprehensives.

Selection 'by ability' and Clough's 'long tail'

We're heavily weighted at the bottom (. . .) the tail wags, the tail wags, yeah.
(Head of technology, Clough GM)

Dominant views of GM schools in the educational press have tended to focus upon two images: one is an image of already 'popular' schools seeking to cement their status and privilege through increased selection at the point of entry (Lepkowska 1998; O'Connor 1996); the other is of schools 'opting out' to avoid closure by the LEA (Dean 1996a). Both images are under-pinned by a sense of injustice at the higher than average levels of financing that GM schools enjoyed for so long under Conservative governments (cf. *Times Educational Supplement*, 7 April 1995: 4). Although these perceptions are undoubtedly based in fact, they over-simplify the varied and complex range of motivations that fuelled schools to seek GM status. As Sharon Gewirtz *et al.* (1995: 62) have noted, for example, in at least one area several schools used GM status to escape the policies of a Conservative local authority: 'These schools were unanimous in seeing grant-maintained . . . status as a way of maintaining their comprehensive identity and avoiding the specialization and selection policies being pursued by Northwark'. The SMT at Clough present their decision to 'go GM' as an attempt to *become* comprehensive.

Senior managers and long-standing members of the teaching staff in Clough report that the school has traditionally received a pupil intake with lower than average 'ability':

> When they came in, 50 per cent of them had a reading age which was below, or *seriously* below, their chronological age, okay? That's about par for the course for us here, has been for many years and I've been here for 25 years so I have quite a sound knowledge of what's what. So the majority of the kids come in, they are not as literate as they are expected to be, they are not as numerate as they're expected to be.
> (Acting head of English, Clough GM)

This skewed intake is in turn blamed for lower than average examination results and the school's perceived lack of popularity among local parents. In the eyes of most teachers, therefore, the school's problems can be traced directly to the nature of its pupil intake, creating a situation that is seen as self-perpetuating and exacerbated by national reforms that have ended school catchment areas and championed parental choice. It is in this context that the decision to opt out is presented: as driven by the demand to enhance pupil recruitment in terms of both *quantity* (number of pupils on roll) and *quality* (that is, overall 'ability'), thereby improving examination outcomes and popularity:

> Because currently we're not a comprehensive school. The intake of the school is such that we have a disproportionate number of pupils who have learning difficulties or who arrive having been ill prepared for secondary school (. . .) 40 per cent of kids typically, 40 per cent of kids on arrival have reading ages at least two years below their chronolo-gical age. They have similar deficiencies in numeracy, basic numeracy, and that kind of intake is reflected in our performance in SATs and GCSE, and the imbalance of the school, in terms of ability, is matched by an imbalance in gender as well. 60:40, boys:girls. (. . .) And so, I mean, that's why we've introduced the 15 per cent selection business that we've just been talking about. In order to try to reduce the size of the sort of lower-ability tail and beef up the top end.
>
> (Headteacher, Clough GM)

The decision to opt out of LEA control, therefore, is explicitly linked to the perceived need to improve the overall balance of attainments on entry: to 'beef up the top end'. This was judged impossible under the direction of an LEA that had made clear its refusal to permit selection by ability for any part of the intake in its schools. In order to take advantage of the right to introduce limited selection on entry, the school had to go grant-maintained.[2] Nevertheless, the head is keen to emphasize the retention of a comprehens-ive *ethos*. Paradoxically, therefore, the dominant view of Clough's intake as 'bottom-heavy' permits the school's senior management to argue that by introducing a measure of academic selection (generally considered antithetical to the comprehensive ideal) the school is in fact becoming more compre-hensive in its character:

> GM schools have the opportunity to make that decision [about limited selection at entry] whereas a local authority school (. . .) decisions about admissions are controlled by the local authority, so it would be dependent upon a local authority decision to go for that. (. . .) we retain our neighbourhood school ethos largely by still recruiting princip-ally siblings and those who live closest to the school. But I'm prepared to spread the net rather wider in order to attract kids who might affect the ability distribution.
>
> (Headteacher, Clough GM)

The newly introduced element of selection on entry is very much seen as a long-term move by senior management. Given the possibility of selecting up to a maximum of 30 pupils (in an intake of 200) it is clear that this move alone is insufficient to challenge the dominant view of the school as held back by a 'long tail' of low-attaining pupils:

> But we do not have a comprehensive intake in this school. We are not a real comprehensive school. In [this borough] the *crème de la crème* are creamed off (. . .) They are going to the prestigious ones which are mainly in the middle-class areas (. . .) We are not a proper comprehensive. We don't have from the brightest to those who struggle most. We are weighted down the lower end, unfortunately, because we are a working-class school.
>
> (Acting head of English, Clough GM)

It is important to note that *social class status and 'ability' are segued in this discourse*. The lower attainment of the pupil intake is assumed to be causally related to the class status of the families that Clough has previously been able to recruit – '*because* we are a working-class school' (emphasis added). This adds another, and older, dimension to the school's view of its pupils and their 'abilities'. This is especially important because such perspectives act to reinforce a series of assumptions that present low 'ability' and attainment as not only predictable but also somehow a *natural* facet of the current pupil intake. The same teacher, for example, draws upon her 25 years in the school to comment on the relative achievements of successive generations of Clough pupils. Although recent cohorts have outperformed their parents, these advances are seen as highly limited and only confirm the overriding judgement of the school and its 'long tail':

> Our main intake, you know, (. . .) feeder schools are on the [local council] estate and we are looking at lots of kids who are coming from families where the parents have never worked, you know, there are no wage earners in the family, they're on social security. They do not have the expectations for their kids from education that your 'middle-class' or your upwardly mobile working-class parents are going to have for their kids, you know. And many of their parents – I've taught them, remember – they were school 'failures' themselves. And in fact many of these kids have done better than their parents, I will say, because I know of so many of the kids who have been coming through whose parents were almost fully illiterate, for God's sake. And these kids come in and they're reading and writing, they can write, read and write to their parents. They are superior to their parents in that sense. But we're not a true comp.
>
> (Acting head of English, Clough GM)

Although a degree of improvement over time is acknowledged, therefore, the dominant perspective among Clough's teachers contains clear judgements not only about the attainment of their pupils in the past, but also about *future* possibilities. This discourse acts to fix 'ability' and possible attainment within tightly constrained parameters; it positions lower attainment among the working class (or at least non-'upwardly mobile' parts of it) as predictable and inevitable. A crude conflation of social class and 'ability' is clear. The headteacher exemplifies this perspective when he anticipates change only within relatively narrow parameters:

> when you consider that something like the Reading Recovery programme for 6-year-olds is only attempting to make up a few months here and there on a 6-year-old. Making up anything up to four *years* on an 11-year-old is not, without the same sort of one-to-one resources, it's not a goer. (. . .) we can't remediate the disadvantage that comes, that kids bring with them in terms of poor basic skills when the scale of the problem is so large.
>
> (Headteacher, Clough GM)

We do not wish to over-simplify how teachers in Clough view the overall make-up of its pupil population. We have already noted that some teachers dissent from the dominant perspectives, and we want to emphasize that the children are *not* seen simply as a homogeneous block – indeed, increasing energy is being directed at identifying and exploiting perceived differences within the pupil population (see below). However, the overriding view is that the 'long tail' of low-attaining pupils is exerting a negative influence across the entire institution:

> all the time that we have this large tail we can't actually help those kids properly but we *are* diverting resources into *trying* to help them which might more reasonably be spent more broadly across the school. So we don't have the (. . .) resource to put into helping the middling and brighter kids. Everyone's affected.
>
> (Headteacher, Clough GM)

Hence there is a deep sense of frustration and of the need urgently to address a situation where everyone loses: according to this view, the 'tail' loses (because it is too big for the school to cope with) and 'the middling and brighter kids' also lose because resources are soaked up elsewhere. In this context the headteacher's view that resources 'might more reasonably be spent more broadly' is hugely significant. The 'long tail' is seen to place an unacceptable (and unquenchable) drain on the school's resources. The school does not reject the inclusion of lower-attaining pupils in its population *per se*, rather it suggests that it is the disproportionately large number of such children that is problematic for all. This is presented in terms of the impossibility of even a well-resourced support service addressing the needs of such a large group of pupils – a support service that consumes resources (that lead to only limited success) that could otherwise be aimed at higher-attaining pupils under 'true' comprehensive circumstances.

This perspective on the nature of the school's present pupil population provides the context within which the following discussion of increased selection within the school can be understood. The 'long tail' is seen as historically given, harmful to *all* children in the school, and as a weight dragging down the school's performance in all externally monitored exercises. The introduction of limited selection at the point of entry is seen as a start but more urgent action is required if the school is to survive:

> it's no coincidence that, year after year, certain schools are at the top of the table and certain schools are at the bottom. It's purely down, not *purely* but it's largely, *principally* due, to the nature of the intake. So, year after year, [particular local schools] are at the top of the table, [other local schools] are at the bottom (. . .) we're just above the bottom.
>
> (Headteacher, Clough GM)

A note on institutional racism: 'race' and selection at age 11

Throughout the late 1980s and 1990s a characteristic of public policy in general, and of education policy in particular, was the tendency to adopt a deracialized discourse (cf. Gillborn 1995; 1997a; Troyna 1993). That is, 'the omission – deliberately or otherwise – of issues of ethnicity and, more particularly, racism, from the interpretive and analytical frames' (Troyna 1994: 326). Policy makers and their advisers (from government through LEAs to individual schools) have adopted a range of targets and performance measures that frequently position 'consumers' (communities, parents and/or pupils) as a homogeneous block, devoid of internal differences and assumed to enjoy equal access to opportunity and achievement. Such a view ignores the real diversity of experience and achievement nation-wide and, perhaps most importantly, serves to remove racism from the agenda, allowing racial inequalities to go unnoticed and unchecked. Within such an approach it is still possible for policy makers to acknowledge that racism exists (few are foolish enough to completely deny its existence); however, when racism is spoken of in policy debates it is usually positioned in terms of individual prejudice and ignorance – as a kind of personal aberration. Such a perspective actually serves to marginalize racism (cf. Gilroy 1987) and, as Barry Troyna argued so powerfully and consistently, denies the socially constructed and officially sanctioned character of the social and economic processes which remake and reinforce racism on a daily basis. It is in this context that the notion of 'institutional racism' has considerable critical importance. The term allows for the identification of racial disadvantage through the routine and unremarkable operation of rules and processes that seem superficially to have no relevance to ethnicity. Even where no explicit reference is made to 'race' or ethnicity it is possible for practices to be racially discriminatory where their consequence is to unnecessarily and disproportionately disadvantage members of one or more minority ethnic groups: 'Racism is . . . expressed institutionally in the form of systematic practices that deny and exclude blacks from access to social resources' (Wellman 1993: 57).[3]

The introduction of selection 'by ability' at the point of entry to Clough provides the first of several occasions in this study where apparently objective (and colour-blind) procedures might have racially specific consequences. Selection at this point has only recently been introduced in the school and it is too early to say with any degree of certainty whether Black or other minority pupils are clearly at a disadvantage. However, the outlook offers real cause for concern. Later in this chapter we consider the racialized nature of IQ tests and formal assessments of 'general ability'; at this stage we wish to note the way in which other aspects of the school's admissions policy might work against pupils from minority ethnic backgrounds. In particular, the decision to give priority to pupils with siblings who have attended the school might be viewed as a form of indirect discrimination. In 1993, for example, the Commission for Racial Equality (CRE) raised concerns over proposed changes to admissions policies in a number of schools that wished to instigate a siblings and/or a parental prior attendance policy (CRE 1993a; 1993b; 1993c). The CRE was especially critical of the attempt to give weight to the fact that *parents* had attended the school and warned of the need to monitor by ethnicity for any discrepancies in acceptance arising from the siblings rule. While the senior management in Clough has to date not suggested a parental attendance rule, the possible impact of the siblings policy has not been lost on at least one member of staff. Drawing on her first-hand knowledge of Britain's *patriality* immigration rules, this teacher (of minority ethnic background herself) sees the siblings rule as highly significant:

> according to the selection they have to take, you know, brothers and sisters who've been in this school. It's again like the government's immigration policy, you know, where they're, you know, this kith-and-kin business.

The Commonwealth Immigrants Act (1968) created a distinction within the previously uniform rights of abode for British citizens. Specifically, right of entry and abode was limited to passport holders who themselves were, or had a parent or grandparent who had been, 'born, adopted, or naturalized in the UK' (Mason 1995: 28). Without ever directly referring to 'race' or colour, this rule served to remove the right of entry and abode for many British passport holders in the New Commonwealth (predominantly Black and Asian people) while retaining it for the so-called 'Old Commonwealth' (Australia, Canada and New Zealand). For this teacher the parallels are clear and direct:

> on a similar basis I think that's how they'll weed out the Black kids because there'll be more white children who've had brothers and sisters, because I think Black people are beginning to move into this area more recently. So the chances that a lot of Black children will have brothers and sisters here, oh there will be some, obviously, but not as many.

As we have stated, it is too early to judge whether the school's siblings rule will have any such discriminatory effect. It is worth noting, however, first, that this teacher is correct in assuming that the minority ethnic population locally is a relatively recent phenomenon (reflecting both social and geographical mobility among part of London's minority communities); second, the school has no clear plans to monitor intake by ethnicity (as recommended by the CRE). For this teacher at least, the possibility of an increasingly racially exclusive intake is not out of step with her perception of other developments in this school and more generally in the locality:

> I don't think that they'll turn away clever Black children because they obviously want their A-to-Cs but I can, I can already, see that there will be huge changes in the composition. And that worries me because in [this LEA] I mean there aren't many schools where there's, you know, the number of Black children like we've got here. I mean there's some schools in [this LEA], you know, you'd think there's no Black people in this country (. . .) I'm not saying that that's what they're going to do but definitely going towards that.

'Ability': definition and measurement

You can't *give* someone ability, can you?
(Headteacher, Clough GM)

We noted earlier in this chapter that in Clough the relationship between 'intake' and final achievement in GCSEs is seen as practically inevitable. The decision to seek GM status was the most obvious of several moves meant to break this cycle. By enhancing the school's status through greater funding, and with the possibility of increased selection at the point of entry, the school attempted to do something about the size of its low-attaining 'tail'. Such moves, however, only promise results in the long term, and more immediate action was judged necessary to address the pressing need to change the school's position in relation to the A-to-C economy. These various strategies are documented in the remainder of our analysis: crucial to each strategy is a particular notion of 'ability'.

With the prior attainment of the pupil intake positioned as of central importance to eventual GCSE outcomes, it is no surprise that Clough prioritizes the measurement of 'ability' on entry: as we will show, these measures play a vital role *throughout* pupils' careers in the school. In order to understand the significance attached to these measures it is also necessary to explore teachers' assumptions about the nature of 'ability'. This is no simple task because discussions of 'ability' often take for granted a series of assumptions that, while exerting a considerable influence on life in the school, are rarely voiced in any explicit or systematic way. The following exchange between the headteacher and a deputy head, therefore, is unusual in exposing some of the deep assumptions informing the headteacher's conceptualization of 'ability':

Head: You can't achieve more than you're capable of, can you? Can you? There are kids who *surprise* you, but I'm not sure that's quite the same thing.

Deputy: If you can *under*-achieve why can't you *over*-achieve?

Head: What does 'over-achieve' mean? That you've done more than you're capable of doing? You can't do more than you're capable of. You can do less than you're capable of, as most of us do most of the time. Don't we? (. . .) if I sat and did that test I'm sure I'd do less well than I *should* do because I frankly couldn't be bothered to do it because I don't like doing them, I find it tedious, so I really wouldn't give it much attention. But I couldn't do better on it. Not absolutely. I might *by freak* do better than I should do but that wouldn't be over-achievement, that would just be a flaw of the test that it allowed me to randomly achieve better than I'm really capable of. Statistically it would be possible for me to guess every answer in that test and come up with 100 per cent. It's a small percentage possibility, but it is possible. So, but that wouldn't mean I'd over-achieved, it'd mean that the test is sort of, well, the test isn't flawed but statistically it's a possibility. But I can't do better than I can do. Can I? (. . .)

Deputy: It's semantics. If you guess and you do better than you should have done you *have* over-achieved, whether it's by guessing, depends how you get there.

Head: But I haven't achieved anything really.

Deputy: You've achieved a result in the test.

This extract is particularly important. First, it illustrates that although the term 'ability' is used frequently by all staff on a day-to-day basis, its precise meaning is hardly ever interrogated: this exchange only arose because the deputy overheard part of a field interview with the head and decided to comment. In the normal run of school business the concept of 'ability' is not subjected to such detailed consideration. Second, it is clear that the head views 'ability' in terms of an intellectual potential that is not only measurable but also relatively fixed. According to such a view a pupil with 'ability' at age 11 is destined for success, assuming they work hard and realize their promise: 'You can do less than you're capable of, as most of us do most of the time'. However, according to this view of 'ability' (as a fixed intellectual potential), by definition, it is simply not possible to exceed these inner limits: 'if I sat and did that test I'm sure I'd do less well than I *should* do because I frankly couldn't be bothered (. . .) But I couldn't do better on it'. It is hard to overstate the importance of this position, not only because the headteacher is the principal policy maker in the school but also because his view seems to us to encapsulate the understanding that informs most teachers' actions in Clough (and Taylor, our other case-study school) regarding the measurement and interpretation of 'ability'. It is a definition that promotes and sustains a series of institutional processes which systematically select pupils for very different destinations.

Clough GM school elicits and makes continuing use of a range of data that are seen to provide measures of each pupils' 'ability'. In practice, the principal indicator of 'ability' is a test produced and sold commercially by the National Foundation for Educational Research (NFER). Within Clough this test is understood to provide an accurate measurement of 'general ability':

> we give every kid in year 7 a standard test. (. . .) And they're *indicators* of ability, whatever that means. And obviously indicators of some sort of *general* ability rather than just sort of subject-specific ability.
>
> (Headteacher, Clough GM)

The year 7 test produces a numerical value, which some Clough teachers refer to as an 'IQ score'. This informal nomenclature is revealing and absolutely in line with how many teachers, including most members of senior management, understand the test. The most traditional and extreme view of 'intelligence' held among psychometricians defines intelligence as a single 'thing' (often referred to as '*g*') that is accurately assessed by IQ tests that 'measure virtually all that's important for school and job success' (Sternberg 1996: 12).[4] This is precisely how the NFER test is viewed within Clough GM. Supplemented by tests taken in the final year of primary school (that produce reading and spelling 'ages' for each pupil) these tests, and the identification of 'ability' that they are assumed to provide, have one ultimate goal – the prediction of GCSE outcomes:

> we have found them [the tests] helpful as indicators of GCSE performance, and in that there is some correlation between the standard tests and the GCSE outcomes (. . .) the correlation coefficient is somewhere between 0.65 and 0.7, which is quite a strong correlation. (. . .) So for a significant proportion you can be confident that the thing *is* a good predictor of their GCSE results.
>
> (Headteacher, Clough GM)

As we have already shown, GCSE outcomes are *the* indicator of success within the A-to-C economy. Given the staff's belief in the predictive power of the NFER test, it is not surprising that pupils' scores (generated in year 7, remember) form a significant part (in combination with gradings from primary school) of the school's attempt to improve performance in the A-to-C economy. The utility of these tests rests upon a particular notion of 'ability'. The school's understanding of 'ability', and its responses to this, are underpinned by two related premises. We have already commented on the first premise, that 'ability' is seen as a relatively fixed potential. Outcomes, therefore, are predictable. As eluded to in the head–deputy exchange (above), an individual pupil cannot, by definition, exceed their ability, although they can fail to fulfil their promise. This then leads to a second premise. If the correlation between measures of ability and future performance fails, that is, a pupil performs *better* than predicted, this is interpreted as a characteristic of the test (a statistical anomaly) within predictable limits. Even in the face of apparently contradictory evidence, therefore, the first premise (that ability is fixed and outcomes are predictable) remains unchallenged. The definition of 'ability' as a relatively fixed and measurable potential remains impervious to contradictory evidence: a pupil defined as 'able' can fail through laziness, a pupil defined as lacking 'ability' who succeeds has not (in the headteacher's eyes) undermined the test (nor the dominant definition of ability) but is simply one of the few anomalous cases that will always occur because no test is 100 per cent accurate:

> there will always be a number for whom the correlation doesn't work, a percentage. But what you don't know is who the individuals are. That's the nature of the statistical analysis. So for a significant proportion you can be confident that the thing *is* a good predictor of their GCSE results. But some kids will score, on a standardized basis, 80 and get good results which they shouldn't, and some kids will score 110 and not get good results and that will happen.
>
> (Headteacher, Clough GM)

Despite some notable failures of prediction, therefore, the school's faith in the overall utility of its bought-in 'IQ test' remains intact. Indeed, when the correlation between a given test and attainment fails, other indicators of 'ability' are invoked as a means of explanation. The means of measuring 'ability' *cannot* be undermined within the terms of this perspective, and the *existence* of a general ability, as a fixed potential, is never seriously questioned:

> There are all sorts of other factors to do with value added to do with whether kids achieve or not like, for example, you can give a kid a standardized non-verbal test on which he or she scores very highly suggesting good basic ability, which should indicate good examination performance. And you can then give them a reading test and discover they can't read.
>
> (Headteacher, Clough GM)

Similarly, the possibility of higher than expected performance in particular subject areas, notably the arts or 'non-academic' subjects, is again explained in terms that preserve belief in the NFER test. As the test identifies 'general ability', in the eyes of the headteacher, it remains plausible, although rare, for a 'low'-ability pupil to have a 'talent' in a specific area:

> These kind of tests wouldn't necessarily tell you that someone's really good at art. So you might get a good result in art. And you might have a particular *talent* in those areas where it's that kind of thing. But, you know, even that, I have to say, is fairly infrequent.
>
> (Headteacher, Clough GM)

Subscribing to a notion of fixed ability might be expected to lead to extreme pessimism in a school with a 'long' and 'wagging tail'. Yet the identification of fixed abilities in year 7 functions in a range of ways through-out pupils' careers in Clough. First, as we shall see, it provides a supposedly fair and scientifically grounded basis for targeting resources differentially (via the sorting of pupils into different classes and subject areas) which holds the promise of maximizing higher-grade GCSE passes. Second, it allows the school to monitor the ongoing attainment of pupils and compare this to what their 'ability' indicates they should be attaining; that is, it enables the identification of pupils who are apparently not fulfilling their promise – these 'under-achievers' are a major concern for both our case-study schools (see Chapter 6). Third, the ascription of particular 'abilities' in year 7 acts to sustain and reinscribe the dominant (though often implicit) notion of 'ability' as both general and fixed – a notion that is crucial for the school's responses to the demands of the A-to-C economy.[5]

A(nother) note on institutional racism: 'race', intelligence and IQ

'An instrument of oppression'

> . . . the IQ test has served as an instrument of oppression against the poor – dressed in the trappings of science, rather than politics. The message of science is heard respectfully, particularly when the tidings it carries are soothing to the public conscience. There are few more sooth-ing messages than those historically delivered by the IQ testers. The poor, the foreign-born, and racial minorities were shown to be stupid. They were shown to have been born that way. The under-privileged are today demonstrated to be ineducable, a message as soothing to the public purse as to the public conscience.
>
> (Kamin 1974: 15–16)

A quarter of a century after Leon Kamin published this damning verdict on the misuses of IQ tests, his words remain as accurate and important as ever. The continued appeal of tests that seem to offer an objective basis for dif-ferentiation is embodied in the eagerness with which the headteacher in Clough has embraced the NFER test used by the school. In this section we wish to reflect critically on how issues of 'race' and racism can operate through the apparently scientific guise of various test instruments and the assumptions that underpin them. As an example, we focus in particular on the marketing and 'standardization' of the *Cognitive Abilities Test* (Thorndike *et al.* 1986; Thorndike and Hagen 1986) widely advertised and distributed by the NFER-Nelson publishing company (an associate company of NFER). Before examining these issues in detail, however, it is necessary to set the scene by outlining something of the broader context of debates about 'race', intelligence and IQ.[6]

In 1994 the issue of 'race' and intelligence hit the headlines. The publica-tion of *The Bell Curve* (Herrnstein and Murray 1994) generated enormous popular interest and debate. Not least as a result of considerable financial and other forms of sponsorship by conservative foundations (Apple 1996: 128), the book became a hot topic for the popular media and a major publishing (and political) success – selling 400,000 copies in two months, featuring on the cover of *Newsweek* and becoming a resident member of the *New York Times* bestseller list (Banks 1995; Kamin 1995). Outwardly the book does not look like a candidate for such popular consumption: initially available only in hardback, it runs to 845 pages and includes 44 tables and more than 90 illustrations (mostly graphs). Nevertheless, its key arguments are presented boldly:

> *Putting it all together, success and failure in the American economy, and all that goes with it, are increasingly a matter of the genes that people inherit.*
> (Herrnstein and Murray 1994: 91; emphasis in original)

> *the average white person tests higher than about 84 percent of the population of blacks . . . job hiring and promotion procedures that are truly fair and unbiased will produce the racial disparities that public policy tries to prevent.*
> (Herrnstein and Murray 1994: 269, 479; emphasis in original)

In Britain also the book featured heavily in popular debate, being hailed by some as a brave rejection of political correctness (Eysenck 1994) that finally spoke out for the interests of 'ordinary whites' (Johnson 1994: 32). Writing in the journal of the Institute of Economic Affairs, one of the country's most influential right-wing organizations, and in the *Times Higher Education Supplement*, James Tooley (1995a; 1995b) suggested that the book offered a scientific basis for the complete restructuring of secondary education. According to him, IQ tests could be administered at age 10 and those revealed as lacking the necessary intelligence could be 'liberated' from the need to attend compulsory schooling that presently sells them 'an egalitarian vision which brings only disappointment' (Tooley 1995a: 7). These debates, of course (like the data in *The Bell Curve* itself), are not new: they revisit, and re-energize, long-standing arguments about nature versus nurture and, in particular, controversies concerning supposed inherent differences in intelligence between 'racial' groups (cf. Eysenck 1971; 1973; Jensen 1969; 1972; 1991).

In an attempt to disentangle some of the claims and counter-claims surrounding IQ debates, Robert J. Sternberg characterizes the views of authors such as Herrnstein and Murray as 'myth' (see Table 3.1). As IBM Professor of Psychology and Education at Yale, Sternberg is writing from the perspective of a confirmed psychometrician. His theory of 'triarchic' intelligence is a prominent addition to current attempts within psychology to isolate and measure different 'types' of intelligence (cf. Gardner 1983; Mayer 1997; Sternberg 1985). Consequently, Sternberg's characterization of 'mythical countermyth' and 'truth' regarding intelligence has to be read as originating from a particular part of the debate. Nevertheless, Sternberg has been openly

Table 3.1 Robert J. Sternberg on 'myths, mythical countermyths and truths about intelligence'

Myth	Mythical countermyth	Truth
1 Intelligence is one thing, *g* (or IQ).	Intelligence is so many things you can hardly count them.	Intelligence is multidimensional but scientifically tractable.
2 The social order is a natural outcome of the IQ pecking order.	Tests wholly create a social order.	The social order is partially but not exclusively created by tests.
3 Intelligence cannot be taught to any meaningful degree.	We can perform incredible feats in teaching individuals to be more intelligent.	We can teach intelligence in at least some degree, but cannot effect radical changes at this point.
4 IQ tests measure virtually all that's important for school and job success.	IQ tests measure virtually nothing that's important for school and job success.	IQ tests measure skills that are of moderate importance in school success and of modest importance in job success.
5 We are using tests too little, losing valuable information.	We're overusing tests and should abolish them.	Tests, when properly interpreted, can serve a useful but limited function, but often they are not properly interpreted.
6 We as a society are getting stupider because of the dysgenic effects of stupid superbreeders.	We have no reason at all to fear any decline in intellectual abilities among successive generations.	We have some reason to fear loss of intellectual abilities in future generations, but the problem is not stupid superbreeders.
7 Intelligence is essentially all inherited except for trivial and unexplainable variance.	Intelligence is essentially all environmental except for trivial and unexplainable variance.	Intelligence involves substantial heritable and environmental components in interaction.
8 Racial differences in IQ clearly lead to differential outcomes.	Racial differences in IQ have nothing to do with differential environmental outcomes.	We don't really understand the relationships among race, IQ, and environmental outcomes.
9 We should write off stupid people.	There's no such thing as a stupid person. Everyone is smart.	We need to rethink what we mean by 'stupid' and 'smart'.

Source: Sternberg (1996: Table 1).

critical of the 'social Darwinism' that figures in Herrnstein and Murray's work (Sternberg 1996: 12). He argues that in key respects *The Bell Curve* is outside the consensus of contemporary work on intelligence. Contrary to Herrnstein and Murray, Sternberg considers that IQ is demonstrably not fixed; that many IQ tests are not generally useful; and that the significance of heritability is widely misrepresented (Sternberg 1995; 1996). With regard to 'racial' differences, he argues that 'Herrnstein and Murray invite the reader to conclude that race differences are due to genetics, even though they have no evidence of that, and they know it' (Sternberg 1995). Nevertheless, the racist discourse that presents Black people as inherently less intelligent continues to figure in apparently credible public expressions of 'expert' opinion. At the height of the furore surrounding *The Bell Curve*, for example, the *Wall Street Journal* published a statement entitled 'Mainstream science on intelligence' (13 December 1994: A18). Signed by 52 'professors – all experts in intelligence and allied fields' – the statement embodied some of the most simple and closed notions of intelligence as 'highly heritable' and well measured by IQ tests. The statement repeated the all too familiar line that ethnic groups 'often differ in where their members tend to cluster along the IQ line', noting that 'The bell curve for whites is centered roughly around IQ 100; the bell curve for American blacks roughly around 85; and those for different subgroups of Hispanics roughly midway between those for whites and blacks'. There has, of course, been a continuing and bitterly fought battle about the impossibility of creating a 'culture-free test' (see Kamin 1981). For many, the entire history of IQ testing is characteristic of 'pseudo-science', that is, the presentation of ideological prejudice disguised as 'scientific inquiry and hypothesis-testing' (Blum 1978: 145). Either way, one might anticipate a little caution from such self-proclaimed experts; the 'mainstream' professors writing in the *Wall Street Journal*, however, have no time for such concerns – the certainty of their belief in the validity of IQ tests is undiminished:

> Intelligence tests are not culturally biased against American blacks or other native-born, English-speaking peoples in the US. Rather, IQ scores predict equally accurately for all such Americans, regardless of race and social class. Individuals who do not understand English well can be given either a nonverbal test or one in their native language.
>
> (*Wall Street Journal*, 13 December 1994: A18)[7]

The breathtaking confidence of such a bold statement belies both the racist history of IQ tests (cf. Gould 1981) and the facts about past, and current, practices:

> With the special status ascribed to IQ tests, little attention was given to the fact that in the development of IQ tests minority children were not included in the standardization of the instrument (Kamin 1974). Further, in actually carrying out research on differences between groups on IQ tests, little, if any, attention was given to social class, inequality

in educational opportunity, language background of subjects, or cultural differences between the groups being compared.

(Padilla and Lindholm 1995: 97)

'Intelligence testing . . . testing . . .'. I began turning the phrase over in my mind and what should have been blindingly obvious (and for that very reason rarely is) hit me. What the pro-differences [in race and IQ] camp were doing was indeed *testing* the intelligence of the group they identified with *against* that of an Other group. It was intrinsically advers-arial, like arm-wrestling – a 'test' of strength. It was, moreover, virtually, the only ostensibly scientific weapon left in the racist armoury.

(Richards 1997: 287; emphasis in original)

It is clear, therefore, that views of intelligence testing and its history con-tinue to generate considerable controversy but little consensus. The relevance of 'racial' differences is especially contentious. Historically, IQ tests have oper-ated as an apparently 'objective' and 'scientific' measure that has, in fact, systematically disadvantaged minority pupils and provided palliatives for a system happy to be reassured that the relative failure of minorities reflects their own inner deficits rather than any unfairness in the system. In view of this history, Clough GM's embrace of such testing as 'a good predictor of their GCSE results' offers considerable cause for concern.

Cognitive ability, progress and GCSE predictions

Figure 3.1 presents an extract from a half-page advertisement in the *Times Educational Supplement*. Under the headline 'Would you find this information useful for your Year 7 intake?', the advertisement promotes the Cognitive Abilities Test (CAT) and speaks directly to the pressures of the A-to-C economy. In a box entitled 'GCSE indicators' the first three items of information offer predictions for the number of GCSE passes (in the ranges A*–C and A*–G) and calculate the 'probability of achieving five GCSE grades A*–C'. Each of these criteria, of course, has immense importance within the construction of the school league tables. The deployment of the all-important benchmark of five higher-grade passes is particularly noteworthy.

According to its authors, '[t]he *Cognitive Abilities Test* provides a set of measures of the individual's ability to use and manipulate abstract and symbolic relationships' (Thorndike *et al.* 1986: 1). Notwithstanding the funda-mental doubts raised in previous work about the possibility of creating a 'culture-fair', non-biased test, we wish to examine the CAT as an example of how the demands of the A-to-C economy might lead users to adopt such an instrument without fully interrogating its technical specifications. First, we examine how recently the material was 'standardized'. Then, we consider the ethnic diversity of relevant sample populations.

The CAT was originally standardized in 1972 using 'a representative national sample' and subsequently 're-standardised' in 1984 (Thorndike *et al.* 1986: 82). More than a decade has passed, therefore, since the test's 're-standardisation'

Figure 3.1   Extract from an NFER-Nelson advertisement

Cognitive abilities test   **Individual pupil profiles**

School: Chalkhead School	*Name*: Anna Petersen	*CAT level*: D
Class/Group: Y7	*Age*: 11 years 10 months	*Date of testing*: September 1995
No. of pupils: 91	*Sex*: Female	

GCSE indicators	
GCSE grades A*–C	7
GCSE grades A*–G	11
Probability of achieving 5 GCSE grades A*–C	85%
Mean overall grade	C
Number of GCSE entries	11
Total points score	59
Mean top 5 points score	6

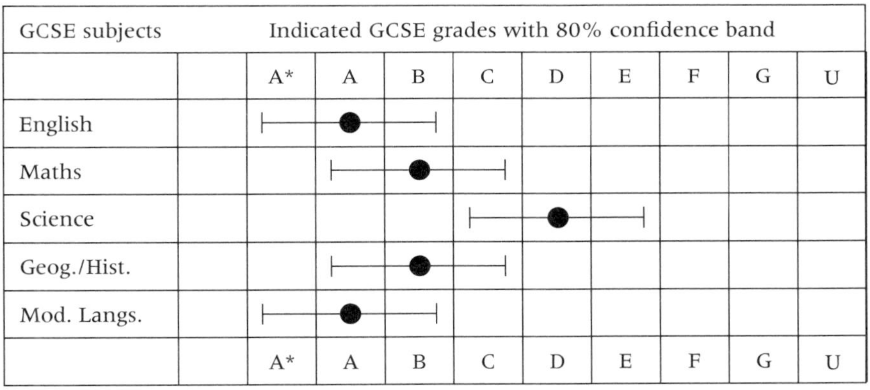

GCSE subjects		Indicated GCSE grades with 80% confidence band								
		A*	A	B	C	D	E	F	G	U
English		├──●──┤								
Maths			├──●──┤							
Science					├──●──┤					
Geog./Hist.			├──●──┤							
Mod. Langs.		├──●──┤								
		A*	A	B	C	D	E	F	G	U

Source: *Times Educational Supplement*, 5 July 1996: 9.

– a period that has seen huge reforms of the educational system and witnessed dramatic changes in overall levels of attainment (see Chapter 2 above). Despite this time period the cover of both the *Administration Manual* (Thorndike *et al.* 1986) and the *Pupil's Book* (Thorndike and Hagen 1986) feature a diagonal flash across the lower right corner that proclaims 'Re-standardised Edition'. A more informative design might read 'Last standardised in 1984'. The covers also feature the faces of six children (represented as two-colour negatives), one of whom appears to be of minority ethnic origin (an African

Caribbean boy). However, the technical appendix does not suggest that ethnic minority pupils necessarily featured prominently in the exercise upon which the test's GCSE predictions are based.

Although the *CAT* documents are dated with a 1986 copyright notice, it is clear that recent reprints (and specifically the one featured in the *Times Educational Supplement* advertisement in Figure 3.1) have been newly amended to include the results of 'The 1995 GCSE Correlation Study' (Thorndike *et al.* 1986: 88–94), on which the advertised GCSE predictions are based. The authors state: 'We can be confident that 80 per cent of pupils achieving any particular CAT score will be likely to achieve the GCSE grade predicted in the tables [provided]' (Thorndike *et al.* 1986: 90).[8] These predictions are based on returns from a sample that the authors admit is neither 'rigorously selected' nor 'nationally representative' (Thorndike *et al.* 1986: 88). Nonetheless, they are confident in their ability to extrapolate on the basis of data from *two* local authorities, described as follows:

> the two LEAs are geographically contrasted and reflect a wide range of school types, ethnic backgrounds and social classifications (. . .) one in the north west of England and the other in the south of England. NFER-NELSON therefore gratefully acknowledges the contribution made by East Sussex and Lancashire LEAs to this study.
>
> (Thorndike *et al.* 1986: 88, 91)

By examining data produced in the 1991 Census, and DfEE returns for 1997, we are able to judge something of the school-age population in these two LEAs:[9] the results *do not* suggest that East Sussex and Lancashire provide a firm foundation for adequately representing ethnic diversity. According to the DfEE, for example, both LEAs have a greater proportion of white pupils than the national average.[10] Compared with all English LEAs in 1991, for children aged 5–15, East Sussex is one of the *least* ethnically diverse authorities, ranked 30th (from more than 100 LEAs) on the proportion of children (97.1 per cent) who are 'white'. Lancashire is somewhat more diverse, ranking 63rd (90.5 per cent). When we compare the LEAs for the representation of the main minority ethnic groups the situation is little improved. For the proportion of 5–15-year-olds classified as 'South Asian' – that is, of Indian, Pakistani or Bangladeshi ethnic origin – Lancashire is ranked 32nd among all LEAs (8.11 per cent) and East Sussex 85th (0.81 per cent). For the proportion of 5–15-year-olds classified as 'Black' (including Black Caribbean and Black African), East Sussex ranks 73rd (0.57 per cent) and Lancashire 83rd (0.45 per cent). These figures mean that neither authority ranks among the upper quartile of LEAs for the relative proportion of ethnic minority pupils. The situation is especially worrying in relation to Black pupils, where both LEAs appear in the lower half of English authorities. These figures raise considerable doubt about the range of ethnic minority pupils who could have been involved in the NFER's 1995 GCSE Correlation Study. These doubts are important because the findings of multi-level statistical analyses in ethnically diverse contexts suggest that pupils in some minority ethnic groups make greater progress during secondary school (all other things being equal) than their white peers.

During the 1980s and 1990s a good deal of attention focused on studies using 'multi-level' statistical modelling approaches to examine pupil progress and school 'effectiveness' (cf. Goldstein 1987; Gray *et al.* 1996; Mortimore *et al.* 1994; Reynolds *et al.* 1996; Sammons *et al.* 1995). The debates about the pros and cons of such work have generated considerable heat (see Chapter 2). There is insufficient space to do justice to the range of debates here; suffice it to say that although some interesting findings have begun to emerge, multi-level modelling is increasingly revealing the complexity of educational progress and raising doubts about the validity of some of the more simplistic claims made on its behalf by policy makers and their advisers (cf. Angus 1993; Drew and Gray 1991; Goldstein 1997). It is clear, for example, that in some ways application of school effectiveness and school improvement findings may actually be antithetical to equality of opportunity: as Geoff Whitty (1997b: 156) has noted 'one conclusion to be drawn from a reading of the pioneering *Fifteen Thousand Hours* research (Rutter *et al.* 1979) is that, if all schools performed as well as the best schools, the stratification of achievement by social class would be even more stark than it is now'. Much school effectiveness and improvement writing has been blind to ethnic diversity (Hatcher 1997; 1998). Where attention has been paid to these issues, however, a relatively common finding is that pupils in different ethnic groups do not make similar progress, especially in secondary school. When issues such as prior attainment and social class background are taken into account, for example, several studies indicate that South Asian and Chinese pupils, in particular, tend to make rather better progress than their white peers in the same schools (Sammons 1995; Thomas and Mortimore 1994; Thomas *et al.* 1994; 1997). The results for Black pupils have tended to be less consistent but also show variability: Pam Sammon's study of pupils' progress over a nine-year period, for example, found that 'in terms of relative progress the Asian . . . and Caribbean groups obtained significantly better GCSE results than their ESWI [English, Scots, Welsh and Irish] peers' (Sammons 1995: 479–80).

These results must, of course, be treated with due caution: none of the projects has dealt with nationally representative samples and the findings for minority ethnic groups have not always been consistent (cf. Gillborn and Gipps 1996: 39–42). Nevertheless, sufficiently large and robust studies now exist to raise considerable concern in relation to the issues that exercise us here. Specifically, we have shown that Clough GM uses a 'standardized' NFER test of year 7 pupils as a basis for predicting GCSE outcomes. Although we cannot be certain precisely which test the school is using,[11] we have seen (in relation to the CAT) that this kind of use is not only sanctioned by test makers, but used as a deliberate marketing ploy (Figure 3.1). We have shown, however, not only that the test advertised in Figure 3.1 is somewhat old (having last been 're-standardised' before the Education Reform Act 1988), but also that the exercise upon which the GCSE predictions are based did not draw upon LEAs likely to provide a sufficiently diverse sample to represent substantially the various minority ethnic groups resident in Britain. The test, therefore, is likely to produce GCSE predictions based largely on the performance of white pupils.[12] And yet multi-level research suggests that pupils in certain minority ethnic groups, including the main South Asian and Black groups, sometimes make relatively *greater* progress (after year 7) than their white peers, all other things being equal. Consequently, GCSE predictions based on white norms are likely to underestimate the GCSE grades of many ethnic minority pupils.

The significance of this analysis is considerable. As we have noted, there is a large body of work on the discriminatory practices that have taken shape under the umbrella of 'science', especially linked with notions of IQ and supposed heritable 'racial' differences. Even if we were to disregard this work (and there is no good reason to do so), there are significant problems with how Clough interprets and uses its tests of year 7 pupils. Clough's senior management read its 'IQ test' results as a good predictor of GCSE outcomes – a position that test makers encourage, but which might systematically disadvantage ethnic minority pupils by underestimating their likely grades. If this underestimation is taking place (and it is difficult to see how we can be certain about this, even within the psychometricians' own terms) this would represent a hugely important case of institutionalized racism. That is, minority pupils stand to be systematically disadvantaged by the very devices upon which selection decisions are based.

Throughout this section we have tried to remain cautious in a field littered with misplaced certainty. The possibility of such institutionalized racism, however, is revealed as particularly serious when we consider the extent to which the various year 7 tests (and especially pupils' 'IQ scores') are used throughout Clough: we examine these practices further in the next chapter.

Conclusions

In this chapter we have set out our understanding of the 'A-to-C economy' and begun to trace how its effects are translated into increasing selection in secondary education. Despite unease on the part of many teachers (and the resistance of some), the pressures of school league tables and public discourses of educational success/failure combine to enforce a situation where GCSE higher grades are all-important. In the A-to-C economy the needs of the school, its pupils and the league tables have become synonymous – as Taylor's headteacher put it: 'the best thing that we can do for our pupils is to strive to get the greatest possible proportion achieving that five high-grade benchmark'.

In order to understand how these pressures are experienced on a day-to-day basis, in this chapter we have focused in particular on Clough GM, a school where teachers have a clear and somewhat depressing picture of their pupil population. They characterize their intake as 'bottom-heavy' and suppose a causal relationship with the school's history of recruiting working-class pupils. This belief has been mobilized to support the introduction of limited selection 'by ability' at the point of entry to the school (in year 7, aged 11) and to justify attempts to recruit greater numbers of middle-class pupils, who are assumed to have a different (and superior) 'ability' profile. In this way social class and 'ability' are linked in the teachers' eyes.

The notion of 'ability' is hugely important in Clough, but is rarely interrogated. In practice many teachers, including the headteacher, adopt a position that equates 'ability' with the crudest and most discriminatory definitions of 'intelligence/IQ', that is, as a fixed and generalized academic potential that can be measured reasonably accurately through certain written tests. This approach assumes that future outcomes (especially GCSE performance) can be predicted with a high degree of confidence and, in fact, provides a perspective that is impervious to counter-argument, even where pupils do *not* achieve as predicted. Hence, if a supposedly 'bright' pupil fails, it is seen as an individual weakness or failure of effort. If a pupil deemed to have little 'ability' actually succeeds academically, this is seen as an anomalous case that is within acceptable limits (since no test can be 100 per cent certain). The possibility that a greater number of similarly labelled pupils might have achieved highly, had the tests not been used to close down opportunities, is rarely if ever considered.

The simplistic and regressive understanding of 'ability' which circulates among teachers in Clough is shared widely in British education. It is a view that rarely finds explicit or conscious expression. It is possible that relatively few educationists would advance such a position if only they realized its full implications. Nevertheless, it is a perspective that shapes policy and practice in both our case-study schools (see Chapter 6 for relevant data on Taylor Comprehensive) and informs national policy making. In 1998, for example, the DfEE wrote 'to around 1 million parents [of children aged 4 and 5] urging them not to try to coach their children for the [newly introduced baseline] assessments as it might "hide the real situation"' (Ghouri 1998: 18). Such a perspective clearly embodies the notion that test results must not be contaminated by 'coaching', they must be free to record pre-existing ('natural'?) differences. The very idea that such tests can be prepared for, in this way, should rationally destroy any belief that they measure innate potential and yet, as we have already seen, these beliefs are impervious to such logic. Indeed, a belief in 'the distinct abilities of individual pupils' is a fundamental assumption at the heart of contemporary education reform (Labour Party 1997: 3–4; see Chapter 2 above). These understandings of 'ability', as a fixed, generalized and measurable potential, are completely incompatible with critical notions of equal opportunities and at odds even with leading contemporary research in psychometrics:

tests of abilities are no different from conventional tests of achievement, teacher-made tests administered in school, or assessments of job performance. Although tests of abilities are used as predictors of these other kinds of performance, the temporal priority of their administration should not be confused with some kind of psychological priority . . . There is no qualitative distinction among the various kinds of measures.

(Sternberg 1998: 11)

Tests of 'ability', therefore, are essentially the same as any other assessment. They measure learnt, mutable skills not fixed and generalized potential:

The fact that Billy and Jimmy have different IQs tells us something about differences in what they now do. It does not tell us anything fixed about what ultimately they will be able to do.

(Sternberg 1998: 18)

The school's belief in the scientific validity and predictive power of its chosen 'IQ test' is especially worrying in view of the historic effects of such approaches, which have systematically discriminated against ethnic minorities and the working-class. Although psychometricians differ in their view of 'intelligence' and its relation to 'race', there is ample evidence of similar tests operating to disadvantage minorities. Indeed, even within the terms of debate set by the testers themselves, there is evidence that claims about 'standardization' and ethnically diverse samples may overstate the representativeness of the populations upon which GCSE predictions are based. The best current evidence on rates of progress in secondary schools, for example, suggests that minority pupils tend to make greater progress than their white peers, other things being equal. Consequently, if the tests make predictions based on white profiles then they will systematically underestimate black and other minority results – a possibility that would represent institutional racism on a grand scale.

The demands of the 'A-to-C economy' and the assumed nature of 'ability' are vitally important. These factors underpin so many aspects of life in our case-study schools that it is difficult to overstate their significance. This chapter has set the scene, therefore, for the following analysis that traces the increasingly widespread, and sometimes hidden, selection that shapes pupils' experiences of secondary education. We begin, in the next chapter, with selection in the first three years of secondary schooling.

4

Selection 11–14

fast groups, 'left-over' mixed ability and the subject options process

Debates about the rights and wrongs of academic selection frequently assume that, whatever a school's chosen approach, it is a fairly simple matter to identify what is happening. Even if pupils and their parents do not fully understand the system, surely teachers (and especially senior managers and headteachers) will have the processes in view and under control. The reality is not so simple.

In the previous chapter we explored the understanding of 'ability' that informs the schools' approaches: in this chapter we begin our analysis of how that understanding is mobilized as our case-study schools begin to use selection to separate pupils with a view to the demands of the A-to-C economy. With a mind to continuity with the previous chapter, we stay with Clough GM as the main vehicle by which to examine the discussions, experiences and perceptions of selection at the school level. Our focus here is on selection in the lower school (years 7, 8 and 9 – Key Stage 3 of the National Curriculum – when pupils are aged 11–14).

Selection has been introduced and extended across the lower school in Clough. The system is changing over time, with so-called 'fast groups' covering a larger proportion of pupils than was planned initially. Nevertheless, there is considerable uncertainty about the specifics of the organization: the term 'mixed-ability', for example, is still used for groups that are markedly less mixed than was previously the case. Additionally, an attempt to better 'target' learning support has led to a situation where the *language* needs of certain pupils are effectively equated with special *learning* needs, operating to select them out of 'fast' groups. The situation does not neatly fit into any simple description: setting by ability is used in certain core subjects, 'mixed-ability' groups remain in name, but are located within a system that in some respects resembles broad-banding or even streaming.

The chapter concludes with an examination of the subject options process: a point of apparent curricular 'choice' that, in fact, operates as a further means of selection with an eye to Key Stage 4 and pupil grouping in the upper school. It is useful to begin, however, with a broad overview of discussions about setting and selection within Clough.

Perceptions of setting and mixed-ability teaching

Clough GM utilizes a range of selection practices at different stages in secondary schooling. Some forms of selection have been used in the upper school for some time, but it is only recently that teaching in the lower school has moved in this direction. One of the most significant recent changes in Clough school policy has been to move away from mixed-ability teaching groups as an assumed norm. Interestingly, many teachers, including several members of senior management, suggest that in some senses 'mixed ability' is considered the 'right' thing to do but is being discarded because it has not produced the desired results. In this sense there seems to be some dissonance concerning the type of pupil grouping that is preferred morally and/or socially and the approach that teachers expect to produce better examination results (necessary in terms of the A-to-C economy):

> We've changed the way teaching groups are organized in recent history to have rather more setting and less mixed-ability approaches. Till a couple of years ago we had a lower school that was almost entirely mixed ability and I suppose we've been through the same cycle as many other people. We thought that it was the right thing to do, in many ways it probably is, but it doesn't work.
>
> (Headteacher, Clough GM)

The criticism of mixed-ability teaching rests on a number of related premises. It is argued that mixed-ability teaching often results in what the headteacher describes as 'teaching to the middle'. This perspective legitimates the move to setting by suggesting that it is in the best interests of both the most and least able pupils:[1]

> we, in common no doubt with every other school in the country, talk a lot about differentiation. And people say: 'Yes it's wonderful isn't it?' And then you look in classes and find that in fact in most mixed-ability classes there's an awful lot of whole-class teaching and an awful lot of teaching to the middle and an awful lot of kids at either end of the spectrum who are really not being catered for. And so we've attempted to narrow the range of people.
>
> (Headteacher, Clough GM)

The failure of mixed-ability teaching, therefore, is positioned as an experience shared by schools nation-wide, adding further weight to the argument against it. Yet the idea that mixed-ability teaching fails due to 'teaching to the middle' allows the possibility that the weakness lies in the application, rather than in the approach itself – that is, that teachers, and by extension the school, might be responsible for this failure. The headteacher draws on the image of the overworked, overstressed teacher to avoid such an accusation. His argument rests on pragmatism – a view that in the real world certain decisions, though perhaps regrettable, *have* to be taken:

> you need superhuman teachers to teach mixed ability (. . .) It's a *pragmatic* decision. When you consider that the average teacher, the teacher who has no [special] responsibility (. . .) teaches something like 35 out of 40 periods a week. So out of five non-contact periods they could quite easily, during the course of their normal week, lose one or two of those. But they have a fairly stressful existence as it is and to expect them to have taught, to have *prepared* differentiated lessons when they're being constantly bombarded by groups of kids, you know, the bell rings every however often it is and they then have another, not *one* lesson prepared but three, four, five, six, seven, however many it takes to do differentiation, differentiated work properly. Differentiation by task rather than outcome. It's just not, it's not, as I said before, you need superhuman teachers and there are very few of those around. You know?
>
> (Headteacher, Clough GM)

The headteacher's criticism of mixed-ability teaching strongly echoes Tony Blair's words when (on 7 June 1996, as Leader of the Opposition) he committed Labour to 'a general presumption in favour of grouping by ability and attainment' in secondary schools because, in his words, 'mixed-ability teaching often makes heroic assumptions about resources, teachers and social context'.[2] This criticism of mixed ability as practically flawed is, therefore, a strong theme in contemporary education policy. It is a theme taken up and expanded upon in Clough. As we have shown, Clough teachers feel that a defining characteristic of the school's present intake is a 'long tail' of less able pupils (see Chapter 3). The size and severity of this situation is frequently cited as making mixed ability *especially* unworkable in Clough:

> Particularly with the range of ability that you might experience with a mixed-ability class here, with everything from a non-scoring on a reading test pupil through to a potential university entrant in the same class. It's just more demanding on teachers than is realistic.
>
> (Headteacher, Clough GM)

> Well, if you've looked at it, I mean, if I walk into a mixed-ability group of 25 pupils, five are very bright, they know the answer before I ask the questions. Five can cope with anything I can give them, five who find anything a bit of a challenge, five who find it difficult and five who can't read and write. Now ideally I should go into that lesson and teach five different lessons or put over five different tasks for them to do and

assess them based upon the work I've given them. Now that can't be done, you know, you might manage it once or twice but you can't, if you're going to put your hand on your heart, you can't do it properly.

(Senior teacher, Clough GM)

Despite the school's adoption of a policy favouring selection and the rationale offered to support this decision, the senior management *does* engage with certain criticisms of setting. In particular, concerns over the impact of setting on pupils in the lowest sets are acknowledged:

The obvious disadvantage of setting is that you end up with bottom sets. No one likes that idea, and it's very easy for the kids in those bottom sets to feel as though they're something apart.

(Headteacher, Clough GM)

Although these disadvantages are acknowledged, they do not prove fatal to the increasing use of selection throughout the school. The headteacher argues that the school is, and must be, vigilant in ensuring that pupils in the lowest sets are not excluded from the school community:

I think one has to be very careful not to encourage them to form that view [that they are something apart].

Members of the school's 'learning support team', which aids those defined as having 'special' learning needs, have been among the most vocal in opposing the extension of selection within Clough. They argue that increased selection will create 'sink' groups and, especially, will lead to pupils deemed to have special needs being 'ghettoized', lesson after lesson, in a stigmatizing and destructive way. These teachers seek to distinguish between targeted support (which they offer) for a part of the curriculum and a continual placement in sink groups across the entire timetable. This distinction is not always accepted by other staff who, in any case, marshal arguments about 'practicality' versus 'ideal world' scenarios. Once again, therefore, pragmatism emerges as a key discursive strategy for defusing opposition: a member of the SMT, for example, observes that 'we can't have your cake and eat it'. By adopting this position, the schools management effectively reduce the issue to an all-or-nothing level and (because of the pressure of the A-to-C economy) inaction is simply not deemed a possibility.

Setting is also defended on the basis that it does not *sharply* differentiate pupils. Rather, it is argued that setting actually retains mixed-ability teaching, it simply *reduces the range* of abilities being taught within any given group:

that's not to say there's still not mixed-ability teaching in class, very much there is, but we've tried to narrow the range.

(Headteacher, Clough GM)

now the benefit of [setting] is that it will reduce the range (. . .) the range of ability will be much closer from top to bottom [in each classroom]

(Senior teacher, Clough GM)

Ultimately, it is argued that the move to various modes of selection across the school is, in the headteacher's words, 'a pragmatic decision' rather than an ideological position. The head appears to concede that mixed-ability teaching would be the 'best' approach if teacher time and skill, as well as resources, were available to do it 'properly'. He argues that these human and financial resources are not available and that, given the restrictions within which the school is operating, the *only* possible way of organizing teaching groups is through setting. In this way, setting is presented as the best approach for *all* pupils in these specific circumstances.

At this point it is useful to reflect on *whose* interests are being served by the move to greater selection within Clough. We have seen that the headteacher argues that mixed-ability teaching 'doesn't work' because it caters predominantly to pupils of 'middle' ability and not the most and least able. When considering possible drawbacks of selection, it is the 'least able' (especially those defined as having special educational needs) who figure prominently in discussions. Two things should be noted: first, the needs of 'the school', as defined by senior management, do not figure explicitly in the debate at this point; second, the position of the 'most able' is assumed rather than explicitly defined. In fact, it is evident that throughout the debate it is accepted that the 'most able' will unequivocally benefit from the move to setting. We have already seen (in the previous chapter) how ability and GCSE outcomes are intertwined within the school discourse. Given the emphasis on higher-grade passes, it seems that the headteacher's assertion that mixed-ability teaching 'doesn't work' may well be made with the A-to-C economy in mind. In this context, the school has to prioritize the attainment of higher-grade GCSE passes by the maximum possible number of pupils: ultimately the move to setting is thought by teachers to facilitate this. We explore teachers' varying assumptions about selection in more detail in the following sections of this and subsequent chapters.

Grouping 'by ability' in the lower school

On initial enquiry Key Stage 3 teaching groups were described to us as being 'mixed-ability'. These teaching groups also act as tutor groups, therefore ensuring that pupils experience both pastoral and academic work in mixed-ability environments. However, when these arrangements were discussed in more depth it became apparent that the groups could not truly be termed 'mixed ability'. As discussed in the preceding section, the school is moving towards greater use of setting by ability. Clough GM's selection practices in the lower school have been under review during the period of our study; consequently, different intakes have experienced slightly different modes of selection. Nevertheless, the guiding principle seems to have remained constant while the selection practices and procedures have been refined over time. There is a continuing trend of escalating selection as pupils move through the lower school (Key Stage 3).

'Fast' groups: streaming by another name?

In relation to the 1993 pupil intake, selection took the form of extracting certain pupils from 'mixed-ability' tutor groups and reallocating them to two *fast groups*, with these groups then remaining constant across all subjects.[3] This mode of selection excludes the possibility of having parallel tutor and teaching groups across the year. Rather, it is a form of *streaming*; where pupils are placed in particular classes 'by ability' and taught all subjects as a single group.[4] In this case, however, the streaming is limited to those pupils allocated to the designated 'fast groups'. The rest of the year group (around two-thirds initially) is taught in groups (based primarily on tutor group membership) that teachers commonly refer to as 'mixed ability'. These are not true mixed-ability groups, of course, since the pupils deemed 'most able' have been removed from the pool. As a head of department puts it: 'in other words, mixed of what's left over'. This 'left over' majority becomes the unnamed and unacknowledged lower stream, which masquerades as 'mixed ability' within the school discourse. This limited form of streaming is subsequently replaced (in year 9, when pupils are aged 13–14) by setting in the core and modern foreign language subjects (see Figure 4.1).

At first sight the relationship between the 'fast' and 'mixed' groups in the lower school might appear to recreate a form of *broad-banding*, where pupils are selected 'by ability' into two or three broad categories, each 'band' containing two or more groups of equivalent standing (cf. Ball 1981). However, in key respects the Clough system is closer to a limited form of streaming where groups are ranked according to a fairly rigid and clearly specified hierarchy. For example, the 'fast groups' are not themselves seen as of comparable 'ability'. Teachers identify a hierarchy of ability between them – as a member of the SMT puts it:

> there are two fast groups (. . .) the fast fast group and the slow fast group.

These distinctions are understood by pupils also (see Chapter 7). Additionally, as we detail below, the 'mixed' groups are not all seen in equivalent terms.

As has already been indicated, the selection practices in the lower school underwent revision during the duration of our study. By the 1996/7 academic year, the year 7 intake had been selected to create four 'fast' tutor and teaching groups, that is, the top stream had doubled in size to include approximately 50 per cent of pupils (see Figure 4.1). Also, the tutor and teaching groups were brought back into line with each other. As a result, pupils in Clough no longer experience genuinely mixed-ability groups in either a pastoral or academic context:

> So we agreed to do something in the lower school which is to identify fast groups. So we're talking about year 7. We divide the year in half, four classes in each half. Two classes, from September, (. . .) on each

Figure 4.1 Pupil grouping in years 7–9 in Clough GM

Years 7 and 8	Year 9	Subjects of Study

For 1993 intake:
Standard practice in
all subject areas:
 	
• 2 'fast' groups, extracted
  from 'mixed' tutor
  groups and taught
  together for all subjects
• 4 'mixed-ability' groups
  (from remaining pool)
• EAL and SEN pupils
  concentrated within
  two 'mixed' groups
	4 top groups
	2 middle groups
	2 lower groups
		English language and
		literature

	2 top groups 2 second groups 2 third groups 2 lower groups	Mathematics
	2 top groups 2 middle 2 lower groups	Science (double award)
	As years 7 and 8	History
	As years 7 and 8	Geography
	Set by ability	French
	Set by ability	Spanish
For 1996 intake: Standard practice in all subject areas: • 4 'fast' groups • 4 'mixed' groups Each group taught together across all subjects Teaching groups act as and determine tutor groups	As years 7 and 8	Technology
	As years 7 and 8	Resistant materials
	As years 7 and 8	Food technology
	As years 7 and 8	Textiles
	As years 7 and 8	Art
	As years 7 and 8	Music
	As years 7 and 8	Drama
	As years 7 and 8	Information technology

> side will consist of fast groups, in other words pupils who have got good SAT results, who are motivated (. . .) and then the others will be mixed ability. (. . .) what we basically said is motivated and able pupils we'll give the challenge of the fast groups.
>
> (Senior teacher, Clough GM)

Notice here the switching between 'ability' and motivation. As we will see, these terms are used in important ways throughout the selection processes that shape pupils' experience of Clough.

English as an additional language and special educational needs:
targeting support or creating a ghetto?

In addition to the limited streaming based upon the creation of initially two
and later four 'fast groups', we need also to consider the school's practices
concerning pupils for whom English is an additional language (EAL) and
those deemed to have special educational needs (SEN). The school reports
that it has a particularly high number of EAL learners[5] and provides a
substantial amount of learning support within classrooms. This support is
concentrated in the lower school, mostly in years 7 and 8. From 1993 the
school has concentrated EAL pupils into two of the eight tutor groups.
Senior management present this change as driven by the demands of the
learning support service, as an attempt to achieve maximum access to
classroom-based learning support for the maximum number of EAL learners.
This is an especially difficult situation for EAL teachers. Section 11 resources
(the principal means by which EAL services were provided at the time of
our fieldwork) were systematically cut by Conservative administrations
and, although an incoming Labour government did not implement a further
planned Conservative cut, the continued status and financing of individual
projects has remained uncertain and often inadequate (cf. Bagley 1992;
Jollife and South 1997; Richardson 1993). In these circumstances, where
even those with the most severe needs cannot all be catered for, EAL co-
ordinators have sometimes used the number of pupils in a teaching group as
a means of deciding which will or will not be supported (cf. Gillborn 1995:
187). One way of responding to this situation, therefore, is to attempt to
maximize the coverage of support staff by concentrating EAL pupils in a
smaller number of teaching groups:

> there's a smaller Asian constituent [in six of the eight tutor groups,
> which] dates back to the demands of the E2L department when the
> tutor groups were made up in the first place, there were two groups
> that had a larger constituent of second language (. . .) slight, you know,
> I didn't accommodate the E2L department 100 per cent.
>
> (A pastoral head of year, Clough GM)

While this approach may have been successful in maximizing access to
limited resources, it clearly has additional consequences for the year group
as a whole. In terms of the distribution of particular ethnic minorities across
tutor and teaching groups, this mode of selection means that certain teaching groups are distinguished by having either especially high, or low, con-
centrations of South Asian pupils. Concentrating EAL pupils in certain of
the 'left-over' mixed-ability classes immediately has the effect of barring them
from any of the 'fast groups'. This is vitally important because it conflates
EAL with lower 'ability' in practice if not in principle. What we see here is
a confirmation of the concerns raised in previous research that suggested
white teachers might sometimes misread Asian pupils' *language* problems as

symptomatic of deeper-seated *learning* difficulties (CRE 1992; Gillborn and Gipps 1996: 56–7; Troyna 1991; Troyna and Siraj-Blatchford 1993).

In addition to the placement of EAL pupils, the use of 'mixed' groups for pupils deemed to have special educational needs also raises equity issues in lower school classes. In our conversations with teachers we noted that issues of EAL and SEN support are often run together, suggesting that organizationally the needs of such pupils are not always identified separately. Certainly, a similar strategy has been adopted regarding the placement of SEN pupils in particular parts of the lower school – again mobilizing the argument that this maximizes use of teaching support:

> The other groups are mixed-ability, which allows us, instead of putting special needs in eight lessons, we are now [putting pupils and support teachers in] four. So the support will be where it's most needed.
>
> (Senior teacher, Clough GM)

In this way, the introduction of a limited form of streaming in the lower school (through 'fast' groups and the concentration of EAL and SEN pupils in certain of the 'left-over' mixed-groups) is presented as beneficial for 'lower-ability' pupils because it allows learning support to be concentrated in fewer groups (where it is most needed). While the practical demands for access to finite resources may have been partially met, this has been achieved through the ghettoization of both EAL and SEN learners – a more pronounced version of precisely the problem that some staff identified when the move to increased setting was first mooted. This differentiation puts EAL pupils in 'slower' groups, among a disproportionate number of SEN peers, and has implications for *all* pupils in the year group in terms of educational and social inclusion.

When the consequences of 'fast groups' and the placement of EAL and SEN learners are put together, therefore, it is evident that what were initially referred to as 'mixed-ability' groups have come to operate as *de facto streams*. The 1993 intake has a higher stream (comprising approximately 25 per cent of pupils), a 'middle' or 'ordinary' stream (comprising approximately 50 per cent) and a 'lower', EAL/SEN stream (comprising approximately 25 per cent). The 1996 intake appears to have a 'higher' stream comprising approximately 50 per cent of pupils and a 'lower' stream comprising the remainder, with EAL and SEN learners again distributed unevenly.

We have suggested that the overall aim of increased selection in Clough has been to enhance performance within the A-to-C economy. Although the changes are presented officially in terms that prioritize the needs of *pupils*, ultimately the needs of the *school* also become evident. Selection of a proportion of the intake on entry (discussed in the previous chapter) is supplemented and extended by a limited form of streaming in the lower school – all designed ultimately to enhance GCSE outcomes, that is, to improve the school's market position within the A-to-C economy. While it is not yet clear that selection in Key Stage 3 is having or will ever have the desired effect, the headteacher is optimistic:

Well, it's made a difference where it's been started early enough (. . .) I mean, I think we've seen the benefits of it in the lower school, now that we have it in the lower school. But it was only introduced in the lower school the September before last. So as far as kids in the higher, upper part of the school are concerned, although they have been in sets in some subjects for a long time, I think too much damage has already been done really. It was difficult to untangle how much kids were not achieving in Key Stage 4 from how much they hadn't done in Key Stage 3, if you see what I mean.

Notice that the possibility that setting in the upper school (Key Stage 4) has failed to enhance performance is not seen as weakening the case for setting. Rather, it is taken as an indication that setting was not introduced early enough: 'too much damage has already been done'. In this way, any lack of evidence of the benefits of selection in the upper school only serves to reinforce the belief in the need for greater selection in the lower school. Hence the effectiveness of selection, as a means of raising achievement, is enshrined in a set of circular beliefs that are impervious to evidence: if the desired results do not emerge, it simply proves the need for *more* selection. As we will see in the next chapter, increased selection is a prominent feature of life in the upper school. Indeed, the year 9 subject options process, to which we now turn, comes to operate as a further mechanism of selection and differentiation, one that helps shape pupils' disparate experiences of the upper school.

The subject options process

Option-allocation is a point at which school careers become
firmly differentiated and at which the informal differences
between pupils in terms of social reputation and their
experiences of the curriculum lower down the school are
formalized into separate curricular routes and examination
destinations.
(Ball 1981: 152)

Before the introduction of the National Curriculum most secondary schools operated some form of subject options system whereby pupils followed a common curriculum for the first three years of secondary education, but then faced a 'choice' as to the kinds of subject they would study for the remaining two years. Remember also that until the late 1980s there was not a unified examination system. The two main examinations at that time, the General Certificate of Education (GCE) and the Certificate of Secondary Education (CSE), were not of equivalent status and, in some cases, schools used the options system to engineer separate GCE and CSE teaching groups (cf. Smith and Tomlinson 1989). The advent of the GCSE and the widespread changes introduced through the 1988 Education Reform Act (ERA), however, signalled the start of a period (from the late 1980s to the mid-1990s) when options processes seemed markedly less significant. The National Curriculum dominated teaching time throughout secondary schools, leaving much less scope for curricular choice and specialization. Schools seem to have retained a smaller, modified version of options during this time (see, for example, Harris *et al.* 1996). Following the reduction in the statutory component of the National Curriculum (Dearing 1994), however, there is now scope for options processes to re-establish their place as a key point of internal selection. Before examining our new data on these issues, it is useful to set the scene by considering research on how options systems operated before the ERA.

Most published research on subject option processes indicates that, despite the rhetoric of 'choice' that commonly features in schools' presentations (to pupils and their parents), the systems usually represent a point of significant academic selection. In particular, pupils identified as 'able' are encouraged to choose high-status options, subjects with a good record of achievement and a wider reputation as 'academic'. Alternatively, many pupils are 'cooled out' (Ball 1981, after Goffman 1952), that is, encouraged to lower their sights, be more 'realistic' and choose 'appropriate' subjects of lesser academic standing (Abraham 1995; Ball 1981; Gillborn 1987; Hurman 1978; Woods 1976; 1977; 1979). Where schools operate some form of internal selection during the first three years of secondary education (streaming, banding and/or setting), previous research suggests that these distinctions are frequently amplified through options decisions (see Ball 1981; Smith and Woodhouse 1982). However, even where mixed-ability teaching was the norm for all or most subjects, before ERA there was clear evidence that options systems continued to operate as a form of hidden academic selection: in particular, working-class pupils, those from minority ethnic backgrounds and girls frequently found themselves 'channelled' towards lower-status subjects and/or non-examination groups.[6] Our research in Taylor Comprehensive and Clough GM provides the first detailed account of how far similar processes are taking shape amid the new pressures of the A-to-C economy.

Options in Clough GM

In our case-study schools the options process begins around half-way through year 9. The decisions taken at this point exert a considerable influence on the shape of pupils' curricular and examination destinations throughout the upper school (in Key Stage 4). Both schools present the options process as a point at which some element of choice is available, but certain constraints are made clear from the outset. These constraints are the result of policy decisions at the level of both central government and the individual school (see Table 4.1). As we look in detail at the options process, the implications of these constraints for the nature and organization of the upper school curriculum will be explored.

Table 4.1 Options and the Key Stage 4 curriculum in Clough GM

Subjects of study	Nature of provision
Compulsory 'core' subjects	The core subjects, that is English, mathematics and science, are compulsory nationally at Key Stage 4. The core subjects account for five subjects of study in the upper school in Clough.
English language and literature	All pupils are required to study English language and English literature although Clough does not expect all pupils ultimately to sit GCSE examinations in both of these subjects.
Mathematics	All pupils are required to study mathematics at Key Stage 4.
Science (double award)	Nationally all pupils are required to study a science course that is equivalent to, and potentially leads to, a single GCSE. Clough has elected to make compulsory a science course equivalent to, and potentially leading to, a double GCSE award.
Other compulsory subjects	Alongside the core subjects there are a number of other areas that pupils are obliged to study. Schools are required to offer GCSE courses in some of these areas, while for other areas accreditation (whether GCSE or in an alternative form) is at the discretion of the individual school.
– with GCSE level courses required	
Technology	All pupils are obliged to retain one technology subject. Clough offers a choice between technology, resistant materials, food technology and textiles.
Modern foreign language	During our fieldwork the study of one modern foreign language was compulsory at Key Stage 4. Clough offers French and Spanish.
– with accreditation optional	
Physical education	All pupils are obliged to follow a course in physical education at Key Stage 4. In Clough optional GCSE physical education is offered in addition to the compulsory course.
Religious education	All schools are required to deliver religious education. In Clough this is a compulsory and unaccredited 'social education' course which runs throughout Key Stage 4.

Table 4.1 (cont'd)

Subjects of study	Nature of provision
Personal and social education	While personal and social education (sometimes also known as personal, social and health education) is not a required programme of study nationally, schools' obligation to cover a range of areas of study (such as sex education and careers guidance) means that PSE is a common area of study. This is a compulsory, unaccredited area of study at Clough.
Optional areas of study	All other areas of study at Key Stage 4 are optional. This includes all humanities subjects, all aesthetics/arts subjects, second modern foreign languages and additional areas of study such as business studies and information technology. While these subjects are not compulsory in terms of national education policy, pupil choice in relation to these areas is not unrestrained. In Clough a variety of practices and processes act to constrain and direct pupils' decisions concerning these areas of study at GCSE.
Humanities	At Clough humanities are a 'constrained' option, that is, all pupils are required to select at least one humanities subject. The school offers geography, history and sociology. A non-GCSE course, known as 'the special option' is placed alongside the other humanities subjects (aimed at pupils deemed to have very 'low ability' or SEN and EAL needs).
Aesthetics/arts	Clough offers art, graphics, music and drama at GCSE as optional subjects.
Other optional subjects	Clough also offers business studies and information technology at GCSE as optional subjects.

The options process in Clough is a key moment in which the legitimacy and centrality of the A-to-C economy is asserted. Through the discursive practices surrounding options, the crucial goal of five higher-grade GCSE passes is conveyed and enshrined. If any lower school pupils were unsure which GCSE grades 'count', by their final term in year 9 they are left in no doubt.

Within Clough the options process is closely linked to work on careers education and guidance. The upper school curriculum is presented as the route into post-16 education, training or employment: education in Key Stage 4 is not viewed an end in itself or an exercise in learning – it is one (early) step towards employability. The 'choices' made at the point of year 9 options, therefore, are commonly related to their assumed implications for future opportunities in post-16 education and beyond. It is interesting to consider this in the context of Clough being an 11–16 provider only: the school does not have a sixth form and therefore has no need to 'recruit' post-16 applications from within its pupil population. GCSE results stand as the final measure of the school's attainment. It is crucial to note here that throughout the options process pupils' potential not only for 'success' in school, but also for post-16 access, becomes synonymous with the achievement of at least five higher-grade GCSE passes, that is, the key benchmark in the A-to-C economy. This is illustrated by Clough's 'Careers Education and Guidance Statement of Entitlement'; a leaflet distributed to all year 9 pupils and their parents/carers. This document promises to 'help young people to identify suitable areas of work and inform them of the various education/training routes they should consider'. It states that 'pupils who have a clear idea of where they are going and *what they need* to get there will be motivated to learn and achieve' (emphasis added). Hence, the school's careers education and guidance is situated in the context of eventual employment destinations. Post-16 education and training is positioned as an intermediary between school and work: as we illustrate below, the achievement of five higher-grade GCSE passes is positioned as an *essential* requirement for successful passage between school and further education or training.

Options and PSE

The importance of the connection drawn between options decisions and the world of work is signalled by the involvement of careers and guidance teachers throughout the process (see Figure 4.2). From the first stage (an open meeting for parents/carers) to the last (making final pupil allocations) the head of careers and guidance plays a central role. Careers education and guidance in Clough is delivered in part through the personal and social education (PSE) curriculum, which is built around a series of topic-based modules. The year 9 careers module booklet, which is given to each pupil, begins by introducing the necessity of options: choosing some subjects to continue to study and some to give up is necessary because of the time needed to study a subject to GCSE level against the limited time available in the school week. In outlining the extent to which pupils can select their own curriculum, the booklet identifies those subjects that are compulsory, including GCSE level National Curriculum core subjects, other compulsory GCSE level subjects and the statutory requirements for non-GCSE-level study of religious, sex and physical education. In explaining the reasons for these constraints the booklet states that 'some subjects are more important than others' and 'you need to be good at these *core subjects* for a great number of jobs' (emphasis in original).

Having outlined and justified the formal limitations to the options process, the module turns to the issue of employment. The booklet offers the analogy of a journey, with options positioned as the first part of that journey. In

Figure 4.2 The options process in Clough GM

Open options meeting for parents/carers

Parents/carers are addressed by the head of careers and guidance. They are given an options booklet (produced by the school) which includes an options form for completion with their child(ren). They are also given an LEA magazine *GCSE Options and Beyond.*

↓

Options assembly for all year 9 pupils

Pupils are addressed by the head of careers and guidance and heads of faculties.

↓

Careers module in tutor-led PSE

Pupils assess their 'ability and interest' in the different curricular areas. Pupil preference and suitability for employment areas dominate.

↓

Pupils interviewed individually by head of careers and guidance or school-linked careers officer

Completed options form, signed by parent/carer and pupil, is to be brought to this meeting. Interview includes a review of pupil's choices, 'ability' and *Jobwise* printout. Changes to the options identified on the form are discussed and either referred (to named teachers and/or parents for further discussion) or made on the spot. Choices are entered into a computerized pupil database.

↓

Head of careers and guidance reviews distribution of subject choices

Head of careers and guidance makes further 'necessary' changes. Preliminary allocation of choices are passed to the curricular deputy headteacher (for timetabling) and faculty heads (for construction of teaching groups).

↓

Curricular deputy headteacher refers any further need for changes (due to timetable or teacher availability restrictions) back to head of careers and guidance

↓

Head of careers and guidance makes final allocation changes

↓

Curricular deputy finalizes timetable

↓

Heads of faculty finalize teaching groups

↓

Pupils informed of final options allocations

making their choices, pupils are asked to consider their final destination, their route, requirements for and duration of the journey. The booklet asks: *'How will you know you have arrived?* – You will be successfully employed in your chosen field of work' (emphasis in original). As such, options, and by extension Key Stage 4 study and eventual GCSE examinations, are firmly positioned as a precursor to employment. With options and GCSEs presented in this way, the module then turns almost exclusively to issues of employment (the module incorporates only two exercises related to the secondary curriculum: self-assessments of ability and interest in each subject). Through a series of exercises, interest in a range of named jobs is translated into a more general interest in particular types of work (to be researched independently) and 'personal qualities' are matched to job types to assess pupils' potential suitability.

Extensive use is made of one particular exercise undertaken as part of the module. A *'Jobwise'* questionnaire is bought in by the school from an external agency which provides an individualized analysis of pupils' completed answers. The questionnaire asks pupils to identify areas of work in which they are interested and rank aspects of work in terms of the activities involved, the conditions under which activities are carried out and the abilities required. In addition, pupils are asked for their expected GCSE outcomes in each named subject (using the grade ranges A*-to-C, D-to-E, F-to-G, and U).[7] The analysis of the questionnaire comes in the form of the pupil's chosen job(s) 'matched' against their questionnaire answers: ranked as 'very good', 'good', 'fair', 'questionable' or 'poor'. Additionally, the computer program generates its own job suggestions based on the pupils' expressed preferences and anticipated GCSE outcomes. Table 4.2, for example, shows the results received by Elizabeth (a girl in one of our case-study tutor groups), who identified herself as expecting A*-to-C grade passes in seven GCSEs and D-to-E grade passes in the remaining four. The *Jobwise* exercise told Elizabeth that the jobs she had targeted most highly were not suitable for her. Her additional selection of jobs faired only a little better. However, on the basis of a short questionnaire, the *Jobwise* program offered her five jobs whose suitability was 'very good' along with a further 13 that were a 'good' match. At age 14, Elizabeth is expecting seven higher-grade GCSE passes and is particularly interested in the very different fields of airline stewarding and engineering. The *Jobwise* exercise tells her she is not suitable for these jobs but should consider employment in advertising, nursing, or teaching, to name but a few of the suggestions.

We are not concerned here with whether Elizabeth is or is not actually 'suitable' for any or all of the areas of employment named in Table 4.2. Rather, we wish to illustrate the degree to which future employment is foregrounded in the options process at Clough. The sum of the various exercises included in the PSE module is to ask year 9 pupils to identify jobs that they are interested in, inform them of their 'suitability' for their chosen jobs and offer alternatives where these choices are deemed unsuitable or a 'poor match'. As such, the PSE careers module, which is ostensibly designed

Table 4.2 Sample results of the *Jobwise* questionnaire

Potential areas of employment	Jobwise *analysis of suitability*
Elizabeth's preferred current job ideas	
Airline	Questionable match
Steward/stewardess	
Professional engineering	Poor match
Elizabeth's additional current job ideas	
Work with children	Fair match
Design	Fair match
Health care	Fair match
Jobwise-provided job ideas	
Advertising art director	Very good match
Residential social worker	Very good match
Art and design teacher	Very good match
Care assistant – children	Very good match
Journalist – radio/television	Very good match
Stage manager	Good match
Public relations officer	Good match
Nurse – mental health	Good match
Probation officer	Good match
Nursery nurse	Good match
Primary teacher	Good match
Secondary teacher	Good match
Special educational needs teacher	Good match
Training scheme manager	Good match
Art therapist	Good match
Music therapist	Good match
Training officer	Good match
Education welfare officer	Good match

to prepare pupils for the decision making involved in the options process, comes to be dominated by concerns over individuals' supposed suitability for specific areas of employment. As we move on to examine another crucial element of this process, the options interviews, we will see further evidence of the school's emphasis on employment as well as indications of why this might be the case.

The options interviews

As part of the options process in Clough all pupils are interviewed individually by either the head of careers and guidance or the careers officer linked to the school (Figure 4.2). Each pupil is required to bring a completed options form indicating their chosen subjects of study, signed by themselves and their parent/carer. The range of choices available is additionally constrained by the school's 'options pattern' (Figure 4.3) which groups certain courses together, adding to the limits imposed by the National Curriculum.

Figure 4.3   The options pattern in Clough GM (as presented in the school's options booklet)

Subjects common to all

No choices to be made		24 periods 5 GCSE's	
English & English Lit.	6	Social Education	2
Mathematics	5	Personal & Social Education	1
Double Science	8	Physical Education	2

Options

Humanities – Choose one 4 periods 1 GCSE	
History	4
Geography	4
Sociology	4

OPTION BLOCK

Choice within the option block **must** include a modern foreign language (French or Spanish) **and** a technology subject (Technology, Resistant Materials, Food or Textiles).

You can **not** choose Information Technology **and** Business Studies.

You can **not** choose three humanities subjects overall.

All courses of 4 periods lead to full GCSE qualification unless otherwise stated. Courses of 2 periods lead to a half GCSE qualification (except Graphics which leads to a full GCSE and PE which is internally accredited). 2 half GCSE's equate to 1 full GCSE.

Choose courses from this block to add up to 12 periods

12 periods – max 3 1/2 GCSE's

MFL – Choose one or two		Technology – Choose one or two	
French	2/4	Technology	2/4
Spanish	2/4	Resistant Materials	2/4
French/Business Studies	4	Textiles	2/4
		Food	2/4

Other options			
Art	4	History	2/4
Music	4	Geography	2/4
Drama	4	Sociology	4
Graphics	2	Business Studies	4
Special Option	4	Information Technology	2/4
Physical Education	2		

We observed more than 20 separate options interviews in Clough, mostly undertaken by the head of careers and guidance. The interviews follow a common format, and usually last between 11 and 13 minutes. First, the head of careers consults a list of results to identify the pupil's year 7 'IQ test' (NFER) and 'reading age' scores (see the previous chapter). Second, the *Jobwise* results are discussed, including consideration of the GCSE grades anticipated by the pupil. Finally, these elements are related to post-16 education intentions, with the entry requirements for post-16 courses being emphasized. While all the interviews we observed followed this same format, there were significant differences between interviews with particular groups of pupils. We will comment on these as we consider each element of the interviews in turn.

Judging 'ability' and motivating further effort

Each options interview begins with a discussion of the pupil's 'ability', as judged by the 'IQ test' and 'reading age' results from year 7. A further measure of the school's faith is these tests (see previous chapter) is that the head of careers does not have access to subject teachers' assessments of how individuals have faired over the last two to three years in Clough. This means that in this respect at least the options process, via the interventions of the head of careers, operates on the basis of dated test results (more than two years old) rather than examining the pupils' more recent, actual attainments while in the school. Not only does this reassert the validity of the tests (and ignore any test biases) but for many pupils it also effectively denies the possibility of raising the school's judgement of their ability by outperforming expectations in the lower school. One of the few exceptions to this is where the test results are not available. For example, the head of careers is left with no official signpost as to the 'ability' of pupils who joined the school late:

HoC: Have you been with us right from the beginning of year 7?
Emma: No.
HoC: No. So we haven't got a reading age for you. You don't have any problems with reading do you? Would you say you're as bright as the next person is? Or *brighter* still? [He smiles.]
Emma: [She smiles but does not answer.]
HoC: Are you being modest?

In this case the head of careers resolved the situation by moving to the second stage of the interview, the *Jobwise* questionnaire. A central feature of these discussions is consideration of pupils' anticipated grades: these become the teacher's guide where no 'IQ' and reading age scores are available. In some cases, however, the teacher has personally taught the pupil and uses his own perception of their 'ability' as a yardstick: telling one pupil, for example, 'you're very able. Your teachers think so, pupils think so too'.

In each of our observed meetings, the pupil is encouraged to raise their sights and work toward good grades. Where year 7 test results are available the head of careers invariably presents them in such a way as to encourage continued effort and optimism. This tone frames the subsequent discussions as he attempts to ensure that the options process acts to increase motivation and maintain pupils' commitment to their work – a common factor in most previous research on options procedures (cf. Ball 1981; Gillborn 1987; Pratt *et al.* 1984; Smith and Tomlinson 1989). Pupils whose test scores identify them as of 'high ability', for example, are told 'your ability score means you're very able – A, B, Cs – has anybody told you this before?' and 'as long as you get six, seven, eight grades A-to-C . . . that's what we expect of *you*'. Their peers with lesser scores are reassured 'your reading age means that your ability score shouldn't hold you back' and 'don't aim low'. In this way, pupils' differential abilities, which are understood as fixed in other school contexts, become a springboard for encouragement, which further enshrines the importance of higher-grade GCSE passes.

'Jobwise' – career aspirations and GCSE expectations

Although a good deal of time and effort (and some expense) are expended on the *Jobwise* questionnaires, their usefulness in the options interviews is often uncertain. In addition to informing work-related curricular decisions, the underlying logic seems often to expect renewed effort from pupils once schooling is linked to the 'real world' of work. In many interviews, however, the *Jobwise* print-outs cause concern to the teacher because of the low grades anticipated by pupils. Wherever pupils have predicted anything below a C grade there is a potential conflict between the teacher's agenda (to motivate and ensure the greatest possible push for higher-grade passes) and the 'advice' of the *Jobwise* package. This is because predictions of grade D or below mean that the package is likely to reject professional aspirations and suggest low-level alternatives. In response the teacher adopts the strategy of reinterpreting the point of the exercise, telling pupils that they should have filled in the grades they *hope for*, rather than *anticipate*:

HoC: [Looks at his copy of the pupil's *Jobwise* print-out] Did you have a look at your print-out?

Alison: Yeah.

HoC: Did you understand it?

Alison: A-ha. (. . .)

HoC: Was it useful?

Alison: Yeah.

HoC: Now you don't have to say 'yes' if you don't mean it (. . .) Now you've indicated that you are not going to get very high grades in your main subjects of English, maths and science. Are you *aiming* not to get high grades, or are you not confident? (. . .) [He recaps her recorded estimates.] That means that you don't expect to get a grade A, B or C, is that still true?

Alison: No. [Laughs.]

HoC: You're hoping to get higher grades – *I should think so as well*.

Similarly, from an interview with a male classmate:

> *HoC*: Do you know what you did wrong? I think all your tutor group have done the same thing. When you came to put in your subjects on the back, you were asked, if you were good at it, and you enjoyed it, to give it an [A–C indication]. You no good at maths?
>
> *Alan*: I'm all right at maths.
>
> *HoC*: Well you gave it [an indication of] below a grade C. Okay? And you didn't fill in a science subject. So you said you're gonna leave with a high grade in English, and *no* grade in science and a *low* grade in maths. So this down here [his chosen job] will have problems won't it? (. . .) If you wanted to do that [the questionnaire] again, you'd get a *totally* different print-out if you put those in.

Pupils who have indicated that they *will* attain higher-grade passes, but who have also expressed an interest in jobs with low or minimal formal entry requirements, are also challenged. This is presented in terms of the pupil aiming too low. One boy, for example, is told that his expected grades are too high for his chosen area of work (car mechanic), while another is told that his grades indicate he should be aiming to be a building surveyor rather than a bricklayer. Alternatively, a 'high-ability' boy who hopes to use his musical accomplishments in his career is discouraged from this and directed towards his second choice of veterinary work, which is identified as demanding high-level academic qualifications throughout and higher-grade GCSE passes initially.

Across the entire range of perceived 'ability', therefore, the head of careers uses the options interviews as a means of emphasizing the importance of higher-grade passes. This provides an interesting point of possible contradiction regarding the dominant notion of 'ability' in the school. As we showed in the previous chapter, Clough GM generally operates on the basis that 'ability' is a relatively fixed and measurable academic potential. This means that 'able' pupils must be encouraged to maintain effort so as to 'do themselves justice', but would, in theory, mean that continually encouraging 'less able' pupils to aspire to GCSE higher grades is, at best, likely to be fruitless and, at worst, likely to store up resentments and disappointments for later. However, the demands of the A-to-C economy are such that this thrust is adopted without teachers reflecting on its consequences for their notion of 'ability'. Within the current constraints every higher grade is vital to the school (and, of course, to individual pupils). As we show in the following chapters, the constraints and pressures of the A-to-C economy are such that at certain points, most especially the run-up to examinations, the schools seem effectively to suspend their view of 'ability' as fixed. At these moments, including the options interviews, the thrust for higher-grade passes is extended even to pupils who at other times are thought unlikely (literally not able) to achieve

Table 4.3 Subject status and selection in the upper school curriculum in Clough GM (cohort entering year 10 in September 1996)

Subjects of study	Years 10 and 11	Additional information
English language and literature	4 higher groups 2 middle groups 2 lower groups	Sets are evenly spread across two half-year groups
Maths	2 top groups 2 second groups 4 third groups 2 lower groups	Taught in two half-year groups
Science (compulsory double award)	2 higher groups 4 middle groups 2 lower groups	In the case of the 1997 year 11, only higher-group pupils took double award – selection was via the options process
History	2 higher groups	Selected through the options process
Geography	2 middle to higher groups	Selected through the options process
Sociology	2 middle to lower groups	Selected through the options process
Special option (non-GCSE)	1 lower group	Selected, as these pupils' sole humanities option, through the options process
French	Set by ability as far as concurrent lessons allow	Compulsory modern foreign language is expected to facilitate setting
French (short course)	Mixed group	Intended as a higher group only but selection through the options process failed to create the desired group
Spanish	Set by ability as far as concurrent lessons allow	Compulsory modern foreign language is expected to facilitate setting
Technology	Higher groups	Selected through the options process
Resistant materials	Mixed groups	Mixed after technology extracted: setting where concurrent lessons allow
Food technology	Mixed groups	Mixed after technology extracted: setting where concurrent lessons allow

Table 4.3 (cont'd)

Subjects of study	Years 10 and 11	Additional information
Textiles	Mixed groups	Mixed after technology extracted: setting where concurrent lessons allow
Art	Mixed groups	Setting where concurrent lessons allow
Graphics (non-timetabled GCSE)	Higher group	Non-timetabled GCSE subject: selection through performance in Key Stage 4 art
Graphics (short course)	Higher group	Selection through the options process
Music	Higher group	Selection via musical proficiency
Drama	Mixed groups	

so highly. This widening of the focus of attention *could* operate to reduce substantially existing inequalities of achievement between different groups of pupils: unfortunately, such moments tend to be somewhat short-lived and relatively inconsequential. In the options interviews, for example, the encouragement for all to 'aim high', is soon tempered by attempts to select certain pupils to particular subject areas and teaching groups.

Selection to 'appropriate' options

The school's view of 'ability' as a fixed and measurable potential is reinstated and reinscribed as the interviews move on to discussions of which particular subjects are 'appropriate' for individual pupils. In several curricular areas there is an informal hierarchization of different options: most notably, humanities subjects, technology subjects, 'short' (half) GCSE courses and non-timetabled graphics (see Table 4.3). Hence, through the options interviews, pupils of differently perceived 'ability' are alternatively 'warmed up' or 'cooled out'.

Among the technology subjects, technology itself is deemed to be a subject requiring high ability while the remaining subjects are believed to be appropriate for those of lesser ability. Pupils are, therefore, directed towards particular technology subjects according to their perceived ability. This viewpoint is strongly supported by Clough's head of technology:

[Technology, as a separate named course is for] the more able pupil, and I aim that course at the top maths and science sets (. . .) they have guidance from [the head of careers] and [the careers adviser] and sometimes it doesn't match up to how I see they should be, you know, they should be set. So sometimes I'll have to tweak the groups a little bit.

The head of careers, therefore, is acting in accordance with the wishes of the head of the technology faculty, in attempting to select different 'abilities' to particular technology options. Where he fails to do so, the head of technology himself acts as a further filter. In this way technology options are partly selected through the options process. A degree of selection in the upper school is possible, therefore, even in subjects where timetabling or a lack of pupil numbers means that subject departments cannot set *within* the subject: effectively, certain subjects are set via the options process itself. A similar selection operates in other curricular areas but not always with the approval of the faculties concerned. The head of humanities, for example, strongly resists the hierarchy of humanities that is applied in the options interviews and the *de facto* setting that is attempted through the process. Yet among senior management such inter-subject selection is deemed appropriate and is justified through recourse to a 'natural' hierarchy between humanities subjects. In the options interviews, for example, 'higher-ability' pupils are warmed up for, first, history and, second, geography: they are cooled out from sociology. For instance, when a high-ability boy decides to choose both geography and sociology, the former is unquestioned while his choice of sociology is resisted on the grounds, first, that the sociology option is full and, second, that an additional humanities subject might not be possible within the constraints of the timetable anyway. In fact, sociology was challenged in every interview we saw concerning a pupil considered as 'able'. Conversely, 'lower-ability' pupils are channelled towards sociology or, in more extreme cases, the non-GCSE 'special option' (which runs concurrent to the main humanities subjects).[8] For these pupils geography and history were routinely queried. Despite resistance from the relevant faculty head, therefore, in the humanities the options process again acts as a form of academic filter, attempting to select pupils into different subjects based on official perceptions of 'ability' and management assumptions about the academic status of particular subjects.

Similar attempts to select between subjects can also be seen in relation to discussions about the 'short' (half) GCSE courses in modern foreign languages (MFL) and graphics. As with the case of technology, the relevant faculties supported the attempt to pre-set groups via the options process through the intervention of the head of careers and guidance. Generally pupils not seen as 'able' are dissuaded from such choices:

HoC: [Reading through the pupil's list of choices.] Modern foreign language: you're doing Spanish at the moment. And you want to do a short course.

Mandy: Yeah.

HoC: Why is that?

Mandy: [Laughs.] I hate Spanish so much. I hate foreign languages.

HoC: So, . . . you've got to remember – who do you think's going to be in this group, if you go for a short course then?

Mandy: [Laughs nervously]

HoC: All the people who don't want to do it. You think what that means. I don't think I'd want to be that group, even if I didn't want to do Spanish. See what I mean? I'd be worried. Do you *really* want to go in a class where people don't want to learn?

Similarly, another pupil is told: 'Nobody knows what two halves mean: what if you get a B and an F?' In contrast, more 'able' pupils are usually allowed the choice without question, the rationale being that only the 'most able' can hope to gain a higher-grade pass in an MFL short course. This decision also frees 'able' pupils to attempt an *additional* GCSE (again the needs of the A-to-C economy are served). However, in the case of selection to MFL short courses the options interviews were not as successful as either senior management or the languages department hoped. A number of 'low-ability' pupils succeeded in retaining MFL short courses – possibly as a result of different selection criteria operating between the head of careers and the attached careers officer (who shared options interviews). Consequently, MFL short-course teaching groups eventually consisted of pupils with disparate perceived abilities. Ultimately, this was considered to be so problematic that, between the relevant faculty and senior management, the decision was made that short courses would not be offered in future.

Sexism and subject options

To date the research literature on options processes has focused a good deal of attention on gender differences in subject take-up (cf. Byrne 1978; Kelly *et al.* 1984; Pratt *et al.* 1984). Even where deliberate interventions have been made to encourage 'non-traditional' choices, familiar patterns of curricular differentiation often emerge (see Kelly *et al.* 1984).[9] Partly this is due to strongly stereotyped assumptions among parents and the pupils themselves. Lynda Measor, for example, has drawn on participant observation techniques to show how 'boys and girls select curriculum areas to act as marker flags for their identities' (Measor 1983: 189). In this way, pupils may use the gendered reputation of particular subjects as a resource to help construct for themselves school-based identities that meet the requirements of dominant notions of masculinity and femininity within a context of compulsory heterosexuality. More recent research shows teenage girls to be adopting relatively sophisticated and multifaceted approaches to school decision making. While their choices might appear 'traditional' (e.g. child care, secretarial studies, etc.), they are not made blindly, but with an eye to local labour market realities – where such gendered roles are seen to offer them a limited opportunity within otherwise non-existent youth labour markets (Mirza 1992; Riddell 1992a; 1992b). Teachers' role in the gendered structuring of different curricular routes has received rather less attention. Nevertheless, there is powerful evidence that, before the advent of the National Curriculum, pupils could find themselves channelled towards markedly different routes depending on teachers' views of the 'appropriate' subjects for either gender (Gillborn 1990b; Measor and Sikes 1992; Riddell 1992a).

The National Curriculum leaves rather less room for the crude structuring of curricular pathways by gender. All pupils must follow a science and MFL subject, for example, imposing key restrictions on two of the curricular areas where gendered 'choices' were most clear. Craft-based and commercial subjects also have largely (though not entirely) thrown off their stereotyped labels, and all pupils now receive some experience across a full range of craft subjects in the lower school. Nevertheless, school remains as highly gendered a social arena as ever:[10] in relation to the options process, even within the limits of the National Curriculum, we could not help but be struck by some very powerful pressures that distinguish teachers' interviews with boys and girls. In relation to the *Jobwise* print-outs, for example, it is noticeable that certain jobs and subjects are rehearsed more often for girls:

> *HoC*: Beautician work. You said it's a *good* match, but not *very* good. And I'd like you to see why it's not *very* good. Now the computer looked at what you'd said elsewhere and came up with some ideas: 'working with children', is that something you're keen on?
>
> *Sally*: Yeah.
>
> *HoC*: 'Catering', possibly.
>
> *Sally*: *Yeah*.
>
> *HoC*: And maybe some 'design'.
>
> *Sally*: Yeah.
>
> *HoC*: Funnily enough, you said 'beautician' there and the computer came up with 'beautician'. And 'hairdresser'.
> Don't worry about the 'butcher' – okay. [Smiles]
>
> *Sally*: [Laughs]
>
> *HoC*: And it also came up with all those other jobs, to do with working with children.

In this extract, certain areas of work are repeated by the teacher and a response sought from the pupil: namely, beautician, working with children, catering and design. In contrast, other areas of work are ignored or even used as a joke: 'Don't worry about the "butcher" – okay'. The possibility of such a non-traditional area of work is assumed by the teacher to be so outrageous as to provide for mutual amusement. In this case the pupil laughs, on cue: we wonder how many pupils would have the confidence to challenge such a situation if they did not share the teachers' perspective. This example is also significant because of the repeated reference to 'working with children'. This became such a frequent part of girls' option interviews that eventually we were surprised when a meeting took place *without* the suggestion being made. 'Working with children' emerged as a common feature of girls' option interviews regardless of their ascribed 'ability' levels. In contrast, we did not see a single boy's interview where this line of work was mentioned.

Similarly, certain technology options retain a strongly gendered identity. Even where new labels have replaced 'traditional' ones, it is clear that old understandings still have currency with both pupils and teachers – though the 'elicit' nature of such terms is sometimes acknowledged:

[The head of careers and the pupil are discussing each of her choices in turn]

HoC: You've gone for food technology. Can you think why that might be suitable? Do you enjoy it?

Kirsty: Yeah. I like cooking things . . . I don't know. I like it better than woodwork.

HoC: Don't let Mr Murray hear you say 'woodwork'. [Smiles]

Kirsty: [Looks puzzled]

HoC: You mean *resistant materials*.

Kirsty: Yeah. Yeah, I like it better than doing that.

HoC: Better than textiles?

Note also that the only other technology option to be raised by the teacher (textiles) is also heavily gendered. Overall, the gendered nature of the technology options remains very strong. We return to the gendered patterns of curricular differentiation shortly.

The push for five higher grades

We have already noted that one of the key features of options interviews in Clough is an attempt to motivate pupils towards continued, or increased, efforts in the upper school. This has been a common feature in previous work on options systems. However, a new feature to emerge in the present study is the emphasis on gaining *five* higher-grade GCSEs. This is a direct reflection of the importance of five higher grades as the key 'benchmark' in the school league tables – the dominant criterion in the A-to-C economy.

The push for five higher grades begins with a concern to stress the 'core subjects'. During our observations, almost without exception, the head of careers and guidance stresses the need to attain higher-grade passes in English, mathematics and science. In Clough this alone translates into five separate GCSEs because, in addition to English language and literature, the science syllabus also leads to a double award.

HoC: Forget about that [the *Jobwise* print-out]. You can still do those [the pupil's chosen jobs] as long as you realize that you've got to get a high grade *there* [indicates English language and literature on the option pattern] and a high grade there [indicates mathematics]. *And* a high grade there [double science].

A further example of the special significance given to five higher-grade passes occurs where the head of careers advises pupils on entry requirements for particular courses in further and higher education. In many cases he asserts, without consulting any specific materials, that five higher grades are a basic requirement for entry. Sometimes, of course, this is not unreasonable: the historic use of *five* passes as an entry criterion, especially in parts of higher education and the professions, is one of the reasons why it has attained such significance in the school performance tables. However, for many pupils there is not necessarily any special significance about the number five. Indeed, there are times in the option interviews when advice on careers or further education would appear to undermine this position. Nevertheless, even on such occasions, the head of careers reasserts the importance of *five* higher grades:

HoC: You've got to aim for five or more grades at C and above. (. . .) You're best to get English, maths and science to start with. The course – pass me that book – the next course that you might consider, if I show you the sort of course that you might go for next, then you can see what sort of qualifications you'll need. [He consults a college prospectus.] Probably that one, BTEC National in childhood studies.

   So if you want to go into teaching, then you would pick A levels, okay? And you need five grades A-to-C for that.

   The other route is to go via a BTEC National course, and just to show that I don't make these things up, [shows her details of the course] what does that say?

Kirsty: [Reading from the leaflet.] Four GCSEs (. . .)

HoC: Now that is the *minimum*, that means that's the least. You *cannot* get on with anything less, so *three* is not good enough. It also means that if they've got 20 places on that course, and you've got four grades A-to-C, if 21 people apply, and all the others have got *five* grades A-to-C, who won't get the place?

Kirsty: Me.

HoC: That's what they mean by minimum. It depends what other people have got: you *will not* get on without them, but even if you've got them you won't necessarily get on. It says *four* there, now you know why I'm talking about *five* or more.

Similarly, in a later interview:

HoC: There aren't that many opportunities which means you've got to be better than the others. The other thing is, you know it said *four* grades A-to-C?

Sally: Yeah.

HoC: So let's say you applied for one of the courses you want to do, like working with children. If you have four grades A-to-C, what they mean is *minimum*. So if there are only 20 places on the course, and you've got four grades A-to-C and everybody else has got *five* – you won't get on. So you've got to remember, when they say *four*, really, your best bet is to aim for *at least* five A-to-Cs.

In this way, whatever the specifics of pupils' post-16 ambitions, the options interviews conclude with a strong restatement of the need not only to maintain effort, but to strive for at least five higher-grade passes. Any contradictions in terms of pupils' preferences or perceived abilities are elided along with any inconsistencies concerning post-16 education and training entry requirements. The PSE careers module presents the options process as the beginning of a much longer education and training trajectory that ends in employment. By placing employment as the point of 'arrival', the school is able to work backwards to the moment of options (via post-16 education and training) and GCSE outcomes. In this way, the most immediate 'goal' for year 9 pupils considering areas of study for Key Stage 4 is the GCSE examination at the end of year 11 and the subsequent progression to post-16 provision. With this progression positioned as largely dependent upon five higher-grade GCSE passes, the options process operates directly to promote the demands of the A-to-C economy among the pupil population.

Conclusions

Selection becomes more overt as pupils move through Clough GM, but is an ever-present aspect of comprehensive schooling in the A-to-C economy. In the previous chapter we saw how the use of limited selection on entry is viewed as a long-term strategy, to reduce the size of the school's 'tail' of less able pupils, and thereby improve its position *vis-à-vis* the A-to-C economy. Selection, by the use of various approaches to pupil grouping, has also been adopted as a strategy for improving 'league table' results in the medium term. In this chapter we have examined the various forms of selection operating in the lower school.

The senior management, and some subject departments, have concluded that mixed-ability grouping does not work. Although they are ambiguous about the rights and wrongs of selection in principle, they are clear that in practice it provides a better way forward. 'Better' for the school, in terms of A*-to-C grade GCSE passes and, they assume, better for pupils. The argument has it that setting is the most pragmatic way of meeting the diverse needs and abilities of pupils: it is an argument championed at a national level by both the major political parties (and enshrined in recent Labour Party policy). At the school level it is given added weight by Clough teachers' belief in the particular problems they face because of the ability profile of its current 'bottom-heavy' intake. Despite this, mixed-ability teaching is still spoken of as the most common approach to pupil grouping in the lower school. On closer inspection, however, these groups are more accurately described, in the words of one head of department, as 'mixed of what's left over': left over, that is, after the selection and separation of 'fast groups'.

'Fast groups' now account for half of the age group in the lower school. From an early point in their secondary careers, therefore, Clough's pupils are being selected into separate groups for which teachers have very different expectations. The 'fast groups' are seen as those with ability and/or motivation, signalling that much less is expected of the 50 per cent of pupils in the 'left-over' mixed-ability groups. Of particular concern is the assumption that EAL pupils are automatically barred from the fast groups. This decision confirms fears raised in earlier studies that, in selective school environments, EAL pupils might be disadvantaged as a result of their *language* needs being misread as *learning* difficulties. This could not be clearer than in Clough's practice of concentrating EAL and SEN pupils in a small number of the 'left-over' mixed-ability groups.

Superficially the introduction of 'fast groups' resembles the practice of broad-banding 'by ability' which was relatively common in the 1970s and 1980s. We have argued, however, that in certain respects the system is closer to fine-grained *streaming*, a practice which drew even more criticism than the banding that often replaced it. The superficial break between 50 per cent 'fast groups' and 50 per cent 'mixed-ability', for example, appears to create a simple bifurcation of the pupil population. However, not only are certain mixed-ability groups distinguished by their higher concentration of EAL and SEN pupils, but the 'fast groups' are also seen as differentiated: not all 'fast groups' are equally 'fast'. In this way, during the lower school years (Key Stage 3), Clough pupils are already experiencing rather different versions of comprehensive schooling depending on their placement in selective teaching groups. The subject options process represents a further point of selection, toward the end of Key Stage 3, as pupils attempt to 'choose' curricular specialisms while 'guided' by teachers and constrained by national and school policy on legitimate choice patterns.

The subject options process is officially presented as a moment of great importance for pupils, where they (with help from their parents) have the opportunity to make curricular choices that will have far-reaching consequences. In reality, however, pupils' 'choice' of subject is heavily constrained both formally and more covertly. Within Clough, pupils face markedly different expectations based largely upon teachers' views of their 'ability', still framed in many cases by 'IQ' and other test scores generated more than two years earlier. The head of careers and guidance plays a particularly important role, especially through his personal involvement in face-to-face option interviews. As we have shown, his guidance embodies many different concerns. In part he has to ensure that workable upper school teaching groups emerge. He is also engaged in various forms of academic selection; some subjects are seen as particularly suitable for pupils of more or less 'ability' and he tries to warm up and cool out choices so that pupils and subjects are matched 'appropriately'. Additionally, in some curricular areas there is an attempt to produce teaching groups in the upper school that are already 'set by ability'. More generally, the interviews also operate as a motivating device, emphasizing the importance of continued effort and relentlessly promoting the significance of five higher-grade passes. It is a cruel irony, therefore, that shortly after the options process is complete, at the beginning of Key Stage 4 (as pupils enter the upper school), further processes of selection get under way which mean that many pupils simply cannot attain this all-important benchmark – no matter how hard they try or how well they achieve in their final examinations. This situation arises from the general selection by ability to different 'sets' in the upper school and, in particular, through teachers' decisions about GCSE tiered examination entries. It is to these processes that we now turn.

5

Selection 14–16

sets, tiers, hidden ceilings and floors

I'm going. I'm going because I've had a lot of freedom of being
a very creative teacher in the classroom and I'm also pleased
that at the end of the day I always feel that my pupils did very
well and they always [reached their] best potential. (. . .) But
I don't think I'm doing justice for my pupils now. Partly because
I feel that I've had to make decisions that I *know* [have]
undermined their self-esteem and, and all those things make me
feel very uncomfortable because I know the children don't
believe it but I was very, very unhappy to do those things.

(Head of faculty, Clough GM, on her reasons for
leaving teaching after more than 20 years)

The increasing use of selection in secondary schools makes demands of
both teachers and pupils. As we will show, pupils are positioned as passive
recipients of decisions taken about them by others. For their part, teachers
are expected to pass judgement on pupils while weighing the various and
sometimes conflicting demands of a system that seems less and less tolerant
of uncertainty. The teacher quoted above is exceptional in deciding that the
demands are no longer tolerable; she speaks for many of her colleagues,
however, when reflecting on the pain that teachers feel compelled to endure,
and inflict upon young people, through their role in the various selection
processes that now shape secondary schooling.

In this chapter we focus on the processes of selection in the final years of
compulsory schooling, covering years 10 and 11 (Key Stage 4) when pupils
are aged 14–16. We have already discussed, in the previous chapter, the
growing use of selection and 'setting by ability' in the lower school (Key
Stage 3). Setting becomes more common in the upper school, and a large
part of this chapter concerns the differing philosophies and practices that
shape setting at this point. A further, and less widely understood, form of
selection also comes into play at this time. The use of tiered examination

papers is little known outside the teaching profession, and yet, by restricting the range of grades available to pupils, GCSE tiering represents a point of considerable selection and separation that has direct and potentially damaging consequences for pupil achievement. Tiering and setting operate in a complex, and sometimes unpredictable, relationship. The chapter begins by examining tiering as the context within which setting decisions are made by subject specialists.

In keeping with our approach in previous chapters, we begin by using Clough GM as the context for a detailed consideration of how tiering is experienced and perceived by teachers. Our focus then broadens to include Taylor Comprehensive, so as to provide for a wider range of issues around the interaction of school-level policies, departmental perspectives and the differing demands of GCSE tiering models (which stipulate either two or three tiers of entry). We conclude by examining some of the consequences of tiering and setting for inequalities of opportunity in the case-study schools. In particular, the processes appear to provide a powerful means of institutionalizing differences in teachers' assessments and expectations that deny equality of opportunity, especially for Black and working-class pupils.

GCSE tiers

Setting is now established in Clough as standard practice during years 10 and 11 as pupils work towards external examinations in their GCSE courses. Although some faculties are reluctant to pursue setting, as we have already noted, the school's senior management have embraced it as the only 'pragmatic' way of catering for the perceived range of abilities in Clough while meeting the needs of the A-to-C economy. Consequently, setting by ability is operated, in the words of one senior teacher, 'wherever there is the possibility' – that is, whenever a subject is taught in two or more groups that are timetabled simultaneously, allowing the faculty to move pupils between groups as they judge appropriate. In fact, some faculties still resist setting (more on this below). Nevertheless, setting is very widely operated in the school. Indeed, as we noted in the previous chapter, even in some subjects where pupil numbers will not allow setting in the upper school (because there will only be a single teaching group) there is sometimes an attempt to introduce a form of *de facto* setting during the options process (by restricting entry to the subject as a whole). It is within this context, of increasing selection by ability within the school generally, that teachers have to face additional selection decisions as the pupils near their final examinations. The *tiering* of GCSE examinations means that teachers are now required to make decisions that can literally place a cap on the maximum grade a pupil can achieve. These decisions must be taken within a system that provides severe penalties should pupils fail to meet the differentiated requirements of the separate examinations.

Figure 5.1   GCSE tiering models, 1998 and 1999

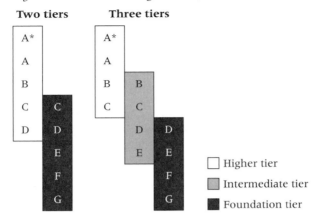

'Tiering' refers to the practice of entering pupils in the same subject for different examination papers. It is justified officially by arguing that in most (but not all) subjects it is not possible to examine adequately the full range of pupils via common question papers.[1] Consequently, pupils are entered for one of two or three tiered examinations (see Figure 5.1). The School Curriculum and Assessment Authority (SCAA) presented tiering as a response to differences in 'attainment' that benefits *all* pupils:

Why is tiering used in some GCSE examinations?
Tiering provides pupils with the opportunity to show what they know, understand and can do by presenting them with question papers that are targeted at a band of attainment.

For example, in English it would be difficult to find unseen reading material for a written examination that is suitable for grade G pupils and would also stretch grade A* pupils.

For each tier of entry, the written question papers will:

• be at an appropriate level of difficulty for the range of grades available at their tier;
• prompt the more able to respond at a greater depth;
• provide opportunities for the less able to show what they know;
• use appropriate language.

(SCAA 1996: 3)

Initially, there was some variation in tiering arrangements between different examination boards. In the late 1990s, however, as part of its remit to oversee examinations nationally, the SCAA (later replaced by the Qualifications and Curriculum Authority) acted both to harmonize and extend tiering (see Table 5.1):

Table 5.1   GCSE tiering subject by subject, 1998 and 1999

GCSE subjects and short courses with **two tiers**: *new tiering arrangements from 1998*
Business studies*
Classical civilization*
Design and technology:
   Electronic products
   Food technology
   Graphic products
   Resistant materials technology
   Systems and control technology
   Textiles technology
Economics*
Electronics*
English
English literature
French
Geography
German
Greek*
Home economics:
   Child development
   Consumer studies
   Food and nutrition
   Textiles
Information technology
Italian
Latin*
Law*
Modern Hebrew
Office studies
Panjabi
Politics*
Polish
Psychology*
Russian
Science:
   Biology
   Chemistry
   Human physiology and health
   Physics
   Coordinated
   Modular
Social science*
Sociology*
Spanish
Statistics
Urdu

GCSE subjects with **two tiers**: *new tiering arrangements from 1999*
Accounting
Agriculture and horticulture
Environmental studies
General studies
Nautical studies
Office applications

GCSE subjects with **three tiers**: *new tiering arrangements from 1998*
Mathematics

GCSE subjects and short courses with **no tiers**
Archaeology
Art
Drama and theatre arts
Expressive arts
History
Humanities
Music
Performing arts: dance
Physical education
Religious studies
Religious education

* Subjects in which this model was introduced in and from 1996
Source: Northern Examinations and Assessment Board (1997: 2)

From 1998, most large-entry GCSE subjects will be examined through a foundation tier covering grades G to C and a higher tier covering grades D to A*. For some subjects, examinations will be tiered for the first time. Mathematics is the only subject that retains three tiers on entry in 1998.

(SCAA 1996: 3)

Before we examine how teachers in Clough approach tiering decisions, it is vital that several features of tiering are clearly understood. First, pupils can only be entered for examination in a single tier. Teachers are not allowed to enter the same pupil in more than one tier per subject, no matter how uncertain they may be as to the 'appropriate' tier for any individual.[2] This restriction is crucially important in view of a second feature of tiering procedures, namely, that pupils cannot exceed the ceiling (the highest grade allowed) for their tier. Guidance from one of the largest GCSE examination boards presents this as follows: 'On the *Foundation Tier (F)*, candidates cannot gain above grade C no matter how well they do' (Northern Examinations and Assessment Board (NEAB) 1997: 1; emphasis in original). In mathematics, which has three tiers, the highest possible grade in the Foundation tier is D.

Third, each tier has a lower grade that acts as a minimum below which pupils are unclassified. This means that a Higher-tier pupil who fails to achieve a grade D (or a grade C in mathematics) effectively falls through the floor of the tier: they are '"unclassified" and will not receive a GCSE certificate' (NEAB 1997: 1). Before the general restructuring of tiers in 1998, some boards made provision for the award of 'exceptional grades': that is, a candidate could be awarded a grade one or (sometimes) two grades above or below the tier limits if 'the Awards Meeting judges that an individual candidate has been entered for an inappropriate tier *and* that there is evidence to support an award outside the tier' (NEAB n.d.: 8; emphasis added). Originally, *all* provision for exceptional grades was removed at the time of the 1998 tiering changes: this was the situation that teachers were getting to grips with during our fieldwork. Subsequently, however, a limited provision for an additional *lower* grade was reintroduced 'to allow higher paper candidates who just miss a D to be awarded an E' (Cassidy 1998b: 5). Officially described as 'a safety net' for a 'very few candidates', this change was given minimal publicity and presented as making little or no difference to how schools should approach tiering decisions.[3]

Tiering in English and mathematics

How tiering works in practice was one of guiding questions in designing this research project: in order to examine the significance of GCSE tiering, and how teachers perceive the decisions they must take, we decided to study two subject departments in some detail. We settled on two of the 'core'

Figure 5.2   GCSE tiering in English examinations before and after 1998
(Clough GM)

Before 1998   1998 and after

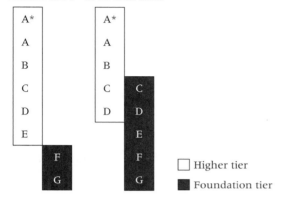

National Curriculum subjects, English and mathematics. We chose these for
a variety of reasons. First, from 1998 mathematics is the only subject to use
a three-tier approach, and we wanted to compare the different models of
tiering. We were also conscious of the expansion of tiering to a wider range
of subjects, and wanted to include a subject still finding its way through the
system. Mathematics has the longest history of using tiered examinations,
and so a good contrast seemed to be English. Tiered papers were first used in
English examinations in 1994: this meant that at the time of our fieldwork
(1996–1997), English teachers would have been able to establish mechanisms
for making the decisions (they would not be floundering with a totally
novel situation) but would still be relatively new to the process. Finally, the
two departments offer a good sample because, as compulsory subjects in the
National Curriculum, both have to make tiering decisions for the entire
range of perceived ability within the school.[4]

English language and literature: two tiers in practice

Now this year there's something happened with our [English
syllabus] which is very scary for us.
                              (Acting head of English, Clough GM)

Before the 1998 changes, English language and English literature examinations in Clough were already based on a two-tier model. The number of
tiers did not change in 1998, but their *composition* did (see Figure 5.2). The
previous model utilized a large Higher tier (grades A*–E) and a much smaller
lower tier (grades F–G).[5] On paper, at least, the new arrangements might
appear to offer some improvement: after all, the new tiers now include an
official overlap of two grades (C and D). Additionally, since the all-important

Figure 5.3   GCSE tiering in English: formal, advised and hidden targeting

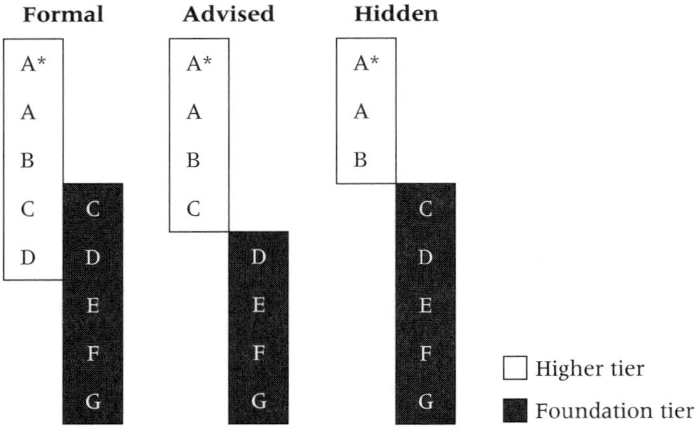

Formal	Advised	Hidden
A*	A*	A*
A	A	A
B	B	B
C C	C	C
D D	D	D
E	E	E
F	F	F
G	G	G

☐ Higher tier
■ Foundation tier

Formal = Actual grade limits to each tier.
Advised = Targeting advised by SCAA.
Hidden = Distinctions adopted by teachers.

grade C is now available in *both* tiers, theoretically *all* pupils can attain a higher-grade pass. Nevertheless, English teachers in Clough see the changes as a retrograde step that makes tiering decisions both more difficult and more dangerous. In order to understand this perspective, it is vital to make sense of how the teachers interpret the nature of the tiers in practice as opposed to their formal presentation.

First, it is necessary to consider the official version of how the tiers are 'targeted' and the formal advice on determining the appropriate tier of entry:

How should the tier of entry for a pupil be decided?
Pupils should be entered for the tier that will give them the best opportunity to show their ability. Teachers will know their pupils' work very well by the time decisions have to be made [initially in January or February for a June examination].

In subjects which have two tiers of entry, grades C and D are available on both tiers. Pupils likely to achieve a grade in the range G to D should be entered for foundation tier and those expected to achieve a grade in the range C to A* should be entered for the higher tier. There may be pupils who produce some work at grade C standard but who find the style, or presentation, of the higher tier questions difficult to respond to consistently. It may be more appropriate to enter such pupils for the foundation tier, where grade C is still available.

(SCAA 1996: 5)

SCAA, therefore, proposed that teachers view the tiers rather more selectively than their formal composition (see Figure 5.3). It is noticeable that SCAA's advice presents the examinations as a chance for pupils to 'show their ability' and appears confident that teachers will have plenty of information upon which to base their assessment of pupils' likely results. SCAA suggests that pupils 'expected' to achieve grade C or better should be placed in the Higher tier, offering them the chance to gain the very highest grades (often essential for entry to degree courses in higher education). SCAA presents the Foundation tier as effectively targeted at 'G to D' pupils and emphasizes that even here 'grade C is still available' – note the crucial weight given to grade C, another sign of the A-to-C economy at work.

Official advice on determining the appropriate tier of entry, therefore, presents the decision as relatively unproblematic. In key respects this calm, rational and confident presentation is at odds with the reality of the situation as experienced by the teachers making the actual entry decisions. It is significant that when she talks about tiering decisions, for example, the acting head of English in Clough often makes reference to danger. A sense of risk and possible harm characterizes her perception of the new arrangements:

Head of English: If [before 1998] it were felt that, with the best will in the world, all the kid was going to come up with would be an F or a G, you were in the lower tier (. . .) And we got used to those, you know, *boundaries*. And there was never, there were never mistakes made as to kids going into the wrong tier or anything.

Researcher: What sort of proportions of kids are distributed across those?

Head of English: In this school the majority on the upper tier, 'cause it's from A-to-E, and the minority on the lower tier.

Researcher: Right.

Head of English: This year it is totally turned on its head for the first time ever and it's very scary. (. . .) The tiers are now as follows: The upper tier A, B and C grades only. So if, on the day, the child does badly, performs badly, there's no 'Oh roll down' (. . .) They've got nothing, nothing for Lang[uage] nothing for Lit[erature]. Now that is a nightmare, you know?

Researcher: How high does the lower tier now go?

Head of English: The lower tier is ostensibly D through to G, but they can roll up, we've been told, and get a C. So now the majority of the school is going to be put into the lower tier, as it's called.

It is clear from this extract that the teacher is unhappy with the tiering changes. The previous Higher tier (A*–E) was seen to cater for the majority of pupils, leaving a lower tier (F–G) for only those who were seen as markedly below the level expected to have a reasonable chance of a higher-grade pass. The teacher seems supremely confident that pupils were not denied the chance to achieve to their potential in the previous tiering arrangements: 'there were never mistakes made as to kids going into the wrong tier or anything'. This confidence is in stark contrast to the uncertainty that characterizes her talk about the new tiers. On first sight the quotation seems to suggest that the teacher may simply have the wrong idea about the grades in each of the new tiers. She seems to be saying, for example, that grade D is not available to higher tier entrants: 'The upper tier A, B and C grades only'. Additionally she appears confused about the possibility of 'rolling' up or down a grade: she tells us that a Higher-tier pupil cannot roll down a grade, but one in the 'lower' (Foundation) tier can 'roll up'. The acting head of English is mistaken if she is using 'rolling up/down' uniformly as a colloquialism for the pre-1998 possibility of some pupils being awarded 'exceptional grades' outside the formal limits of the tier: as we have noted, this provision was largely removed in 1998. However, as the interview progresses it becomes clear that something more complex, and significant, is happening here.

The phrase 'rolling up/down' is an echo of the pre-1998 provision for exceptional grades but is now used with reference, not to the *formal* composition of each tier, but the *informal* limits being imposed by the English faculty. The threat of a Higher-tier pupil falling through the floor of the tier, and being ungraded, introduces a degree of uncertainty and danger unlike anything the English teachers have previously faced. The official provision for Higher-tier pupils to get a grade D, *and no lower*, is seen as completely redefining the nature of the upper tier. It is no longer 'safe' to enter a pupil on the Higher tier if there is any doubt that they are more than capable of a higher-grade pass:

> Unless we could swear and put money on the fact that they're going to get an A or a B we can't risk them in that top tier. So they've got to be very bright, they've got to be highly motivated, they've got to be permanent attenders, you know, the wind's got to be blowing in the right direction on every count. And so, for example, out of my English group, this is the Key Stage 3 group. I've got 30 kids in that set. When we have our meeting, which will be this summer, to put them into their groups for Key Stage 4, I will be going through with a very fine-toothed comb that they fit the criteria in every way, shape or form. (. . .) If I have any doubts I can't risk it or else the kid's going to have nothing, no Lang, no Lit.
>
> (Acting head of English, Clough GM)

Consequently, the danger of a Higher-tier entrant being ungraded (if they fail to merit a grade D) is seen as so great that the teacher simply 'can't risk it'. In practice, therefore, the Higher tier shrinks to become suitable (in the teachers' eyes) only for pupils destined for grades A*-to-B. The Foundation tier (previously used for a minority of pupils) now becomes a 'safe' home for the majority – 'safe' because the all-important grade C is at least available to all, even though the tier is officially targeted at those likely to gain grades D-to-G. It is in this sense that Foundation-tier pupils can still 'roll up' to a higher-grade pass (in this teacher's terminology) if they achieve better than predicted by staff.

The English teachers, therefore, have reinvented the new tiers in view of their perception of the danger involved in entering anyone for the Higher tier unless, in the words of the departmental head, 'the wind's (. . .) blowing in the right direction on every count'. *Any* suggestion of a deficit in terms of ability *and* attitude ('they've got to be highly motivated, they've got to be permanent attenders') is taken to define the pupil as material for the Foundation tier. This means that, for the very best intentioned of reasons (with a particular view of the pupils' interests in mind), the English teachers in Clough have remade the Higher tier into a much more selective environment, even than envisaged by SCAA (see Figure 5.3). Foundation-tier pupils have no opportunity to gain grade B or above – a restriction that could prove costly in the competition for entry to further and higher education. Nevertheless, because of the weight placed on grade C (historically and in the terms of the A-to-C economy), such a limitation is seen as nothing compared to the danger of being ungraded on the Higher tier. In this way, a system of *hidden* tiers is in operation – hidden in the sense that (like the 'hidden curriculum') the informal system adopted by teachers defines the reality of access and opportunity within the school but differs markedly from the formal presentation in policy documents.

Despite the assured tone of official pronouncements on tiering, therefore, in reality the situation is considerably more complex and, in teachers' eyes, dangerous – dangerous because of the disproportionate weight attached to higher-grade passes in general and the significance of the C grade in particular. An ideal situation would seem to be one where all pupils, as they begin answering their examination papers, retain the opportunity to achieve the highest possible grades. This is especially important where teachers' assumptions about 'ability' and motivation can be skewed by stereotypes attached to certain social class, ethnic and gender groups. As we have already indicated, our case-study schools use setting and other forms of selection (for example, in the options process) progressively to differentiate pupils according to their perceived ability and motivation. Even so, where they are examined by a common question paper there still remains the possibility that pupils might confound their second-class labels, might buck the trend of increasing selection and demotivation, by surprising their teachers and outperforming expectations.[6] For many pupils tiering, by definition, removes this opportunity by placing a ceiling on the grades it is possible for them to achieve. In this context, teachers must balance their desire to give pupils the chance to achieve as highly as possible against the possibility that they might lose everything by falling through the floor of the Higher tier. This is a gamble not only for the pupil, but (within the terms of the A-to-C economy) for the teacher, the department and, ultimately, the school. Playing 'safe', in this

Figure 5.4   GCSE tiering in mathematics examinations before and after 1998 (Clough GM)

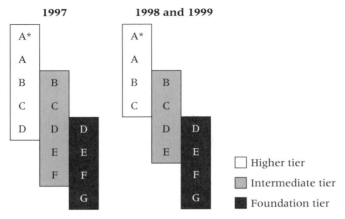

context, translates into placing increasing numbers in the Foundation tier, sacrificing the possibility of the best grades for the sake of avoiding unclassified results while retaining access to a grade C.

As Figure 5.3 indicates, although the two-tier model seems to present plenty of scope for overlap (grades C and D are common) the true situation is somewhat different. SCAA advises teachers to be more selective about the Higher tier, using an expected grade C as the lowest point of inclusion. As we have shown, however, in practice a system of hidden tiers operates so that the Higher tier shrinks still further, with the Clough English department using grade B as a cut-off point. The message of the diminishing Higher tiers in Figure 5.3 is clear: the closer tiering moves to the chalk face, the more exclusive is access to the highest-grade examination passes.

Mathematics: three tiers in practice

I dislike this *tiered* exam. I think it would have been better if there was one exam.
                                     (Head of mathematics, Clough GM)

Mathematics is the only GCSE subject to operate three tiers after 1998. During our fieldwork Clough GM already used a syllabus based on three-tiered entry. However, the withdrawal of the provision for exceptional grades, and the tier/grade compositions stipulated for 1998 and 1999, mean that (like the English department) mathematics teachers face changes to the formal tiering arrangements (see Figure 5.4).

As with the two-tier system, SCAA provides guidance for teachers on how to decide pupils' tier of entry:

Figure 5.5 GCSE tiering in mathematics: formal, advised and hidden targeting

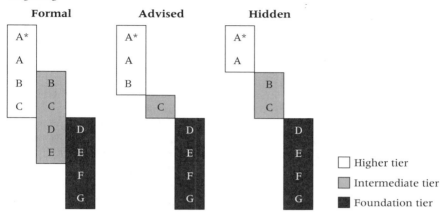

In mathematics, which has three tiers of entry, the range of grades available in the higher tier is narrower than in other subjects. Pupils whose estimated grade is C should be entered for the intermediate tier, and only those likely to achieve grades B to A* should be entered for the higher tier. Grade C is available on the higher tier for pupils who perform less well than expected.

(SCAA 1996: 5)

As was the case with English examinations, therefore, in mathematics there has been a shrinkage in the size of the Higher tier. In formal terms the Higher tier changed from five grades (A*–D) in 1997 to four grades (A*–C) in 1998. Equally important, SCAA's advice on determining pupils' appropriate tier of entry reduces the Higher tier by a further grade (advising entry only for those 'likely to achieve grades B to A*'). Again, this echoes the situation in English examinations, where SCAA advises teachers to treat the Higher tier as one grade more exclusive than is officially the case. Similarly, when we turn to the perspective of mathematics specialists in Clough, we find that teachers are restricting entry to the Higher tier still further: again, a hidden tiering system is in operation (see Figure 5.5). In contrast to the English case, however, the mathematics department did not associate this increased selection with the altered tiers in 1998 – having *already* adopted this approach when the Higher tier was, in formal terms at least, more inclusive than is now the case:

In the Higher level you get A*, A, B and C. They may award them a D in the Higher level but, you know, otherwise it's unclassified. This is where there's a big problem about children who you, I mean you only really put kids in the Higher level if you're sure they're going to get an

A, which is very difficult. So you, if you *think* that somebody's going to get a B, instead of putting them for the Higher level, you put them in for the Intermediate because you're going to guarantee a B. Which, again, I don't like doing that because, you know, it would be nice to encourage children to do the higher level but it's, it's this kind of thing, which I am forced to do, is to play the system, you know?

(Head of mathematics, Clough GM)

In Clough GM, therefore, the mathematics department restricts the Higher tier to those pupils they are confident will attain grade A or A*: this system of hidden tiers was in place even before the 1998 amendments, when the Higher tier still officially included grade D. This is more exclusive than recommended by SCAA and, like their colleagues in English, reflects the mathematics teachers' judgements about the risks involved in entry to the various tiers:

Researcher: How does the Intermediate *guarantee* a B for the same kids who might not get a B if you put them in higher?

Head of Mathematics: Well because you see, I mean I'm not saying that it does *guarantee* them a B but they're answering a question paper that starts from questions on [National Curriculum] level 5 and level 6 (. . .) which probably is easier for them. 'Cause some children just freeze in exam times, so they get easier questions to start off with, so by the time they're getting on to questions on level 7 and 8 they seem to be able to cope better with it. Whereas if they're on the Higher level they might not have enough easy questions at the beginning of the paper to put them at ease. So they're starting straight away with levels 7 and 8 questions (. . .) I think it is very important because I think, if we just think of ourselves, you know, if you just think about doing an exam, you know, you want the first couple of questions to be something you can do just like that. And then later on, you know, once you're into it, you've got over your fear, your first few fears of exams.

As the departmental head explains, therefore, the particular structure of GCSE mathematics papers is also seen as a key factor. This teacher places considerable importance on pupils being able to settle into their question papers without feeling immediately intimidated: 'you want the first couple of questions to be something you can do just like that'. This view of the particular dangers posed by mathematics papers has important consequences. First, it means that the Higher tier becomes very exclusive. Additionally there is a knock-on effect, through the Intermediate and Foundation tiers, such that even pupils thought to be destined for a grade D come to be seen as a risk in the Intermediate tier (which extends to a grade E and offers their last chance of a higher-grade pass):

> a lot of kids want a C and so we have kids who we know they'll probably get a D if they do the Foundation. But if they did the Intermediate they might again, for the same reason, not get a D.
>
> (Head of mathematics, Clough GM)

The teacher's concern that pupils have the chance to settle 'into' their question papers, therefore, leads to a situation where 'playing safe' actually means placing some children in the lowest tier (where a grade C is not available) despite their expectation that the pupil will miss the C grade quite narrowly. This decision pits the teacher's desire for pupils to do as well as possible (and the pupils' hunger for grade Cs) against the teacher's fear that the structure of Higher- and Intermediate-tier papers, by beginning with relatively difficult questions straight away, might lead the pupil to 'freeze' or 'freak out'. This is seen as a problem for both genders but especially girls:

> Well, I just think, you know, that a lot of children, and especially girls for some reason, I don't know why, I mean again it's just my gut feeling, I don't think there's any scientific research to show this. But just from my gut feeling I just feel that girls always let themselves down more in exams. I mean like for instance just today, this [test] they had, you saw yourself how worked up they were. And when I went round, which you may not have noticed, when I went round to talk to some of the girls, they make silly mistakes, you know? (. . .) Kelly, I was talking to her and she just did a hash of things and she just said, 'Oh miss, I'm just so nervous'. And I said, 'What for? It's just [for] me, it's just practice!' You don't get nervous in a practice. But if you just take that as an example of how nervous they get. So this is one of the reasons why I feel that if they do the Intermediate they would warm up to the more difficult questions and answer the questions on levels 7 and 8 better, because it comes at the end of levels 5 and 6, than they would if they started off with them. And then *also*, you know, what a lot of children do, even though you tell them not to, I mean they look at other questions before they start answering, which is not a bad thing, I don't think. And then they'll look at some questions in level 9s and 10s and they'll think 'Oh my God, I don't understand this!' And it freaks them out.
>
> (Head of mathematics, Clough GM)

It is important to recognize that this teacher is not only a woman, but one of the most active members of staff when it comes to issues of equal opportunities across the school. Her view of the increased likelihood for girls to 'freak out' in mathematics examinations, therefore, cannot simply be dismissed as narrow sexist stereotyping by an uninformed male head of department. It may hint at something more fundamental about gendered perspectives within mathematics as a subject sub-culture. Certainly, there is a good deal of research to suggest that certain subject specialisms tend to support particular ideological positions (cf. Ball 1987; Lacey 1977; Sikes *et al.* 1985): often mathematics and science departments, for example, have been found to be somewhat more traditional and authoritarian than colleagues in English or the humanities (cf. Ball 1981; Ball and Lacey 1980; Gillborn 1994). It is interesting to reflect that one of the earliest studies of inequity in tiered GCSE entry raised concerns about the position of girls in mathematics. Gordon Stobart *et al.* (1992) found that a desire to 'play safe' interacted with mathematics teachers' uncertainty about the performance of girls so that tiering decisions tended to accentuate differences in maths performance between the genders. Since then, of course, the UK has witnessed a moral panic about boys' under-achievement (cf. Epstein *et al.* 1998a; 1998b) that, while promoting anti-anti-sexist positions in the media, may actually have fed into a raising of teachers' expectations about girls' 'ability'. Interestingly, data on the final tiers of entry in Clough do not reveal any significant difference between boys and girls in mathematics (see below). Unfortunately, there is evidence that other inequalities are not only reflected in tiering decisions, but may even be accentuated by the process.

Tiers and tears

Our examination of tiering in GCSE English and mathematics reveals some fascinating and disturbing trends. Teachers in both departments tend to view tiering decisions as difficult, distasteful and dangerous.[7] The language of risk dominates. At greatest risk in these decisions is pupils' opportunity to win the highest pass grades in GCSE examinations: for many, the ceiling on Foundation (and, in maths, Intermediate) tiers means that the very best they can hope for may be less than they need or want. Their teachers are aware of these possibilities but weigh them against another risk: the risk of falling through the tier 'floor' and being ungraded. This risk jeopardizes both the pupil and the teacher: for the teacher (and the department and school) higher-grade passes are all-important in the A-to-C economy.

GCSE tiering decisions therefore create a maze of risk and counter-risk. In both departments the teachers' response is to restrict entry to the Higher tier, even more than suggested in official advice. The result is a system of hidden tiers: the teachers redefine tiers in ways that are more precise and exclusionary than both the formal structures presented in GCSE syllabuses and SCAA guidance.

The major difference between the departments seems to be that mathematics have remained unmoved by the 1998 tiering changes: they had already adopted a highly selective approach to tiering. In English, by contrast, the 1998 changes are seen as reversing the balance of pupils so that the majority will now enter the Foundation tier: 'it is totally turned on its head'. The reasons for this difference between departments are not certain. It may be a reflection of the longer history of tiering in mathematics, but it also seems likely to reflect, at least in part, something of a mathematics subject sub-culture where knowledge has long tended to be viewed as hierarchical and structured according to a clear linear progression: this, of course, is part of the very reason for mathematics being the only subject where three tiers are felt necessary and justifiable.

It is clear that, despite some differences, GCSE tiering decisions are viewed as painful and dangerous by both English and mathematics teachers in Clough. As the next part of our analysis suggests, however, the distribution of pupils across GCSE tiers indicates that it is certain pupils who currently pay the highest price.

Setting and tier entry

Having outlined the formal and hidden restrictions that result from GCSE tiering procedures, we now focus on the details of pupils' placement in particular teaching and examination groups. To this point we have used one school (Clough GM) as the principal context within which to examine the minutiae of selection processes: it is now useful, however, to broaden our area of concern by drawing explicitly on data from both our case-study schools. This is revealing because the two schools operate somewhat different philosophies of pupil grouping in the upper school. An analysis of pupils' set and tier placements across the two schools, therefore, offers an interesting comparison between different philosophies and practices, and allows us to examine a sample of pupils that is larger than possible in most qualitative studies.

The relationship between sets and tiers is neither uniform nor simple. As we have seen, Clough's overarching policy (led senior management) is to set pupils 'by ability'; in contrast, Taylor's overall policy is to retain mixed-ability groups. Yet as we move closer to the chalk face, we find that school-level *policies*, concerning the nature of teaching groups, are not necessarily reflected in *practice* at faculty level. In exploring the complex and multiple relationships between tiers, sets, policy and practice we will continue to focus on the English and mathematics departments. As will become evident, there is no single or predictable relationship between the structure of GCSE tiers and teaching-group composition during Key Stage 4. Nevertheless, the structuring (and restructuring) of the tiers is deeply implicated in senior managers' and faculty leaders' decisions concerning the organization of teaching groups. In turn, set composition places certain pupils in a markedly disadvantaged position in relation to their final tier of entry in GCSE exams.

Mathematics departments

Taylor Comprehensive

There is a clear and deliberate link between setting and tier entry in mathematics at Taylor. Despite the school's general commitment to mixed-ability grouping, in this faculty teaching groups are set by ability and inextricably linked to tiers from the beginning of year 9 through to GCSE examination. Furthermore, mathematics is timetabled across the year group, rather than in two half-year blocks as is the case for all other GCSE subjects in the school. This organizational decision was made with the express purpose of enabling maximum differentiation within mathematics. This runs directly counter to the school-level commitment to mixed-ability teaching and is explained by the headteacher with explicit reference to GCSE tiering:

> what has led to our setting for maths and science is mainly the National Curriculum requirements and the tiered entry for GCSE. In other words, in those two subjects it's much more external pressure than internal desire.

Two related aspects of the tiered system lead the school to view setting as its only available response – namely, the differences in *content* between each tiered syllabus and the subsequent *pace* at which the higher syllabus must be covered:

> it is all a question of volume of content and therefore of pace moving through the syllabus (. . .) If you want children to get up to the highest levels, National Curriculum levels, then they've got to work at a particular pace to cover the necessary ground. And you either have an individualized learning scheme, with no whole-class teaching, which would allow the average of five or six kids in each class who are aiming at the highest levels to work on their own, or you set them.
>
> (Headteacher, Taylor Comprehensive)

Although the school has judged that setting in mathematics is the only practical option available in the context of tiering, it remains firmly opposed to both tiering and setting in principle. The introduction of tiering is perceived as a direct attempt to impose setting upon schools and reinscribe the divisions inherent to the old bipartite examinations system (between GCE O-level and CSE examinations) which the GCSE was initially promoted as abolishing. Asked 'How do you see a tiered GCSE?', Taylor's headteacher replied:

> I think it's condemnable. I think it's been an attempt to do two things. First of all, to reintroduce the dual [exam] system by the back door. Secondly, to impose a system of internal organization on the schools, to wit: streaming. (. . .) When it was first mooted I was completely baffled because, after all, it's not long ago that we went through that extensive exercise with research consultation, tons and tons of literature

on criteria-based GCSE gradings. Now that's all gone clean out the window. It's again to up the ante of league tables.

This analysis is echoed by the head of mathematics:

I mean, the whole purpose for a GCSE when it was originated was ideal because, in a subject like maths they immediately then contradicted all that and had tiers. And the whole purpose of GCSE was everybody followed the same course and everybody did the same exam and you came out with your grades. But in, that doesn't work in maths. It doesn't work in science, I don't think. It doesn't work in English. In English they only have two tiers but at least they all still follow the same work in English, they achieve at their own level in English I believe, but in maths *we have to predetermine their level before we even start teaching them*. (our emphasis)

It might be assumed that within Taylor, the headteacher and the head of faculty are the best placed to determine the way in which teaching groups are organized. Yet despite their strenuous criticism of tiering, and the setting it demands, neither of these members of staff feels able actively to resist this move within the confines of the A-to-C economy. In practice, set placement relates directly to tier placement in Taylor's mathematics faculty from year 9 onwards, when mixed-ability, tutor group-led maths groups are replaced by a hierarchy of eight ability- and tier-based maths sets. Each set is ranked; identified as studying for a particular tiered GCSE examination; and syllabuses and resources are selected to enable teaching for the relevant tier. The head of mathematics in Taylor represents the set/tier relationship as a clear organizational one, which we reproduce here as Figure 5.6.

The head of faculty states that pupils are allocated to a set/tier that will 'stretch' them and asserts that movement between groups remains possible into year 11. However, when this is examined in detail, it appears that set movement is most unusual beyond the middle of year 10 and is commonly restricted to movement between sets of the *same tier*. Movement between different tiers is rare and usually limited to *downward* movement (demotion). Teachers explain this with reference to the discrete nature of the syllabus for each tier:

Head of mathematics:	And then through the whole of year 9, 10 and 11 there are loads of opportunities, or loads of times during those three years, where children can change in and out of the tiers – in and out of the *groups*, sorry. (our emphasis)
Researcher:	Right. So when you say they can move between groups, can they move between *tiers*?
Head of mathematics:	Yes. That's what we tend to do. Once you get to year, middle of year 10, towards the end of year 10 and you realize that, the change inter-tiers tends to

Figure 5.6   Mathematics sets and GCSE tier entries: a schematic representation (Taylor Comprehensive)

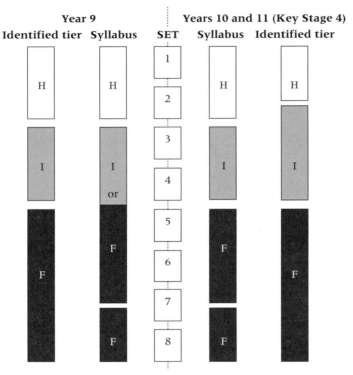

Year 9   **Years 10 and 11 (Key Stage 4)**
Identified tier Syllabus   SET   Syllabus Identified tier

Source: Diagram sketched by Taylor's head of mathematics during field interview.

happen less often. In year 9 and year 10 we're very flexible about, but late year 10 and early year 11 to change a tier is a big – 'cause you haven't really followed that course.

Researcher: Right.

Head of mathematics: Downwards yes, but not very often upwards.

Our discussions with other mathematics teachers in Taylor suggest that movement *between tiers* is limited even before the middle of year 10. For example, towards the end of year 9 (a full 12 months before the head of mathematics says that movement becomes unworkable), the teacher of set 6 (the second of the four year 9 Foundation sets) explains a number of recent movements into and out of her set. These include movements up and down, but they are all *within* the cluster of Foundation sets:

this boy here has just come up; that boy just come up from the very bottom set; there were a couple of girls who have come down. There are four Foundation groups and this is the second, so she's moved down from another one (. . .) there are two that I've just pushed up . . .

As we can see from Figure 5.6, during year 9 there are pupils in five different maths sets all studying the same syllabus (in the sets numbered 3–6, and including part of set 7): a separate Intermediate syllabus is only introduced in Key Stage 4. As such, upward *tier* movement remains viable *in principle* until the end of year 9 for pupils in sets 5 and 6, and some in set 7. In *practice*, however, this does not appear to be the case. For example, in year 9 the teacher of set 6 (above) explains that she will continue to teach this group as a Foundation tier group in the upper school. Hence, towards the end of year 9, the tier for which these pupils will be entered has in fact already been determined. In outlining the relationship between the year 9 Intermediate/Foundation syllabus and the distinct syllabuses for Intermediate and Foundation pupils in Key Stage 4, this teacher demonstrates that the rigidity of tier allocation in the upper school is viewed as inscribed in the very nature of the tiered syllabuses and their associated teaching resources:

Maths teacher: The structure of these [text]books is that, if you think of the four [Foundation] classes and the kind of middle [the two Intermediate sets], in the third year [year 9] they all do [books] B1 and B2 and from there they either do R books – which leads on to Intermediate – or the B3, 4 and 5 books – which will lead them on to Foundation. (. . .) So in fact, B3 is easier than these [B1 and B2] because they take them up to Foundation. So in fact, the paperwork will be quicker, the work will be slightly easier and when they will come back to this it will be in a much simplified, a much, much simplified form.

Researcher: So is this work they're doing [in year 9] the hardest stuff they're going to do?

Maths teacher: Ermm . . . yes, but they'll still carry on doing it. This is level 6 and when they do the Foundation, that will be the limit, you know, level 6 will be the top . . . and that's the way we do things, and I've found it really works well, to start with this and work back.

This early cementing of tier allocations can be seen in the contrasting ways in which year 9 pupils in particular sets/tiers are warmed up or cooled out for GCSE. For instance, in maths set 1 (the first of the two year 9 Higher tier maths sets) lesson content is already related *directly* and *explicitly* to the demands of the Higher tier GCSE examination paper:

[Teacher to the class (year 9, maths set 1)]:
Now lets learn a noun that you'll need to be familiar with for GCSE.
[The teacher dictates.]
That's the GCSE Higher level way of writing that question, the simpler way is [explains in more direct language]. Unfortunately they won't write it like that.

(Observation fieldnotes)

In contrast, maths set number 6 are following a syllabus that *could* lead to Intermediate- or Foundation-level study, but they have in fact already been identified as a Foundation set. Here pupils are 'reassured' that the Key Stage 4 syllabus will be *easier* than the one they are following at present:

[Teacher to the class (year 9, maths set 6)]:
When you go on to the next book in the series, which might be before the end of term, you might find that it starts off in a slightly easier way than this book ends up, for those members of the class that have recently joined, if you're looking at these equations and some of these formulas and thinking 'Oh my God, I've never seen anything like this before', don't worry, you will see things like this again plenty of times – it will get easier.

(Observation fieldnotes)

It is worth reminding ourselves of the belief of the head of mathematics that pupils are placed in sets that will 'stretch' them (above). This notion, that different tiers allow all pupils to be 'stretched', is a common theme in arguments proposing the benefits of differentiated grouping. Indeed, as we have already seen (above) it is a reason given in official justifications of tiering (SCAA 1996: 3). And yet, in Taylor we have a situation where year 9 maths pupils (a full two years from examination) can look forward to work that 'will get easier'. This confirms the point that arose through an interview with the faculty head (quoted earlier) that 'work they're doing [in year 9]' is 'the hardest stuff they're going to do'. In Taylor, therefore, we have a school dedicated to an inclusive comprehensive philosophy (including the retention of mixed-ability teaching) but where the mathematics department (with the full support of the headteacher) not only operates a policy of setting 'by ability', but where sets relate directly to GCSE tiers and pupils destined for the Foundation tier can expect little or no 'stretching' in Key Stage 4. Patently, Foundation tier pupils are not the priority within the A-to-C economy.

By the end of year 9, therefore, upward inter-tier movement (promotion) is only considered possible (although rare in practice) for pupils in the highest sets of the Foundation and Intermediate tiers. By Key Stage 4 no such upward movement is possible. Promotion into a higher set, it seems, is precluded not by a lack of will or vision on the part of faculty staff but, rather, by the nature of the tiered syllabuses themselves: 'you haven't really

Figure 5.7 Mathematics sets and GCSE tier entries (Taylor Comprehensive)

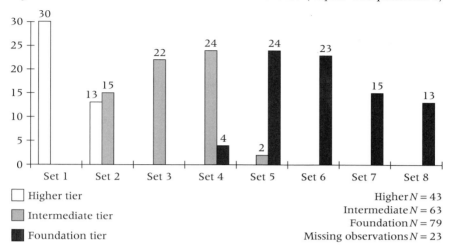

☐ Higher tier

▨ Intermediate tier

■ Foundation tier

Higher $N = 43$
Intermediate $N = 63$
Foundation $N = 79$
Missing observations $N = 23$

followed that course'. In contrast, downward inter-tier movement (demotion) remains possible. For instance, Figure 5.6 shows that only a part of set number 2 (the second Higher tier set) is expected to be entered for the Higher tier examination (despite having followed the appropriate syllabus through year 9 and Key Stage 4). Analysis of the actual tier allocation of year 11 pupils demonstrates that the rigidity of sets/tiers identified by teachers is reflected in practice almost without exception.[8] In this case set number 2 was eventually divided approximately equally into Higher and Intermediate tier examinations, as anticipated by the head of faculty. The only unpredicted tier entry was seen in set number 4 (the lower Intermediate set) and set number 5 (the highest of the Foundation sets), where a very small number of pupils experienced downward or upward tier movement respectively (see Figure 5.7).

The marrying of sets to tiers, and the almost blanket preclusion of upward tier movement in the upper school, has serious implications for pupils' access to passes of both the *highest* and *higher* grades. The headteacher is all too aware of the patterns of inequality that may emerge: he anticipates, for example, that outcomes for Higher tier pupils may be enhanced but at the expense of depressed outcomes for pupils in the Foundation and Intermediate tiers – the latter would certainly coincide with much previous research in the field (cf. Gillborn and Gipps 1996; Hallam and Toutounji 1996; Hatcher 1997; Oakes 1990; Slavin 1996):

Headteacher: I think it's highly likely that the kids in the top tier will do somewhat better than they would have done in mixed-ability classes. (. . .) I think, however, you may get a worsening,

Figure 5.8　GCSE mathematics tiers by ethnic origin (Taylor Comprehensive)

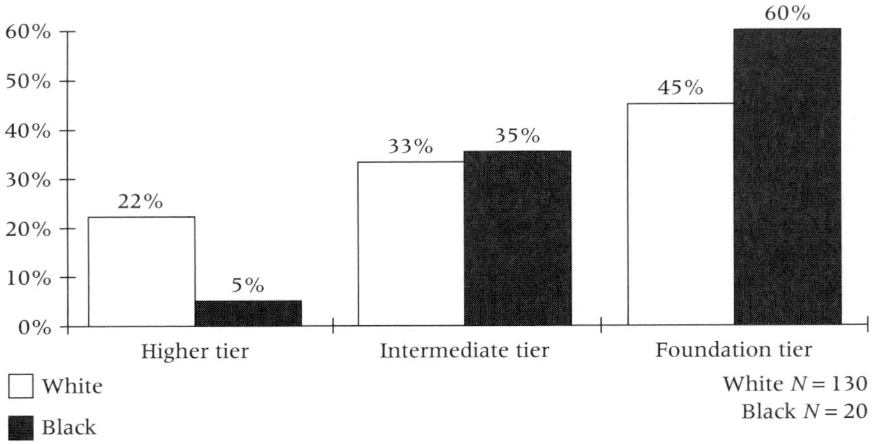

☐ White　　　　　　　　　　　　　　　　　　　White $N = 130$
■ Black　　　　　　　　　　　　　　　　　　　Black $N = 20$

deterioration of the results in the lower streams. I imagine
you might also get that in the middle. In other words, I
think the overall result could be a depression. (. . .) So the
beneficiaries will be a very small proportion of children.

Researcher:　Those children who were going to get Bs or As anyway?

Headteacher:　That's right. Which is a funny economy.

Analysis of the actual mathematics tier allocation in year 11 suggests that
Taylor pupils do not enjoy equal opportunities. In particular, there is a
striking association between ethnic origin and pupils' chances of entry to the
Higher tier. White pupils are four times more likely to be entered in the Higher
tier than their Black peers, meaning that African Caribbeans are almost
completely absent from Higher tier mathematics in Taylor (see Figure 5.8).
Simultaneously, Black pupils are significantly more likely to be entered in
the lowest (Foundation) tier, where a higher-grade pass is literally not possible.
When we consider indicators of social class a similar, though less pronounced,
pattern of inequality emerges.[9] Pupils in receipt of free school meals (FSM),
a crude proxy for social class (indicating those living in poverty), also experience a disproportionate likelihood of being in the Foundation tier and absent
from the Higher tier (see Figure 5.9). In contrast, the discrepancy between
genders is considerably less marked in the Higher tier: here the main contrast is between Intermediate (where girls predominate) and Foundation
(where boys are the majority): see Figure 5.10.

Mathematics in Clough GM

As we have already seen, setting is promoted as school policy in Clough.
However, the head of the mathematics faculty asserts that she resists setting
as far as possible. The success of her resistance is limited somewhat by senior

Figure 5.9 GCSE mathematics tiers by free school meals (Taylor Comprehensive)

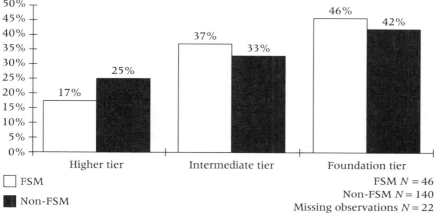

FSM *N* = 46
Non-FSM *N* = 140
Missing observations *N* = 22

Figure 5.10 GCSE mathematics tiers by gender (Taylor Comprehensive)

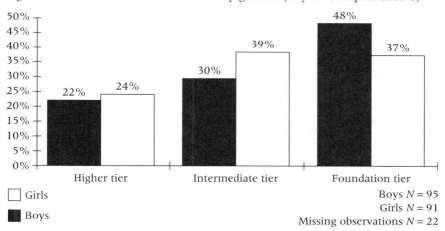

Boys *N* = 95
Girls *N* = 91
Missing observations *N* = 22

management's pressure to set and by the operation of 'fast' groups across the curriculum at Key Stage 3 (discussed in Chapter 4). In this context, the head of mathematics concedes that setting is practically unavoidable but maintains that 'all the groups are mixed-ability to a degree':

the year 9, 10 and 11, their maths lessons are in two [timetable] blocks and in each block we've got what we call an 'express group' or 'fast group'. And the rest, I like to keep them mixed-ability because I don't like too fine a setting because that, if you do that, you would then end up with a group of children who, perhaps, would, you know, be of very low ability and they won't have the opportunity to interact with children who are a little bit more able than themselves (. . .) and this goes against my own personal belief because I think that – I know that there's a lot of talk about, against mixed-ability teaching, but I think if you've got the resources and, you know, skilful teachers, then mixed-ability teaching can work, even in mathematics, you know. In my own experience I've had it work for me. But with the constraints of the National Curriculum, you know, all sorts of other things, the school policy and since we've gone grant-maintained, I mean, we now have setting from year 7 onwards. So we're forced to do that. But at the same time, though you have setting or banding or whatever you want to call it, in my opinion all classes are still fairly mixed-ability.

Despite feeling under considerable pressure (both from outside the school and from her own senior management), therefore, the head of mathematics at Clough takes solace in the notion that most groups retain *some* element of mixed-ability teaching, although (in her words) 'the ability may be in different ranges'.

The mathematics faculty in Clough uses a GCSE syllabus that supports individualized learning; the head of mathematics argues that this allows a degree of flexibility over tier allocation to be maintained until examination entries are finalized in January of year 11. In contrast to Taylor, therefore, in Clough teaching groups/sets are said *not* to relate directly to GCSE tiers. Similarly, maths teachers in Clough do not identify sets based on tier allocations. Rather, National Curriculum assessment levels are frequently drawn upon when indicating the supposed range of ability in any set.

The headteacher in Clough, like his head of mathematics, asserts that mathematics sets do not relate closely to tiers. Unlike his head of faculty, however, the headteacher considers this to be regrettable. This supposed lack of fit between maths sets and tiers in Clough is said to be due to two factors: first, the need to timetable mathematics in two separate half-year blocks; and second, the perceived ability profile of the pupil population (the 'long tail' we saw in Chapter 3):

> I'm not sure that we have sufficient bright kids in a sense to suggest that it [set and tier placement] is directly related (. . .) we couldn't say that the top set is top tier, or Higher tier or whatever its called, and the Intermediate and Foundation, or whatever their names are . . . There are cross-overs between groups. We operate half-year blocks as well which kind of in a sense dilutes the sets; not all the best kids are in one group.
>
> (Headteacher, Clough GM)

It is significant that when discussing the set and tier arrangements, it is 'the best kids' in the 'top set' who receive most attention from the headteacher: this contrasts with the concern of the head of mathematics for those 'of very

Figure 5.11 Mathematics sets and tier entries in practice (Clough GM)

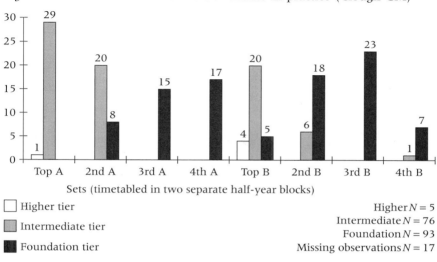

Sets (timetabled in two separate half-year blocks)

☐ Higher tier

▨ Intermediate tier

■ Foundation tier

Higher $N = 5$
Intermediate $N = 76$
Foundation $N = 93$
Missing observations $N = 17$

low ability' (see above). In a school with a supposedly 'long tail' of less able pupils we might expect a sizeable proportion to be entered in the Foundation tier, thereby allowing a number of lower maths sets to be matched directly to tiers. Yet this does not feature in the headteacher's commentary: his main concern is the school's inability to match precisely the higher sets and the Higher tier. Once again, the demands and reach of the A-to-C economy are clear.

Despite fundamental differences in their attitudes towards setting, therefore, both the headteacher and head of mathematics maintain that sets and tiers are *not* directly related in Clough. However, when we look at the actual set and tier allocation of year 11 pupils, we find that both of these key members of staff underestimate the extent of this relationship (see Figure 5.11). While the intersection of sets and tiers is not as uniform as in the case of Taylor (Figure 5.7), there is nevertheless a strong relationship between set and tier allocation. Although the head of faculty asserts that she endeavours to maintain mixed-ability groups, only one of the eight sets includes pupils finally entered in each of the three tiers: this group ('Top B') is taught by the head of faculty herself and comprised in this way largely as a result of a change in teaching staff. Four of the remaining seven sets are solely (or almost solely) composed of Foundation tier pupils. It is clear, therefore, that in practice the faculty head's resistance to setting has only limited success and the relationship between sets and tiers is stronger than either the head of mathematics or the headteacher believes or cares to admit.

The relationship between maths sets and final GCSE tiers in Clough GM, therefore, is stronger than anticipated by Clough teachers, but weaker than

Figure 5.12   Mathematics sets by ethnic origin (Clough GM)

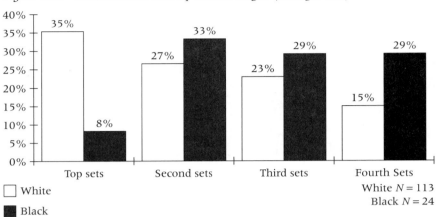

that observed in Taylor (where the relationship was deliberate and fairly precise). We have already noted that access to the Higher tier was especially limited for Black pupils in Taylor, but how do their peers in Clough fare? In answering this question, it is interesting to compare first, Black pupils' placement in Clough maths sets, and second, their eventual representation in GCSE tiers: since their teachers claim no direct set/tier relationship, is there any difference in Black pupils' experiences of setting and tiering in Taylor? Figures 5.12 and 5.13 compare the ethnic breakdown of the maths sets and tiers respectively.[10] It is clear that, as in Taylor, Black pupils are relatively unlikely to be placed in top maths sets: more than one in three white pupils appear in the 'top' maths sets, compared with less than one in ten of their Black counterparts. In contrast, more than half of the Black pupils (58 per cent) are placed in the bottom half of teaching groups – the 'third' and 'fourth' sets (Figure 5.12). These inequalities are even more pronounced in the eventual tiers of GCSE entry. The Higher tier seems extraordinarily restrictive in Clough, regardless of ethnicity: just two white pupils are entered at this level and not a single Black pupil. Perhaps most revealing, however, is the number of pupils entered in the Foundation tier. As in Taylor, Black pupils are considerably more likely to be entered at this lowest level: 71 per cent of Black pupils are entered at Foundation (denying even the possibility of a higher-grade pass), compared with just over half of white pupils. In terms of ethnicity, therefore, it seems that Black pupils in Clough face restricted opportunities through the use of setting, and that these inequalities of opportunity are further cemented and extended by their eventual tier of entry.

An analysis of maths tiering decisions by free school meals in Clough raises further concerns about equality of opportunity. As in Taylor, FSM pupils appear to fare badly in tier allocation, where they are significantly

Figure 5.13 GCSE mathematics tiers by ethnic origin (Clough GM)

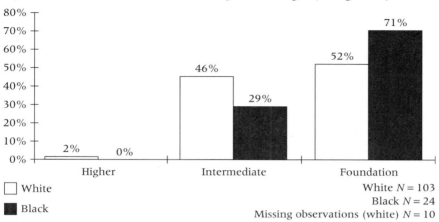

White *N* = 103
Black *N* = 24
Missing observations (white) *N* = 10

☐ White
■ Black

Figure 5.14 GCSE mathematics tiers by free school meals (Clough GM)

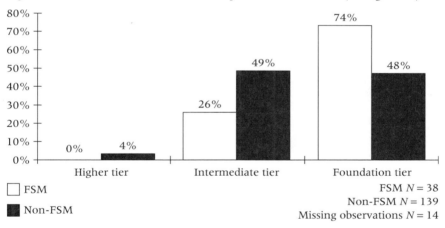

FSM *N* = 38
Non-FSM *N* = 139
Missing observations *N* = 14

☐ FSM
■ Non-FSM

over-represented in the Foundation tier (74 per cent, compared with 48 per cent of non-FSM pupils); and completely absent from the Higher tier (see Figure 5.14). In contrast, and despite the concerns of the head of mathematics regarding girls' examination performance (see above), tier allocation appears to be relatively balanced in terms of gender.[11]

English departments

Clough GM

In line with the school management's overall approach to pupil grouping, in Clough, English groups are set by ability.[12] At Key Stage 4 the English sets are explicitly linked to the pupils' eventual tier of entry. During our field-work the situation appeared relatively positive, with a majority of pupils entered for the Higher tier: almost nine out of ten year 11 pupils were entered for the Higher tier (89 per cent) and all of the Foundation tier pupils were concentrated in two sets (labelled internally as 'Lower A' and 'Lower B').[13] It must be remembered, however, that (as we discussed earlier in this chapter) English teachers in Clough anticipate that the new tiering arrange-ments will invert this situation, so that only a small minority of pupils will sit Higher tier exams in the future. As the acting head of English puts it, they expect to

> scrape two [Higher tier] groups (. . .) and the other six will be this lower tier as it's called, might not even get two groups.

Furthermore, and as is the case for mathematics in Taylor, inter-tier move-ment is limited in practice. With the expansion of the Foundation tier under the new tiering arrangements, it appears that the majority of pupils may soon be locked into the Foundation tier from the beginning of year 10. Asked 'Will there be any chance for movement?', the acting head of English replied:

> Moving betwixt and between? Absolutely, yes absolutely. Well, I'm not sure it will happen really. Unless, you know, teachers see 'Oh God, this really is an error, there's no way I could guarantee this kid's going to get a C, this kid is a C–D borderline, lets put them into the lower tier'. And I suppose, yes, it could work the other way, teachers would say 'My God, something miraculous has happened to this kid over the holiday. He or she has improved so stunningly I think we could guar-antee a C' – 'cause you can't put them up there unless you're saying 'I guarantee an A-to-C'.

The acting head of English in Clough clearly wants to retain the possibility of inter-tier movement ('Absolutely, yes absolutely'), but in practice seems to think it unlikely ('Well, I'm not sure it will happen really'). Interestingly, the option that seems most likely, and is discussed first, is demotion to the Foundation tier, rather than upward movement into the Higher tier. It may be, therefore, that even where movement does occur, the likeliest destination is downwards.

Any analysis of current patterns of tiered entry must be informed by an awareness that the English teachers predict only a minority of pupils will be entered at the Higher tier in future, because of the new tiering arrange-ments (see above). Black pupils are currently over-represented in the English Foundation tier at Clough: compared with their white counterparts, they are twice as likely to be entered at that level (16 per cent compared with 8 per cent). Currently this still affects only a small minority of pupils, but if the overall ratios change as the English teachers predict, the result seems likely to have a disproportionately negative impact on Black pupils. Similarly, FSM pupils currently face a much higher probability of appearing in the Foundation tier (21 per cent compared with 9 per cent of non-FSM pupils). In terms of gender, however, boys and girls in Clough currently enjoy roughly equal chances of Foundation tier entry: 12 per cent of boys and 11 per cent of girls.

The pattern of set placement and tiered entry for English in Clough, therefore, indicates that those at greatest risk of Foundation tier entry at present are pupils in receipt of free school meals and those of African Caribbean ethnic origin. The numbers involved are relatively small at present but the English teachers themselves predict that a majority of pupils will soon experience this: the class- and ethnic-based inequalities, therefore, would seem likely to worsen still further.

English in Taylor Comprehensive
Mixed-ability grouping remains the dominant approach in English at Taylor Comprehensive, in line with the school's overall policy. Tier entries are distributed fairly evenly across groups, with every set including some pupils from each tier. Both the head of faculty and the school's GCSE coordinator have expressed concern over the implications of tiering, but the faculty remains committed to mixed-ability teaching and is supported in this by the headteacher:

> it is the judgement of the English staff that they would much prefer to remain mixed-ability and despite the requirement for tiered entry they feel that they can sustain that.
>
> (Headteacher, Taylor Comprehensive)

The reasons why Taylor's English faculty can sustain mixed-ability teaching, while the mathematics faculty in the same school cannot, is signalled by the head of mathematics. As we saw above, the head of mathematics feels that the English faculty has two particular advantages when attempting to retain mixed-ability groups under a tiered system – two, rather than three, tiers; and the retention of a common syllabus:

> In English they only have two tiers but at least they all still follow the same work in English, they achieve at their own level in English I believe.
>
> (Head of mathematics, Taylor)

This is significant because it signals that whatever the school (and department) commitment regarding pupil grouping, externally controlled factors (the curriculum and the number of tiers) can have a critical effect at the school level. Within the current organizational structure for English, all pupils have access to the same Key Stage 4 English curriculum and all year 11 pupils are able to take the Higher-tier mock examination. Performance in these mock exams is used by teachers when making final decisions on tier of entry. This practice, and the reasons for it, are made explicit to pupils:

[English teacher addressing a year 11 teaching group]:
this is an opportunity for you to do your best and help me to know what paper will best suit you – so do your best, otherwise it's difficult for me to know. I have got an idea anyway but this will help.

(Observation fieldnotes)

Under certain conditions, therefore, tiering allocations can be postponed, and the possibility of the highest-grade passes for all pupils can be retained until late in year 11. Nevertheless, there are indications that all pupils may not actually enjoy equal access to the Higher tier, even where these conditions pertain. As in Clough GM, in Taylor Comprehensive Black pupils are more likely to sit Foundation tier English than their white counterparts (25 per cent compared with 16 per cent of whites) – although the degree of over-representation is not as severe as in the GM. The degree of over-representation of FSM pupils, however, is much the same, with FSM pupils twice as likely to be entered at Foundation level.[14] In relation to pupil gender, however, whereas Clough showed a balance of pupils at Foundation level, in Taylor boys are considerably over-represented: a quarter of boys (26 per cent) are entered for Foundation tier English in Taylor, compared with less than one in ten (8 per cent) of their female peers.

The experience of Taylor's English faculty demonstrates that tiering does not inevitably lead to setting and highlights the important influence that faculty heads and other key teachers can have over the way that national policies are translated and resisted at faculty level. The importance of the headteacher's support for continued mixed-ability teaching must be stressed here – Taylor's successful resistance to sets/tiers in English contrasts sharply with the very limited retention of mixed-ability teaching in Clough mathematics where policies and practices imposed school-wide by senior management place significant limits on the head of faculty. Yet while practices in Taylor's English faculty may offer some encouragement to those seeking to retain mixed-ability teaching, this is not the end of the story. The head of English and GCSE coordinator anticipate that the imminent changes to the English tiers, discussed above in relation to Clough, may threaten the continued retention of mixed-ability teaching and postponement of tier allocation in their faculty. Teachers in Clough expressed their concerns about the new tiers in terms of the changes to tier boundaries. The head of English in Taylor likens the new English tier boundaries with those that already exist in mathematics and, drawing upon the experience of the mathematics faculty, suggests that the relatively exclusive nature of the Higher tier demands selection in these subjects:

Maths and science have worked with that kind of system for some years now (. . .) Simply, you've got to kind of allocate kids, and they've moved to streaming to target kids and slot them into pigeonholes of grades, or, you know, batches of grades.

The same teacher argues that the new English tier boundaries, alongside changes to the syllabus in English language and literature, and the increased volume of coursework, may 'push faculties into having to very more specifically define groups of kids at an earlier stage (. . .) and having to identify, earlier I think, where a kid belongs in that tiering'. The GCSE coordinator predicts that, in future, this will have to happen *before* the year 11 mock examinations – all pupils will no longer retain access to the highest-grade passes throughout Key Stage 4.

Setting and tiering in practice: reinforcing selection and deepening inequalities

Our case-study schools and choice of departments offer a varied and complex view of the relation between setting and tier allocation. At this point it may be useful to recap briefly on what they tell us about selection in the upper school during Key Stage 4.

First, the mathematics departments exist in very different contexts and have faculty heads who proclaim contrasting approaches to pupil grouping. Nevertheless there is a clear and direct relationship between mathematics setting and tiering in both schools. In Taylor, despite the school's commitment to mixed-ability grouping, both the headteacher and head of mathematics acknowledge a close and clear relationship between set placement and eventual tier of entry. As with so many decisions within the conditions of the A-to-C economy, the teachers view these developments as largely unwelcome but necessary as a pragmatic response to the demands they face. In Clough GM the situation is outwardly different but the consequences are much the same. Although Clough's headteacher and head of mathematics are in disagreement about the merits of setting, in practice the relationship between set placement and eventual tier of entry is again relatively clear and consistent. Despite the apparent variety of philosophy and practice, therefore, we find that in practice Key Stage 4 mathematics is taught in selective pupil groups that translate into even more selective GCSE tiers. For most pupils their mathematics destinies seem quite fixed; even as early as year 9 their set placement offers a strong guide to their eventual tier of entry in two years' time.

The pattern in the schools' English departments is somewhat more varied. Unlike their colleagues in mathematics, the English department in Taylor *has* successfully resisted the external push for greater setting and selection. Mixed-ability teaching groups have been retained across the subject and decisions about tier entry are postponed as late as year 11. The support of the headteacher appears to have been the crucial factor here, although changes in tier arrangements are thought by staff to threaten this situation. Specifically, Taylor's English teachers anticipate that the more exclusive nature of the new Higher tier may lead to earlier tiering decisions and, potentially, threaten the continued use of mixed-ability teaching across the department. In contrast, Clough already operates a system whereby English set placement and tier allocation are closely matched. This will continue, but here too the new tier descriptions are expected to have a clear negative consequence so that the majority of pupils will now be placed in sets that lead to the Foundation tier. It appears, therefore, that the externally generated changes to the tier definitions in English GCSE will have regressive effects in both Taylor Comprehensive and Clough GM. Although the two English departments have markedly different approaches to setting and tier entry at present, both anticipate that the new arrangements will make the Higher tier more exclusive and force earlier decisions about tier of entry.

It seems, therefore, that the external structuring of GCSE tiering is a strong factor in determining school-level practice. Despite differences in ethos, both schools operate closely allied systems of setting and tier entry for mathematics (where three tiers are in operation). In English, where a two-tier model operates, there appears more scope for variation. However, it is important to note that English teachers in both schools view new tier descriptions as likely to strengthen set/tier links and lead to earlier and more final differentiation in the upper school.

In addition to examining *how* set and tier allocations are made, we have also interrogated *who* is allocated *where*. The findings make for depressing reading. Both setting and tiering appear to institutionalize inequalities of opportunity, especially those based on ethnicity and social class.

Among the most consistent and pronounced inequalities of opportunity are those suffered by Black pupils: in both schools and in both subject departments, Black pupils are less likely to be entered in the Higher tier and most likely to be placed in the Foundation tier. In both schools a majority of Black pupils were entered in the Foundation tier in mathematics, where they cannot attain a C grade: an inequality that is likely to have very serious consequences for their eventual levels of achievement and post-school educational and labour market opportunities (cf. Gillborn 1997b; Rasekoala 1998). A similar pattern of inequality is evidenced among pupils in receipt of free school meals. Without exception, in both mathematics and English FSM pupils were more likely to be in the Foundation tier, and less likely to be in the Higher tier, than their more affluent peers. The patterns of gender-related placement were less consistent. In Clough pupils experienced relatively similar chances of placement in the various GCSE tiers, regardless of gender; in contrast, within Taylor girls are over-represented in the mathematics Intermediate tier. In both English and mathematics, boys in Clough are disproportionately placed in the Foundation tiers.

Conclusions

I think it's condemnable

there's something happened with our [English syllabus] which is very scary for us.

I don't like doing that because, you know, it would be nice to encourage children to do the higher level but it's, it's this kind of thing, which I am forced to do, is to play the system, you know?

These quotations give a sense of teachers' unease about the decisions they are asked to make as part of GCSE tiering arrangements. These are not the views of beginning teachers or junior staff, they are from a headteacher, a head of English and a head of mathematics, respectively: they convey something of the teachers' frustration at being caught (as they perceive it) in a system that requires them to act in ways they do not believe to be in the best interests of pupils but which are practically necessary in view of wider constraints. The demands of the 'league tables', the requirements of GCSE tiers and syllabuses, are all seen to define a context where to be pragmatic is to deny equality of opportunity to some pupils. There are, of course, exceptions. In Taylor Comprehensive, where school-level policy supports mixed-ability grouping, the English department (unlike their colleagues in Clough GM) have resisted the trend towards setting. However, even here the outlook appears bleak, with teachers anticipating negative changes as GCSE tiers are redefined in the immediate future. Worse still, regardless of pupil grouping approaches, it appears that GCSE tiering provides for the institutionalization of inequality in ways that seem remarkably consistent between our case-study schools.

Unlike the old dual examination system, where pupils could sit GCE and/ or CSE papers, the current system of GCSE tiering is little known or understood outside education: certainly most of our pupils conveyed the sense that their parents would know nothing of it (see Chapter 7 for the pupils' own thoughts on the system). Tiering decisions are completely in the hands of teachers and are final – no dual entry is permitted. Most importantly, as we have shown, there is evidence that tiering may operate to institutionalize inequalities of opportunity earlier and with greater finality than at any time in the recent history of the British educational system – not, in fact, since the tripartite system of 11-plus exams and selective admissions which arose following the 1944 Education Act (and was largely phased out during the 1970s and 1980s).

Our data show that teachers perceive tiering as a stressful and 'dangerous' process that requires them somehow to reconcile conflicting views of the interests of pupils, the subject department and school. Teachers' desire to 'play safe' with pupils can lead them to close down the opportunities that are available: in practice, teachers operate a system of 'hidden' tiers that is even more selective and elitist than that suggested by official pronouncements.

Setting and tiering decisions are sometimes seen as intimately related. Where subjects set by ability at Key Stage 4 we find a clear and somewhat fixed relationship between sets and tiers. Where they set earlier, as in Taylor's mathematics department, these decisions can be taken for most pupils as early as year 9. Where a department resists setting, and where a two-tier model is in place nationally (for example, English in Taylor) the final tiering decisions can be postponed, even into pupils' final year (as is officially assumed by examination boards). However, recent changes in the composition of tiers are thought by English teachers (in both our schools) to threaten earlier and more selective tiering in future.

So far as winners and losers are concerned, some of our worst fears are realized. In particular, Black pupils are, without exception in our case-study schools and departments, most likely to be in the Foundation tier and least likely to be in the Higher. Pupils in receipt of free school meals are similarly disadvantaged by the dual selection processes of setting and tiering at Key Stage 4. These conclusions are distressing. They confirm that the introduction of tiering across a greater range of GCSE subjects may well be associated with deepening inequalities of opportunities: first, by stimulating greater use of setting by ability; and second, by placing a disproportionate number of pupils from Black and working-class backgrounds into second-rate teaching and examination groups. However, there is a possible ray of light. The pressures of the A-to-C economy are such that our case-study schools are consciously targeting greater resources at pupils who might previously have failed to reach the five A-to-C benchmark. Given that Black and working-class pupils are traditionally over-represented in this group, it could be that such moves will help finally to redress the balance of opportunities. It is to this question that we turn next.

6

Educational triage and the D-to-C conversion

suitable cases for treatment?

triage n. of action f. *trier* to pick, cull . . . 1. The action of
assorting according to quality . . . 2. The assignment of degrees of
urgency to wounds or illness in order to decide the order of
suitability of treatment.

(Oxford English Dictionary)

The demands of the A-to-C economy are felt across our schools, in each
year group and by all teachers. We have already seen how so many areas of
activity, throughout secondary schooling, have come to reflect a concern
with maximizing the proportion of pupils who eventually attain the benchmark level of five or more higher-grade passes in their GCSE examinations.
The multiple selection and setting practices, that we have described above,
represent the main school-wide strategies adopted (with varying degrees
of enthusiasm, regret and concern) within our case-study institutions. The
pressures of the A-to-C economy are such, however, that both Clough GM
and Taylor Comprehensive have sought to identify additional means by
which they can further target resources on a limited number of pupils in
one last push to maximize their scores in the nationally published school
performance 'league tables'. In practice these strategies often focus on pupils
seen as heading towards grade D passes, where an improvement of a single
grade could potentially figure significantly in the school's final results. In
effect, the schools seek to convert likely grade Ds into grade Cs.

In this chapter we will examine the D-to-C conversion strategies utilized
in each of our case-study schools. These strategies appear to be very different, reflecting the ethos and established practices and procedures within
each school. As we will show, however, at a deeper level the strategies share
similar characteristics and can be understood as a form of *educational triage*
– a means by which scarce resources are rationed, leaving some to perish

Figure 6.1   Educational triage: the rationing of educational opportunity

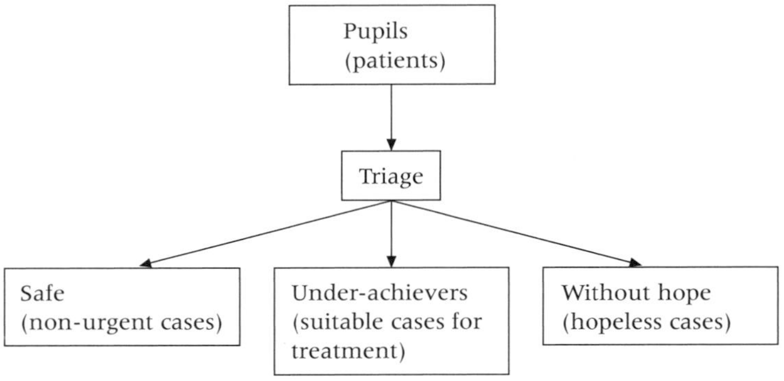

while others survive. As we will show, like medics in a crisis, teachers are increasingly seeking to identify those individuals who will benefit most from access to limited resources. In a medical emergency *triage* is the name used to describe attempts to direct attention to those people who might survive (with help), leaving other (less hopeful) cases to die. In school, educational triage is acting systematically to neglect certain pupils while directing additional resources to those deemed most likely to benefit (in terms of the externally judged standards). These strategies seek to maximize the effectiveness of scarce resources but their effect, in practice, is to privilege particular groups of pupils marked especially by social class and 'race'.[1] The process is represented schematically in Figure 6.1.

In making sense of the processes of educational triage, it is useful to draw on Foucault's understanding of disciplinary power. Foucault suggests that, rather than being something that is held or possessed by one individual or group over or against another individual or group, power should be understood as something that circulates through the deployment of discourses. No particular discourse is intrinsically imbued with more or less power than another. Yet, through drawing on particular discursive practices, in the specific context and in the light of the exigencies faced, certain discourses do become dominant and, therefore, come to bound what counts as legitimate knowledge and, indeed, what is knowable. The making of individuals, who are knowable and known, is central to this technique of power. Foucault identifies a series of technologies or instruments of disciplinary power – specifically, hierarchical observation, normalizing judgement, and the examination – which enable the simultaneous making and surveillance of the individual who is, in turn, self-surveillant (Foucault 1991).

Three key discourses, and a set of concomitant technologies, are essential to the functioning of educational triage. First, a particular understanding of 'ability' as fixed and measurable. Second, the predictability and subsequent prediction of pupils' likely GCSE grades, which are underpinned by, and draw heavily upon, this understanding of ability. Third, the notion of 'under-achievement', again underpinned by a particular understanding of ability as fixed and measurable, and the subsequent identification of, and intervention with, 'under-achieving' pupils. In subsequent sections of this chapter we examine each of these discourses in turn. We begin, therefore, by returning to the notion of 'ability', a discourse that has already featured heavily in our account of life in Clough GM and Taylor Comprehensive.

'Ability' in teacher discourse

As we saw in Chapters 3 and 4, in relation to setting and selection practices, Clough operates with an underpinning discourse of ability as a fixed and generalized academic potential. In turn, a series of technologies for the measurement of ability are mobilized, including 'IQ' testing and reading and spelling 'ages', that feed into (and help shape) the school's understandings of individual pupil's performance throughout their school careers. On the basis of this understanding of ability, and the concomitant techniques for measuring it, we saw that the notion of 'under-achievement' – performance below the level expected – is a staple of the school's discourses surrounding ability and attainment.

A similar situation persists in Taylor. While the school does not make use of generalized-ability testing, it does draw upon a range of other measurement tools. We have already mentioned, for example, the banding system used by the now abolished ILEA and still current in several London authorities: this assigned pupils into one of three ability bands, on the basis of tests undertaken in year 6, with an optimum 'comprehensive' banding ratio of 1:2:1. Taylor, in line with its LEA, continues to make extensive use of these bands and, in these terms, continues to argue that it is 'truly comprehensive'.[2] Alongside these bands, which act as the key general indicator, Taylor utilizes year 9 SATs levels and tests within individual subject areas to assess the 'ability' of each member of its population. As in Clough, these tests, and the ongoing reference made to them, indicate an adherence to an overarching notion of ability as fixed, generalized and measurable. No single or precise relationship between 'ability' (as defined by banding on entry) and potential GCSE outcomes is explicitly offered by the school. This does not mean, however, that no such relationship is thought to exist. Taylor's headteacher, for example, believes that band on entry acts as a good general predictor of eventual GCSE outcome. As in Clough, however, this relationship is far less clear at the level of individual pupils:

> We analyse their GCSE results also by banding on entry. And, not surprisingly, there are very big differences in the overall performance, the average performance of band 1, band 2, band 3. If you looked at individuals then you get a much cloudier picture. You know, you get the occasional child who entered in band 3 and finishes up getting

five-plus As-to-Cs. You get children who entered in band 1 who drop out completely. Not many, but you get one or two each year. (. . .) On average they are pretty good predictors (. . .) After all, that banding is done on their London Reading Test, their reading is a fairly basic skill, their reading age at 11, or 10 when they take the test, also correlates quite well with their social background, parental income level, the whole lot.

(Headteacher, Taylor Comprehensive)

For this headteacher, therefore, there is a clear and predictable relationship between reading on entry to Taylor (tested at age 10 or 11 and translated into bands) and subsequent GCSE outcomes at age 16. The reliability of this relationship is not seriously disrupted by the 'one or two' pupils whose performance contradicts it. For band 1 pupils, low performance is understood in terms of 'able' pupils 'dropping out'. For band 3 pupils, 'finishing up' with benchmark grades remains an unexplained anomaly. Significantly, the headteacher also views these differences as marked by social class. He does not assert that pupils from different social class backgrounds have different levels of 'ability', nor does he suggest that this relationship highlights a possible area of inequity which the school might endeavour to redress, rather he simply states that a correlation exists – its origins and wider consequences go unremarked.

In this 'truly comprehensive' school, in line with the old ILEA banding system, band 1 pupils make up roughly 25 per cent of the population, but, in line with the national average, over 45 per cent of the school population actually attain benchmark grades (of five or more higher-grade passes). We have seen that the headteacher subscribes firmly to the banding system and its relationship with GCSE outcomes. As such, we might expect the school to include at least the upper quartile of band 2 pupils in those it anticipates will attain the benchmark level. It seems, however, that this is not the case. Drawing comparison with the educational opportunities and subsequent outcomes available within the old tripartite system (where test performance at 11 placed pupils into different types of school) the headteacher points out that the many band 2 pupils who now attain the benchmark would not have enjoyed access to the equivalent GCE O-level examinations in a selective grammar school:

[If] we go back to the days of the old grammar school, strictly speaking no child in band 2 or band 3, no child should finish up with five A-to-C grades. They wouldn't have got to the grammar school so they wouldn't even have taken the old O level. As it is, lots and lots of them do. And you do see advances in children who entered in band 2 and finish up performing as if they were in band 1.

(Headteacher, Taylor Comprehensive)

This might be taken to indicate a belief that inequitable opportunities and outcomes, along with gross underestimations of the potential maximum performance of large groups of pupils, were embedded in the old tripartite structure. Yet the headteacher's assertion that these pupils are 'performing as if they were in *band 1*' (emphasis added) illustrates a continued belief in a particular set of relationships between 'ability' bands and GCSE outcomes – namely, that it is only really band 1 pupils who can be expected to attain the benchmark. This view persists despite evidence to the contrary within the school itself. As such these related practices of labelling, differential treatment and contrasting teacher expectations remain intact (through the measuring of 'ability' via reading ages, allocating pupils to bands and the assumed relationship between bands and GCSE outcomes).

Heads of year, as we have already seen (for example, in Chapters 4 and 5) play a key role in applying these judgements of 'ability' to real-life questions such as setting, options allocations and, as we discuss below, identifying pupils for additional support. In comparison with senior staff, especially the headteacher, year heads appear less confident of the relationship between early test scores and likely GCSE outcomes – nevertheless, they ultimately continue to subscribe to it. Asked 'does a particular reading age tell you a particular kid should be getting certain grades?', Taylor's head of year 9 replied:

> Not necessarily. I mean, it depends [on the] subject. But certainly a kid with a reading age, taking on GCSE English for instance, with a [current] reading age of 9.6, 10 or lower is going to have difficulty achieving a benchmark of E, which is just below the national average.

This reference to variation across subjects could be viewed as a move *away* from a notion of generalized ability. However, it might also reflect a subscription to the division of (high-status) 'academic' subjects and (lower-status) 'practical' or 'arts' subjects. Furthermore, the identification of reading as the means of access to one particular (high-status, academic) curricular area is easily extended to all such curricular areas, thereby reducing dramatically the range and nature of subject areas across which this variation might be seen. Ultimately, despite the assertion that reading age does not 'necessarily' relate to anticipated GCSE outcomes, this head of year feels confident in drawing a relationship between a specific reading age and a specific GCSE outcome. The head of year 11, when asked whether it is possible to relate ability bands to expected GCSE grades, answered:

> Loosely. Very loose. I mean it is loosely 'cause don't forget that was five years, well four years ago. That gives you a rough idea. And they are compared back to that in some of the figures, how the girls have achieved in [band] 1, 2 and 3 and how the boys have achieved. So they are, they do refer back to them. (. . .) It's roughly. There's the odd hiccups, but not that many.

It appears initially that this teacher does not subscribe to a notion of fixed ability; pupils' performance can change over time, thereby diminishing the utility of bands on entry. Yet the description of this relationship is shifting – 'loosely' becomes 'roughly' and, ultimately, the relationship seems fairly secure: there are 'the odd hiccups but not that many'.

The situation appears to be further confused when we look specifically at the GCSE outcomes of pupils in band 2. We have seen the headteacher attempt to explain the benchmark attainments of many band 2 pupils while simultaneously retaining the notion that such grades 'should' be restricted to band 1 pupils. We find a similar lack of clarity and consistency with this head of year:

> *Researcher*: So you can't say that sort of [band] 2 will get between . . . ?
> *Head of year 11 (Taylor Comprehensive)*: No, I don't think so. No. I mean they are average, [band] 2. So the average is meant to be, I think it's an E isn't it? For GCSE? Which, some of those will get, a lot of those will get higher than that.

Here we find the incommensurability of 'average' in terms of band on entry and 'average' in terms of GCSE outcomes: an 'average' band position does not translate into the official 'average' GCSE outcome. Yet the discursive strength of these measures/labels is such that this teacher, and indeed the school, is unable to either separate or discard them. Furthermore, this lack of 'fit' does not mean that the teacher cannot ascribe GCSE outcomes on the basis of bands, rather, it means that the outcomes might not be the ones most readily expected. It seems, therefore, that understandings of the nature of the relationship between band and GCSE outcome vary both within and across key members of school staff. Yet despite this apparent incoherence and inconsistency, the overarching belief in the relationship itself remains intact.

Predicting GCSE grades

So far, in this and preceding chapters, we have detailed numerous contradictions, incongruities and potential inequities bound up in discourses of 'ability', and the tools used to measure it, in our case-study schools. Despite the problematic nature of these discourses, whether acknowledged or unacknowledged, both schools continue to predict GCSE outcomes for their year 11 pupils based substantially (though not exclusively) on these measures of ability.

Making predictions in Taylor Comprehensive

Given the relationship that is believed to exist between band on entry and GCSE outcomes, it is not surprising that these bands are the starting point for the year head charged with the task of assessing pupils' predicted grades in year 11 (their final year of compulsory schooling). The predicted GCSE grades utilized in Taylor are supplied in the first instance by individual subject teachers and collated by the head of year. This is done following 'mock' GCSE examinations taken in the autumn term of year 11. Given the time and effort expended on 'mock' examinations, however, it is perhaps surprising that the 'mock' results do not translate directly into predicted grades. Rather, these are used in conjunction with a range of other indicators of varying degrees of formality:

> Well it's a gut feeling for a start, I have to say, in all honesty. But then there's [a system used across the school for evaluating pupils' effort and performance] (. . .) And there's also comments you get back from staff. It's just an overall picture you get. And reports, I mean you get the yearly reports. And year 10s' were only done at the end of last year so they're quite new. So it's quite interesting to see. I mean it is a gut feeling.
>
> > (Head of year 11, Taylor Comprehensive)

In view of these other indicators, therefore, pupil's predicted grades may differ from the actual grades they have only recently achieved in subject specific 'mock' examinations.

Making predictions in Clough GM

As we have already seen, NFER test results (referred to by some teachers as 'IQ' results) and reading and spelling 'ages' on entry are considered to be effective indicators of GCSE outcomes in Clough: the headteacher argues strongly that 'for a significant proportion you can be confident that the thing *is* a good predictor of their GCSE results'. As in Taylor, these sources are drawn upon when predicting GCSE outcomes. While Taylor predicts GCSE grades only once during year 11, however, in Clough the GCSE predictions are revised throughout the year. Again, no single indicator is relied upon totally. Rather, a variety of data are drawn upon in an attempt to divine the future:

> we use all the data that's available so we use, we use their SATs testing in year 9, we use their NFER scores, where they're tested internally, we use their reading ages and spelling ages, any data.
>
> > (Head of technology, Clough GM)

Problems with predictions

Both schools make considerable use of predicted grades, but they are not universally seen as unproblematic. In Taylor, as we have seen, the use of 'gut feeling' in predicting grades is clearly acknowledged. And whereas the accounts of teachers in Clough tend to emphasize the range of tests drawn upon, in interview one head of faculty (technology) also cites 'gut feeling' while another (modern languages) describes predicted outcomes as a 'shot in the dark at the moment'. One of the difficulties identified is the range of approaches taken, and different intended impacts, when individual teachers predict GCSE grades:

> different teachers use different ploys for estimating the grades as well. So you get that inaccuracy built into it as well. 'Cause if you look at it there are very few As. Teachers won't commit themselves to giving a grade A as an estimated grade 'cause they're wanting to err on the side of caution. Then you've got the teachers who use them to underestimate to try and motivate. So, although you've got a kid that you think might get a grade C, you think if you tell him he's going to get a C he'll sit back and won't do any more work. So you give him a D in the hope . . . So some teachers use that as a ploy.
>
> (Head of technology, Clough GM)

The use of such 'ploys' renders predicted grades even more uncertain than would otherwise be the case. Notwithstanding doubts about the validity, reliability and usefulness of predictions based on particular test results (of different styles and ages), the range of approaches among teaching staff serves to render predicted grades of even less use as a serious measure of pupils' attainment and guide to future achievement. Despite teachers' willingness to acknowledge such problems in certain circumstances, it is nevertheless the case that predicted grades carry very real significance within schools. Predicted grades are not only a tool used by school managers or faculty heads: wide-ranging discussions concerning individual pupils are suffused with references to such predictions. In both our case-study schools, tutors who were asked to briefly describe members of their tutor group readily offered such predictions (without reference to the basis on which they were being made) alongside references to family background, relationships with teachers and peers, and judgements about personality, motivation and behaviour.

Racism and problems with predictions

In preceding chapters we have already raised several concerns about the possibility that pupils of minority ethnic backgrounds might be especially disadvantaged in processes of selection and the attribution of different academic categories. This can occur through the use of formal tests as well as featuring in a range of informal judgements about 'ability' and 'motivation'. The production of 'predicted grades' provides yet another context within which such processes might come into play. The apparently concrete nature of each predicted grade, when presented in written form on reports and elsewhere, belies the uncertain and subjective nature of the processes that lie behind its production. There is considerable scope for racialized interpretations of 'ability', motivation and effort inadvertently to influence the kinds of grade produced, quite apart from any discrete 'ploys' adopted by individual teachers. This infuses the process with additional possibilities for predictions that are inequitable or even discriminatory. This is clearly demonstrated by the following account, by a senior teacher in Clough, which concerns Black pupils' attempts to improve these predictions:

> I found that quite strange that the kids had their estimated grades because they then came back at you and gave you earache, you know, would challenge you in the corridor and so you were under threat. You know, 'why have you only given me that grade', you know? Because kids, you know, have different perceptions of themselves, they have no understanding, you know, and some of them live in Cloud-cuckoo-land. I mean we've got, we had a whole period where we had Afro-Caribbean kids running around with gold rimmed glasses on with plain glass in them because they thought it made them look more intelligent, you know, they really had highly inflated opinions of themselves as far as academic achievement, and this is fact. I mean there were a whole group of kids that put on glasses and wandered round the corridors with gold rimmed glasses on because they really felt that they were sort of A/B . . .
>
> (A faculty head, Clough GM)

On the basis of this teacher's account it is clearly impossible to discern whether Black pupils were wearing non-prescription glasses and, if they where, what their motivations for doing so might have been. Nor is this quotation evidence that this or any other teacher was actively or unwittingly making poorer predictions for Black pupils than for their peers from other ethnic groups. Nevertheless, this account does give a worrying insight into several issues relevant to the production and use of predicted grades. It shows quite clearly, for example, that this teacher recognizes that the predicted grades are important to pupils but that he is dismissive of their protests that the estimates are too low: 'kids, you know, have different perceptions of themselves, they have no understanding'. The quotation seems especially dismissive of protests by Black pupils: 'they really had highly inflated opinions of themselves as far as academic achievement'. Furthermore, it is noticeable that the pupils' concerns (which *could* have been interpreted as a sign of motivation, a thirst for achievement and success) are experienced negatively as 'challenge' and 'threat'. There is a strong echo with previous research that has suggested teachers' readiness to impute a challenge into the actions of Black pupils (cf. Gillborn 1990a; Gillborn and Gipps 1996; Sewell 1997; 1998; Wright 1992).

It is clear that the processes of GCSE grade prediction are multiple and inconsistent. Even if we were to accept the particular view of 'ability' (as fixed, measurable and generalizable) that underlies so much of the schools' approach, we would still surely have to accept that these predictions are of limited utility in view of the numerous, uncoordinated and personal judgements and ploys that come into play. Nevertheless, these predictions are formally the key to the D-to-C conversion strategies mobilized in both of the schools, that is, they are the core means by which triage assessments are made.

'Under-achievement'

We have seen that understanding ability as a fixed, generalizable and measurable attribute underlies schools' attempts to predict levels of performance and eventual GCSE outcomes for individual pupils. In this and previous chapters we have discussed the problematic nature of this notion of 'ability', the tools used to measure it and the subsequent prediction of pupil performance. Yet despite all the contradictions and inconsistencies, both of our study schools continue to draw heavily upon these techniques. More worrying still, they are mobilized to support the notion of 'under-achievement', to identify pupils who are considered to be 'under-achieving' and who are seen, therefore, as ripe for additional support.

Before examining the forms of additional support that are provided, it is important to understand the ways in which the case-study schools construct and mobilize notions of 'under-achievement'. In educational contexts where demands for equality of opportunity continue (albeit in sometimes diluted forms), any disproportionate allocation of resources to particular groups of pupils can be called to account. If pupils are identified as *already* suffering or losing out in some way within the current system of resource distribution, however, a justification for 'special treatment' becomes available. In this way, within the particular constraints and demands of the A-to-C economy, discourses of 'under-achievement' serve to justify the privileging of particular pupils by presenting the action as remediating existing disadvantage, thereby allowing inequitable resource allocation while retaining a construct of equity and comprehensiveness. As we will see, the schools operate quite specific notions of 'under-achievement' that do not replicate previous academic understandings of that term. In both Taylor and Clough, two pupils could have identical attainments and yet only one of them might be seen as 'under-achieving' and therefore deserving additional support.

'Under'-achievement in Clough GM

In Chapters 3 and 4 we explored notions of ability and 'under-achievement' as they are understood within Clough. We saw that ability is seen to be fixed, generalized and measurable and that assessments of performance are compared with measured ability in order to identify 'under-achievement'. We also saw that, in making sense of performance that *exceeds* expectations based on measured ability, the school was not able to consider seriously any possibilities that challenged either its understanding of fixed ability or the utility of the measurement tools it employs. It is in this context that assessments of 'under-achievement' are made in the upper school:

> The heads of department, I would then go through the estimated grades and look where I feel that kids are under-achieving within the department, so they're identified. So the pupils that are on Ds and they're getting Bs and As anywhere else, I then identify those children, we'd

discuss them at a meeting and look to see if individual teachers, because when you do your estimated grades you do it isolated. So you, once you can get an overall picture of how a kid's performing elsewhere, you may look at a pupil and think well that's a, he's only ever going to achieve a level D, but then by looking at his other grades and maybe he's picking up As and Bs in history and English, that can then raise teacher expectations of the kid. 'Cause we're all only human.

(Head of technology, Clough GM)

Here again we see the significance of the teachers' belief in 'ability' as fixed and generalizable. If a pupil's predicted grade in one subject does not match the profile of grades elsewhere, there is an assumed under-achievement. Because ability is thought to operate across subject boundaries, a pupil predicted a grade D can be elevated in teachers' eyes through attainment elsewhere: 'by looking at his other grades (. . .) that can then raise teacher expectations of the kid'. Being identified as 'under-achieving', therefore, is not simply a matter of performing badly in a subject: performance elsewhere can influence such decisions (confirming or challenging expectations). Other aspects of pupil identity can also come into play. We examine these in detail below with reference to decisions made in Taylor.

'Under-achievement' in Taylor Comprehensive: gender, class and 'race'

When teachers in Taylor talk about 'under-achieving' pupils, it is clear that ideas about several indicators are in play simultaneously. For example, notions of 'ability' and gender interact in important ways, and the precise consequence for different groups of pupils is not always as clear as first described by senior teachers. The headteacher suggests that under-achievement is found most commonly among boys from band 2:

severely under-achieving is something we have seen among pupils of all levels of ability, our biggest concentration of such problems being among boys who entered the school in [ability band] 2.

Turning to the description of 'under-achievers' offered by one head of year, however, we see a somewhat different picture of which pupils might be allocated to this group. Boys are once again focused upon, but issues of social class and 'race' are also brought into play. The notion of boys' under-achievement is given authority and validity through recourse to national examination patterns and prominent coverage in the popular media (see, for example, Woodhead 1996).[3] However, the ways in which ability and identity categories are drawn into and out of the frame indicate a sense of contradiction and confusion. In the following quotation, for example, the teacher switches continually between class and ethnic categories:

And boys generally are under-achieving. *White middle-class boys.* (. . .) And *Black Afro-Caribbean boys.* I think there's been a fair amount of energy put into the problem, you know the challenge of *Black middle-class, um, Black Afro-Caribbean boys,* but I think *white working-class boys* have been kind of a little bit left behind. (. . .) I am very aware that *boys* do under-achieve (. . .) of those 23 boys [whose parents/carers did not attend parents' evening] they're nearly all under-achievers, they're nearly all *middle, um, working-class white boys,* I think there were two *Afro-Caribbean boys* in that group. The rest were *white working-class boys* with poor attendance whose parents we very rarely see, for whatever reasons.

(Head of year 9, Taylor; our emphasis)

From this quotation it can be seen that the *gender* of under-achievers remains stable while their *'race'* and *social class* is shifting. The class background of under-achieving white boys is frequently identified as being middle-class and then changed (corrected?) to working-class. In addition, a racialized understanding of social class also appears to be expressed. The social class of white boys, while unstable, *is* continually expressed. However, the social class of African Caribbean boys is all but absent: 'Blackness' appears to act as a totalizing signifier (of a homogenous group) of which further elaboration is unnecessary (or one in which social class is understood as self-evident)(cf. Mac an Ghaill 1989). Ultimately it seems that African Caribbean boys are assumed to be uniformly classed: it is only in the case of white pupils that social class emerges as a key axis of differentiation in the teachers' eyes.

The situation becomes increasing complex (and revealing) when teachers are invited to give concrete examples of these general patterns of experience. The movement from the general to the particular can reveal processes of which the teacher may be only partially aware: in this case, the head of year offers an example of an individual boy from year 9 who has been identified as under-achieving. While it was not claimed that this boy was necessarily representative of all under-achievers, it is interesting to note that the example concerns a white, middle-class boy from ability band 1, who is deemed to be performing to the level of ability associated with band 2 and therefore under-achieving in relation to the school's expectation of a band 1 pupil:

It's a bit subjective really. But it means, for instance, in science, say, that he's coming up to taking science SATs and they're undergoing science assessments which, potentially, they could be at level 6 [of attainment] if they're at the very top, level 6 or level 5 in science. *I would expect this boy to be somewhere in level 5 or 6 because he's intellectually, you know, one of the top echelon. He's actually performing at below 4.* So I picked that up from his science reports. Now if that's happening across the board then, and I know it is because I've looked at his books. So I know, as an English teacher, what a year 9 student achieving level 5, say, which is the higher end of the National Curriculum, what he should be writing and the kind of level of his writing and the level of his oral work. And that boy is not producing it, in terms of effort, it's just not going down on paper, and I think it is mainly effort.

(Head of year 9, Taylor Comprehensive; our emphasis)

As we discussed earlier, test results that act as indicators for ability, combined with teachers' own judgements, enable the identification of particular groups of pupils who are assumed to be capable of attaining A*-to-C grades in GCSE examinations. Hence, while this ability band 1 boy is *under*-achieving (in relation to teachers' expectations for his ability band), a peer classified as ability band 2 performing *to the same level* in their SATs would be deemed to be achieving appropriately to their potential (that is, *not* under-achieving).

It should also be noted that while the headteacher asserts that under-achievers are primarily *band 2* boys, and the head of year appears to have the intention of suggesting that they are primarily white *working-class* boys, the pupil in the proffered example is a white, *middle-class* boy from *ability band 1*. In the particular instance that the teacher chooses to use as an exemplar, therefore, strategies to achieve D-to-C conversions are reworked from an imagined target clientele of working-class pupils in ability band 2, and refocused (via the particular definition of under-achievement) to highlight a middle-class pupil in band 1. While the ability and class nature of the clientele may have shifted upward, however, the ethnic and gendered character of the target group remain stable: white boys.

The racial and social class dimensions of 'under-achievement' (as defined by the school) go largely unremarked and unexplained by teachers: however, its gendered nature is discussed. Extending the code of pupil pathology and deficit to families, one head of year suggests a connection between boys' under-achievement and parental interest – a connection that might be read as simultaneously indicating that these boys are positioned as being working-class – and uses this to absolve the school of any active role in pupil failure by asserting 'there's a strong link between parental interest and boys'. Furthermore, when there is an acknowledgement that the school, or at least the education system more generally, might be culpable in boys' under-achievement, this is related not to current school-level practice but to earlier curricular changes that are said to have disadvantaged boys:

there's a lot of research that says that, you know, the curriculum has moved in the '70s and '80s when there was that whole feeling that girls needed to, we needed to address the curriculum in comprehensive schools for girls. And then they did skew it slightly then. (. . .) But, the curriculum is now perhaps more girl-biased, I don't know, I don't.

(Head of year 9, Taylor Comprehensive)

It is interesting that in this teacher's commentary on curricular change the pre- and post-National Curriculum eras are conflated, with pre-National

Curriculum practices presented as continuing to impact within the very curricular reorganization that was, at least in part, designed to undo those changes associated with the 'progressivist' project (cf. Ball 1994). This teacher claims authority for his claim that the current curriculum favours girls by reference to 'a lot of research', in contrast to the 'feeling' which led to the earlier moves to enhance girls' access to the curriculum. This juxtaposing of the researched-based 'facts' of boys' current curricular disadvantage, with the implicit questioning of the basis upon which earlier efforts to improve girls' access to the curriculum were made, acts to validate the subsequent claim that it is this which has led to boys' under-achievement. Hence, even where educational practices are identified as being a partial cause of boys' under-achievement, it is not current practice that is responsible. At fault, rather, are the supposedly over-zealous changes of earlier progressivists (and by extension even girls themselves). Despite the contradictions within the analysis offered by this teacher, therefore, it is a discourse that operates to give further credence to the category of 'under-achieving boys'.

These assertions of under-achievement act to validate the school's focus upon, and demand for, D-to-C conversions. Through the practice of identifying pupils as under-achieving, the school avoids the appearance that it is attempting to get 'natural' grade D pupils to convert their grades to Cs – a move that would, of course, deny the very notion of 'ability' enshrined in the school's actions. Rather, within the dominant view of fixed and generalized ability, the school sees itself as attempting to get 'natural' A*-to-C grade pupils to increase their performance so as to fulfil their intellectual potential. As such, implicit to the school's notion of 'under-achievement' is an understanding of 'ability' as stable and predictable, while also being mutable enough to be unfulfilled or unmet. It is already clear that targeting pupils on the D/C borderline intersects conveniently with the school league table demands for higher-grade passes in the A-to-C economy. The key to understanding the iniquitous effects of these processes lies in the nature of the interventions made with appropriate 'under-achieving' (but supposedly capable) pupils. The understanding of 'ability' mobilized by the school enables those pupils thought to be most likely to make the D-to-C conversion (that is, those pupils considered most valuable to the league tables) to receive particular attention. In practice, it is an approach that embodies familiar biases against pupils of working-class background, Black young people (regardless of class) and girls.

These decisions represent a central element in the processes that we identify as educational triage. The school is seeking to identify those for whom additional resources might prove the difference between life and death/success and failure. In this instance, however, it is clear that the professional judgements that identify 'suitable cases for treatment' are deeply scarred by social class, gendered and racialized perspectives on the health/ability/potential of pupils. In order to understand the ways in which triage, underpinned by these notions, is constructed and deployed, we will examine one key strategy in each school: the 'Achievement Initiative' in Taylor and the target setting and internal competition embodied by the 'pupil league table' in Clough.

The 'Achievement Initiative' in Taylor

We have seen that in Taylor Comprehensive, as in Clough GM, there are key interrelated discourses that circulate within the staff body and inform decisions on pupils. Ability is believed to be fixed and generalized, it is assumed to be measurable and is, therefore, measured. Similarly, GCSE grades are seen as predictable and so they are predicted. Finally, and relatedly, 'under-achievement' is both identifiable and identified. These interconnected discourses, and their facilitating technologies, provide both the conceptual and practical basis for those strategies deployed in the pursuit of D-to-C conversions and maximum school attainment at the five A-to-C benchmark.

Since the 1995/6 academic year, one strategy by which Taylor has sought D-to-C conversions has been through an *Achievement Initiative*. The main component of this initiative is the establishment of 'Achievement Groups' in which final-year pupils (selected by their head of year) are mentored by individual teachers and given additional support and assistance in preparation for the GCSE examinations. Selected pupils are invited to attend these groups, which meet outside school time and are led by members of the teaching staff on a voluntary basis. It is interesting to observe in this regard that the pastoral is 'ministering' to the demands of the academic.[4] An indicator of the importance attached to this initiative is the status of the teachers involved; in addition to some year 11 tutors, the volunteers also include the headteacher, both deputy headteachers and the head of year 11.

For the headteacher, the express aim of the Achievement Groups is to raise the number of pupils attaining five higher-grade passes. Recall his assertion that 'the best thing that we can do for our pupils is to strive to get the greatest possible proportion achieving that five high-grade benchmark' (Chapter 3). He goes on to say: 'In this regard, our Achievement Initiative is being tested in its first year of operation'.

The processes whereby pupils are identified for inclusion in the initiative draw upon the notion of fixed and measurable ability and the subsequent prediction of GCSE grades and assessment of 'under-achievement'. As such, triage principles are applied in order to identify those pupils who are 'safe' (non-urgent cases), those who are 'without hope' and those for whom treatment might make the difference (pupils defined as 'under-achieving' in the school's particular sense of that term). These processes, however, are neither straightforward nor uniformly applied. Analysis of teachers' accounts of these groups and the actual membership of them shows that both formal and informal selection criteria are in operation. Furthermore, the head of year's resistance to the dominating focus on five A*-to-C grades adds a further dimension of inconsistency to these groups.

Figure 6.2   Extract from a memo by the head of year 11 identifying pupils for inclusion in the Achievement Initiative, Taylor Comprehensive

Thank you for the lists of predicted grades for pupils whose grades fall below the 5 A–C threshold. (. . .) I have also picked out a further 29 pupils who could achieve the 'target' if they raised their levels by one grade –

[pupil name] [tutor group]	B C C C D D D
[pupil name] [tutor group]	C C D D D D
[pupil name] [tutor group]	A A B C D D
[pupil name] [tutor group]	B C C C D D D
[pupil name] [tutor group]	A C D D D D D D
[pupil name] [tutor group]	A C C D D D
[pupil name] [tutor group]	B C C C D D D D
[pupil name] [tutor group]	C C C C D D D
[pupil name] [tutor group]	C C C C D D D D
[pupil name] [tutor group]	C C C C D D D D D
[pupil name] [tutor group]	C D D D D D
[pupil name] [tutor group]	A C C D D

. . .

Officially, the criteria for selection are based on the intersection of pupils' predicted grades and teachers' assessments of 'under-achievement'. The following constellation of characteristics formally marks out a pupil for inclusion in the initiative:

1 The pupil is *entered* for five or more GCSE examinations.
2 The pupil is assessed as having the *ability* to attain five or more higher-grade passes.
3 The pupil is currently predicted to *fall short* of the five A*-to-C benchmark by one grade in one or more subject(s).
4 This predicted shortfall is seen as an indication that the pupil is 'under-achieving'.

These criteria for inclusion and the objective of the initiative are illustrated by an extract taken from a memo sent to the deputy head (curriculum) by the head of year 11 (see Figure 6.2).

The central concern of the Achievement Groups is to maximize the proportion of the school population attaining the benchmark level through the D-to-C conversion. Formally, this implies that outside the Achievement Groups will be pupils in two categories: a 'safe' group of pupils already predicted to attain at least five higher-grade passes (non-urgent cases in the metaphor of medical triage); and those pupils (seen as hopeless cases) who are not expected to attain the benchmark even with extra support. The latter group will include a wide range of pupils: some may be expected to attain no pass grades at any level, while others may be predicted to attain a string of D grades but *not* be assessed as 'under-achieving' in the school's terms (see above).

Our analysis of the actual composition of the groups, however, shows that both the third and fourth criteria for selection, that is, those restricting

Table 6.1 Educational triage by ethnic origin, free school meals and gender (Taylor Comprehensive)

	Safe (non-urgent cases)		Suitable cases for treatment		Without hope		Total	
	%	N	%	N	%	N	%	N
White	43	(64)	41	(60)	16	(24)	100	(148)
Black	29	(6)	52	(11)	19	(4)	100	(21)
FSM	25	(14)	49	(28)	26	(15)	100	(57)
Non-FSM	49	(74)	37	(56)	14	(21)	100	(151)
Boys	33	(34)	45	(46)	22	(23)	100	(103)
Girls	51	(54)	36	(38)	12	(13)	99	(105)

Based on the composition of the Achievement Groups in Taylor.

selection to pupils performing *below* the benchmark and concerned with 'under-achievement', are frequently discarded. In addition, pastoral heads of year move through the school with the same cohort of pupils. This means that the head of year 11 (a key player in implementing the Achievement Initiative) changes annually. A recent head of the year 11 makes it clear that effecting D-to-C conversions was the original aim of the Achievement Initiative (and remains an important aspect of it) but, in selecting pupils from her year group, she broadened the scope of the Achievement Groups to include pupils from across the perceived ability range, thereby effectively refusing the dominant definition of 'under-achievement' in Taylor. Furthermore, she states that she selected pupils to ensure that the groups had an equal gender balance:

> They're kids who are under-achieving (. . .) it tends to be across the curriculum (. . .) on my list it was mainly kids who are not getting five A-to-Cs, but there are other kids who are under-achieving, and kids with special needs who'll get a little extra attention, and I tried to make it equal boys and girls (. . .) the intention is to improve their grades, it's not just about A-to-Cs (. . .) to me there's more to achievement than five A-to-Cs.

By the early part of year 11, a proportion of pupils (42 per cent of the year group: n = 88) are defined as safe/non-urgent cases, that is, they are predicted by teachers to be on track to attain five or more A*-to-C grades without further need for any formal additional or special support.[5] While this group includes boys and girls and individuals from the range of ethnic and social class groups, it is the case that girls, white pupils and those not in receipt of free school meals are disproportionately represented (see Table 6.1 and Figure 6.3).

By the same point, and in stark contrast, a proportion of pupils (17 per cent

Figure 6.3   Pupils designated 'safe' by triage at Taylor Comprehensive

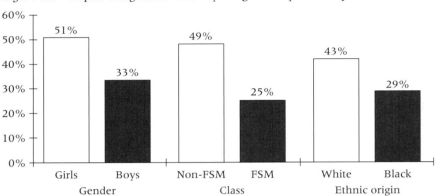

Figure 6.4   Pupils designated 'without hope' by triage at Taylor Comprehensive

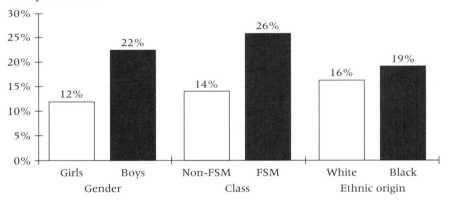

of the year group: n = 36) are treated as *beyond help*, that is, five or more A*-to-C grades are predicted by teachers to be beyond their reach. Again, this group of pupils encompasses both boys and girls and the range of ethnic and social class groups. In this case, however, it is boys, Black pupils and those in receipt of free school meals who are disproportionately represented (see Figure 6.4).

Together these two groups represent 60 per cent (n = 124) of the year group. The remaining pupils are included in the Achievement Initiative. Given the multiple processes by which pupils are identified for inclusion, it is unsurprising that few of these pupils actually fulfil the official inclusion criteria outlined above.

Superficially, membership of the Achievement Groups appears to be relatively equitable, that is, no particular groups of pupils (in terms of class, gender or ethnicity) dominate.[6] Given the inclusion criteria and the ethnic and class profile of the 'safe' group, we should expect to see a disproportionately high representation of Black pupils and pupils in receipt of free school meals in the initiative. Pupils in these groups are somewhat more likely to appear; in practice however, entry into the group does not make good the under-representation of Black pupils and pupils in receipt of free school meals in the 'safe' group. Furthermore, it also includes 28 pupils (33 per cent of those in the Initiative) who are *already* predicted to attain the five higher-grades benchmark. In this way we can see that the Achievement Initiative (equivalent within the triage model to a 'treatment' group) does not make up for the disproportionately small chance of being 'safe' experienced by Black pupils and those in receipt of free school meals. In addition, some pupils judged 'safe' (non-urgent cases) according to the school's own criteria are included in any case as an insurance policy.

We have seen that, at the point of prediction and inclusion, the composition of the treatment group reflects the range of ethnic and social class groups, but that this does not of itself denote equity (since some groups are markedly under-represented in the 'safe' category). More revealing still is an examination of the *outcomes* of the process. As we have noted, some teachers (like the recent head of year 11) are not only aware of inequalities in the identification of likely candidates for D-to-C conversion, but are also prepared (so far as is possible given their location in the staff hierarchy) to modify (subvert?) the systems. It is equally clear, however, that such individuals are in the minority and that their views (of under-achievement and the school's priorities) are out of step with the dominant position that currently informs most academic and pastoral moves in the school.

Our analysis of outcomes in the school suggests that of all the pupils included in Achievement Groups, white pupils and pupils not in receipt of free school meals are more likely to attain the benchmark (five higher grades) than Black pupils and pupils in receipt of free school meals. Furthermore, the majority of those who do finally achieve the benchmark have in fact already been predicted to do so. Of those in the initiative, 18 pupils attained five or more higher-grade passes; of these 16 had been predicted to do so. Of these pupils only a minority were Black and/or in receipt of free school meals.[7] In total, only two Achievement Group pupils achieved the benchmark in contradiction of teachers' previous predictions. Even here, where it might reasonably be suggested that the initiative had helped support a D-to-C conversion, both of these beneficiaries were boys, one white and one defined officially as 'other'. Not only did the Achievement Initiative fail to make good existing inequality in its composition, therefore, it also delivered results that replicated existing trends in the disproportionate success of white pupils and those not in receipt of free school meals.

It appears that despite the best efforts of teachers and a high-profile formal concern with those on the C–D borderline, in practice Taylor's Achievement Initiative is neither concerned with effecting D-to-C conversions nor able to do so. Rather, it is an insurance measure, that is, it acts to ensure that pupils already expected to attain the benchmark do indeed do so. Although the year head's personal concerns over inclusivity extended the catchment of the group somewhat, it had little or no impact in terms of D-to-C conversions. These outcomes seem to confirm that the Achievement Initiative, despite laudable intentions, does little to equalize opportunities in the school; indeed, it is implicated in further cementing, or at least playing out, existing inequalities.

Surveillance and self-surveillance in Clough

In Clough a very different technique is deployed in pursuit of the same outcome – maximizing attainment of the benchmark through D-to-C conversions. In contrast to the Achievement Initiative in Taylor, which is predicated on notions of comprehensiveness and equity (however flawed) and delivered within an ethos of supportive pastoral care, in Clough the strategies are predicated on a market model of individualized competition that does not pay even rhetorical attention to issues of equity and diversity. In Clough the strategies and their underpinning discourses are resolutely blind to issues of 'race', class, gender and the differential outcomes between such groups.

Target setting and the monitoring of teachers

This internal marketization in Clough is manifest through targets pertaining to the proportion of pupils attaining A*-to-C grades at GCSE. These targets are set by the school's governing body and the headteacher. The targets are multiple and include:

- the proportion of pupils attaining the five A*-to-C benchmark across all subjects, responsibility for which lies with the headteacher;
- the proportion of pupils attaining A*-to-C grades across the subjects making up each faculty, responsibility for which lies with the relevant faculty head;
- the proportion of pupils attaining A*-to-C grades within each individual subject within each faculty, responsibility for which lies with the head of faculty and the subject coordinator, where one exists;
- the proportion of pupils attaining A*-to-C grades across groups taught by each teacher, responsibility for which lies with the individual teacher;
- and the proportion of pupils attaining five A*-to-C grades within each group taught by each teacher, responsibility for which again lies with the individual teacher.

The level of disciplinary surveillance is clear. In addition, these targets are not static; teachers and faculties are under pressure to produce year-on-year improvements:

> So we're not naive enough to not think that, you know, the pressure's not on to improve those. 'Cause, you know, that stops the teacher sitting back thinking . . . well I don't, see I personally hit 66 per cent last

year which is well above national [A*-to-C] average (. . .) So that's well above national average. The national average is what, something like 50, isn't it? So I could actually sit back and say well, you know, I'm above, but I haven't I've had to set 70 per cent this year . . .

(Head of faculty, Clough GM)

Faculty heads and teaching staff within Clough take a range of positions in relation to these targets. The head of technology traces the pressure for benchmark grades from the headteacher, to the school's governing body and ultimately to education policy nationally:

I don't think we're getting much understanding from senior manage-ment over that sort of thing but, you know, they've got targets to hit 'cause they're set targets by the governors. So they then put the pres-sure on us (. . .) the whole thing's motivated by league tables now, isn't it? That's what's motivated everybody.

(Head of technology, Clough GM)

Within Clough it is made explicit that the targets might be met through concentrating on 'borderline' pupils (again, the D-to-C conversion):

Well if you look at my estimated grades now, my estimated grades are about 51, 52 per cent. So that means to hit those targets I've got to put the pressure on, on the Ds, what I've estimated to be a D. And I won't hit my 70 per cent [target] unless I can *convert those Ds into Cs*.

(Head of faculty, Clough; emphasis added)

Not all teachers, however, see this conversion as a real possibility. The head of English at once confirms the school's understanding of ability and alludes to its implicit shift in focus from D grade 'under-achievers' to *all* D grade pupils:

You give them [senior managers] the names of the Ds, the borderline people, who if they whip themselves a bit harder possibly could go to a C, but the other thing is this, a lot of those Ds they're there, that's as high as they can go.

(Head of English, Clough)

While still confirming the school's notion of fixed ability, the head of year 11 goes further in identifying the contradictions and incoherence of the demands for A*-to-C grades in general and the D-to-C conversion in particular:

you're teaching for results, it's almost, you know, you must get the results. I think you've always wanted to get the results but I think there's more pressure on pushing everybody and I think if you push everybody at the same speed some aren't going to make it. I mean, does that make sense? (. . .) And this is something which, as a teacher, you know. You are always going to have a proportion of children who aren't going to reach the average. Or you bring the average down so low that everybody, you know, it is, that's the problem isn't it? You can't do it, you're never going to be able to get everybody to achieve the average, it's unrealistic. But you in the classroom can understand, and you presumably looking at statistics can understand that but some people can't. They think that every child coming into school, every child coming in must get five A-to-Cs. And if you try and explain to them that it's not possible for some to get that they say, well, it's because you're not teaching them well enough. And that's soul-destroying as a teacher because you can get them up to a certain level but you can't get them all to get A-to-Cs, it's meant for everybody to reach an A-to-C. (. . .) So, you know, you're on a, whatever you do you're going to be judged as not succeeding. And that, to me, is crazy.

(Head of year 11, Clough GM)

Expected performance in relation to each of the staff targets in Clough is subject to ongoing monitoring through repeated analysis of pupils' predicted grades throughout Key Stage 4 and during year 11 in particular. These are compared across faculties, subjects (with the core areas of English, maths and science subject to particularly heated competition) and individual teachers. This is understood to allow 'discrepancies' in performance between faculties, subjects and teachers to be identified. Furthermore, it facilitates the identification of 'discrepancies' in the performance of individual pupils across and within faculties and subjects. Again, the process takes for granted that 'ability' is relatively fixed and generalized:

So [the senior teacher] calculates all the deviation scores. We do a deviation for individual teachers and we do it for, for, you know, teaching groups, so I can look at each teacher's deviation score. And then whole department, the whole of food [part of the faculty] will be looked at as a deviation score or the whole of resistant materials [another part of the faculty] (. . .) to see whether kids are scoring a grade lower or a grade higher. (. . .) and then when you get kids like who are performing in art and get two grades higher than they've got everywhere else, you know, that puts you under the cosh a little bit. (. . .) we can get a kid who is maybe performing at a grade B with us and, but he's only achieving Es and Fs in English and . . . so you can get that skew, you know. Which can be a pain in the neck because when you look at the final grades, 'cause then departments are actually compared, so you have, every grade a kid gets is awarded a number so I think if he gets an A, A* it's 10, 9. And then you'd get, the norm is worked out, you know, from that listing.

(Head of technology, Clough GM)

This same head of faculty goes on to put these results into the context of performance nationally:

But then what we found interesting is that last year the *Daily Mail* published the deviation scores across the whole country and technology and physics and I think mathematics are scoring 0.8 of a grade lower nationally, across the whole country. And the same with art and drama are scoring, you know, I think it was one-plus, one point something above deviation. I found that quite interesting. So I think really, to get a true deviation score you should take those into deviation. So, for example, if I come out −0.8 I'm doing okay 'cause . . . It's at the national level 'cause that's across the whole country, they're scoring a lower grade in our subject than in English, maths or . . .

It is important to recognize what all this calculation and recalculation represents so far as issues of power and control within education are concerned. Here we see attempts to instigate complex and multiple systems of hierarchical observation, examination and categorization, that is, *surveillance*, through the establishment of multiple parameters of internal competition within the school. These permeate all levels and sections of the school community (literally from the headteacher, through every member of staff, to any given individual pupil) and engender an unprecedented degree of *self-surveillance*. These technologies find their most public and extreme expression in a regularly updated league table of year 11 pupils.

A league table of pupils

The Clough 'pupil league table' reflects the performance indicators deployed in the nationally published league tables of schools and LEAs; it is posted in a key public space within the school. This league table ranks year 11 pupils on the basis of their predicted GCSE outcomes, as collated through the teacher/subject/faculty/school target monitoring processes already outlined (above). A ranking of the entire year group is produced but only the top 150 pupils are listed on the publicly posted version, with the bottom 40 pupils being omitted. As the table is regularly updated pupils may, in principle, not only move up and down the rank order, but actually move on and off the public version. An extract from the table is reproduced in Figure 6.5.

The rank placement on the pupil league table is based on a mean score calculated on each pupil's *predicted* GCSE performance. Calculating exam scores (for GCSE in this instance) involves the assignment of a numerical score to each grade (eight points for an A*, seven for a grade A and so on down to one point for a grade G) which can then be added together to derive an overall exam score for each pupil. It has been noted that calculating exam scores in this way enables examination passes at all grades to be included in assessments of performance. At the same time, however, a single overall exam score might be arrived at through varying collections of grades. A score of 25 might indicate attainment of five higher grades (by achieving five passes at grade C) but it can also indicate a combination of GCSE passes that does *not* meet the five A*-to-C criterion (such as one grade B, three Ds, two Es and a G); see Gillborn and Gipps (1996: 15). In Clough

Figure 6.5 Extract from Clough pupil league table

Rank	Given name	Family name	GCSE average	A	B	C	D	A–C	Attendance	NFER score*
53			4.70	0	1	5	4	6	93.4	121
54			4.67	0	2	4	2	6	99.3	92
55			4.67	0	2	3	3	5	98.1	97
56			4.67	1	0	3	4	4	98.1	0
57			4.67	0	3	2	3	5	93.9	0
58			4.63	0	3	1	3	4	94.6	97
135			3.29	0	0	0	4	0	54.7	0
136			3.25	0	0	0	3	0	97.5	103
137			3.25	0	0	1	4	1	93.1	75
138			3.25	0	0	0	3	0	79.5	95
183			1.88	0	0	0	0	0	91	77
184			1.88	0	0	0	2	0	64.9	101
185			1.83	0	0	0	0	0	87.7	94
186			1.75	0	0	0	1	0	98.7	72

* NFER test results are included in the version used by senior teachers but omitted from the table that is displayed publicly in the school. A score of 0 denotes that no test was taken (usually because the pupil joined the school later in their secondary education).

these predicted overall exam scores are then transformed into an average grade score across all subjects for each individual pupil: where an average grade score of five is assumed to be equivalent to a grade C (i.e. the grade for which five points would be allocated). However, this technique does not alter the range of possible routes to single scores: an overall exam score average of 5 may or may not reflect the benchmark criterion in exactly the same way as an overall raw score of 25. This means that it is technically possible, though unlikely practically, for a pupil *not* predicted to attain five higher-grade passes to appear higher on the table than one who *is* expected to reach the benchmark.[8]

The various routes through which a single exam score can be attained (be it a raw figure or an average) means that ranking in the Clough pupil league table does not reflect directly predicted performance in terms of the single most important measure of the A-to-C economy. Nevertheless, the influence of the A-to-C economy is clear; the use of an aggregate exam score measure does not mean that Clough has rejected this economy in favour of an arguably more inclusive mode of monitoring and representing predicted performance. Although ranking on the table is based on exam score averages, the table also includes a number of other indicators of pupils' predicted performance (see Figure 6.5). Pupil by pupil predicted grade score averages are supplemented by the number of GCSEs predicted at each grade between grades A and D (D being the conversion grade) and the total number of GCSEs predicted at grades A-to-C. Predicted GCSE passes at grades E-to-G do not appear on the table. Pupils' NFER scores (or 'IQ' results as many staff refer to them) also appear on the version of the table retained by senior managers but are removed from the version that is publicly displayed in the school. It is interesting to note that, in guiding us through the table, the senior teacher with a leading role in its production highlighted as evidence of 'under-achievement' those cases (pupils) where there were 'discrepancies' between high NFER scores and low GCSE averages. He did not, however, either highlight or attempt to explain those cases where there were 'discrepancies' between low NFER scores and high GCSE averages.[9]

The inclusion of multiple yet selective indicators of predicted performance belies Clough's overriding concern: the A-to-C economy. Ranking by predicted grade averages rather than the benchmark could reflect a push for greater inclusivity within the competitive model. It could also reflect a 'failure' to make best use of the available information within the terms of the market model employed. As already noted, ranking by grade averages allows some pupils to occupy an 'artificially' high rank in terms of the A-to-C economy. This may function to 'keep hold' of pupils who might otherwise become disillusioned and 'drop out' of the race for benchmark grades. It should also be noted that the information technology used to generate the pupil league table has the capacity to sort and resort by any of the indicators included in it. Ultimately, it is clear that Clough GM is utilizing every available and 'relevant' technology (in both statistical and Foucauldian terms) to survey, judge and classify each individual pupil and, in turn, promote pupils' self-surveillance.

In discussing the basis for inclusion in the public version of the pupil league table, and the rationale for making it public, the headteacher restates the school's mobilization of particular notions of fixed ability, 'under-achievement' and the implicit adoption and extension to pupils of a market model of competition:

> Well, we reckoned that that left about 30 kids or so, 30-plus who, for one reason or another, were never going to change their position in that they were always going to be right at the bottom, not necessarily through their fault. (. . .) there are kids down in the sort of 120s who really with, in terms of their ability, could easily be in the top 25 or 30. So the idea was to provide a spur to all those who had it in them to do a bit better really. There is always a group of kids who can't, for one reason or another.

The head of year 11 also explicitly says that the table was designed to engender competition between pupils inside the school. She also suggests that the table seeks to raise pupils' and teachers' sense of competition with other schools. In this way, this head of year notes a lack of consensus among staff concerning the extent to which pupils should be exposed to their own educational 'success' and 'failure':

> It was to get them, the ones who are not being so successful, to get them to realize that they could do better and that they were letting themselves down. And the other problem is that schools don't realize that they're in competition with other schools. (. . .) So it's to try and place them within society as well as within the school I think. You might think that getting five GCSEs, yeah five A-to-Cs here is good but if you went to somewhere else you'd be down the bottom. (. . .) there are still within the school those who want to cushion the children and only let them see their successes and those who say, 'Yes, let them see their successes but also prepare them for the fact that there are also failures', that you aren't going to achieve necessarily what you want to.

The headteacher is confident that pupils' have received the table well and that it has succeeded in engendering competition and prompting further effort from pupils, as demonstrated by improved grade averages when the table was updated:

> They certainly found it interesting and are keen to see where they are. Most of the kids in year 11 will tell you where they are in the league table and who's top and where their friends are relative to them and when the tables were revised most kids, the vast majority of the kids had better estimated grades than previously.

The headteacher reports that he was unaware of the responses of those pupils whose ranking was too low to be featured in the table. In discussing this he shifts from his previous assertion that these pupils are almost certainly not able to improve their position to suggesting that withholding their ranking is simultaneously a protective and a motivating factor. Finally, he moves his attention back to the top of the table:

> Well the message that went to the year group as a whole was that we would put up the top 150, we didn't say the rest of you are duffers, or useless, or whatever. (. . .) And I guess that's the sort of message that they received. So the fact that they don't know whether they're 151 or 150-something or other might be an encouragement to some of them to try and leap into the table. What we didn't want to do was to put up a list which had, I remember [pupil name] was 190, and have it there all the time, you know, and that person become the object of some ridicule amongst his peers or whatever. Being 150 isn't quite so bad, is it? For some of those kids being first would be quite bad as well.

The head of year for these pupils does not share the headteacher's confidence concerning the impact of the table:

> The 50 that don't appear on there are going to be ridiculed, I feel. Now you can ask them, maybe you can come back and tell me what they say. I feel that they're maybe being ridiculed a little bit. Some of them who have got the ability and see themselves as 147 think 'Oh God that's shameful', and hopefully . . . So that's obviously where it's going to work. Some of them will make excuses, 'Oh the computer's wrong', 'Oh I mean really interesting', 'Oh that's a mistake'. They won't face up to the fact that they're not achieving. I've got one boy who, you'll probably not meet him. He is the greatest, he's amazing, he's got such an impression of himself and he just thinks he's wonderful and he didn't appear on the lists. I think he was 152nd. And he was just so outraged, he just said, 'Oh well the system doesn't work because I should be there. The machine's wrong'. And that was it. You know, he has no recognition of the fact that he was under-achieving at all.

Dominant models of an inclusive school ethos, embedded through pastoral care and the development of a collective and cohesive school community, are difficult to reconcile with the explicit institution of such overt competition between pupils (and teaching staff). Yet as the discussions of the pupil league table outlined above demonstrate, at the level of senior managers at least, such a notion has been sacrificed to the greater demands of the A-to-C economy. While resistance to this move remains among some pastoral middle managers, many members of teaching staff appear to have accepted, if not embraced, this internal market. As we will see when we move on to examine pupils' experiences of the A-to-C economy, it is the pupils themselves (in formal terms the least powerful members of the school community) who represent the main locus of resistance, however ineffectual, to such market strategies.

Table 6.2   Educational triage by ethnic origin, free school meals and gender (Clough GM)

	Safe (non-urgent cases)		Suitable cases for treatment		Without hope		Total	
	%	N	%	N	%	N	%	N
White	33	(38)	38	(43)	29	(33)	100	(114)
Black	4	(1)	58	(14)	38	(9)	100	(24)
FSM	7	(3)	44	(19)	49	(21)	100	(43)
Non-FSM	35	(52)	42	(62)	22	(33)	99	(147)
Boys	23	(23)	49	(49)	28	(28)	100	(100)
Girls	36	(32)	36	(32)	29	(26)	101	(90)

Based on positions in the pupil league table and GCSE predicted grades as formulated by Clough.

Drawing once again on the notion of rationing opportunity through the practice of educational triage, we can identify three relatively discrete zones or areas within the Clough pupil league table (see Table 6.2):[10] first, a 'safe' group, where all pupils are predicted to attain the benchmark of five or more A*-to-C passes (this would include ranks 1 through 55: n = 55: 29 per cent of pupils); second, a group without hope, pupils who cannot attain the benchmark level because they are entered for too few subjects (ranks 137–190: n = 54: 28 per cent of the year group). This produces a maximum size 'treatment' group of 81 pupils (ranks 56–136, 43 per cent of the year group) for whom attaining the benchmark grades is seen to remain at least a possibility, that is, they are entered for at least five GCSE examinations. In the light of the conceptual contradictions between notions of inclusivity and competition, the inequalities played out through setting and selection in the school, and the broader evidence concerning differential outcomes at GCSE nationally (Gillborn and Gipps 1996), it is perhaps not surprising that pupils' positions within this league table and their eventual actual GCSE outcomes are marked by 'race', class and gender. Dividing the table into these triage groups once again highlights considerable inequalities of experience and outcome.

Black pupils and pupils in receipt of free school meals are unlikely to be predicted grades that allocate them to the 'safe' group (see Figure 6.6). And while this under-representation is made up to some extent in the treatment group, Black pupils and those in receipt of free school meals are over-represented in the group judged as without hope (see Figure 6.7).

Furthermore, those Black pupils who do feature in the treatment group are far less likely than their white peers ultimately to attain five or more higher-grade passes. Almost all pupils in the safe group ultimately attain the

Figure 6.6 Pupils designated 'safe' by triage at Clough GM

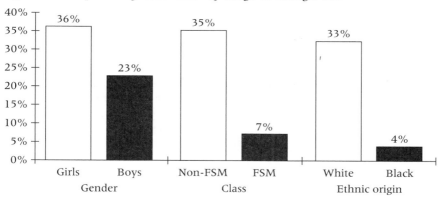

Figure 6.7 Pupils designated 'without hope' by triage at Clough GM

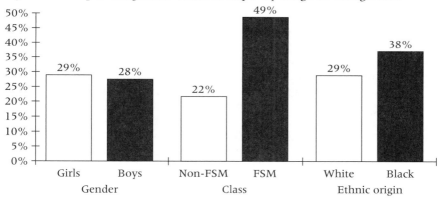

benchmark – the exception to this being pupils in that category who were also in receipt of free school meals: only one of three such pupils did so. In addition, there is a strong general correspondence between pupils' position in the league-table groups and their 'ability' ranking as defined through the NFER tests administered on entry to year 7 (which we discussed in Chapter 3).

The pupil league table in Clough GM, therefore, embodies the processes, products and outcomes of those inequitable setting and selection practices discussed earlier (see Chapters 3–5). Given the strength of the school's adherence to notions of unequal and fixed ability, which guide its practices, it is not surprising that its measurements of ability and subsequent GCSE grade predictions prove to be so prophetic. Indeed, based on our data and analyses in this and previous chapters, we suggest that these discursive practices *produce* the very effects that they claim to *predict*.

Conclusions

Despite pockets of staff unease and even resistance, both Taylor Comprehensive and Clough GM have largely succumbed to the demands of the educational market place and its A-to-C economy. They exist in a marketized situation where they compete not only with other schools (for pupils and resources) but also with themselves (striving for year-on-year improvements in the performance tables both overall and within each subject area). Amid all this, the percentage of pupils attaining at least five higher-grade passes has become the paramount concern. Schools' responses, however, are not predetermined; Taylor and Clough are very different schools, and in pursuit of improved performance against the national benchmark they mobilize different technologies, reflecting the broader ethos, mechanisms, skills, capacities, and beliefs within and about each school. Nevertheless, there are strong similarities between the underlying assumptions and discourses that shape the measures taken in each school in pursuit of converting predicted grade D passes into final grades of C and above.

First, both schools adopt a view of 'ability' as if it were fixed, generalized and measurable. There is often an interesting contradiction when teachers speak of the relationship between 'ability' and outcome. Initially they seem reluctant to sanction a clear and reliable relationship; they speak of 'loose' fits and do not accept simple relationships when posited. Nevertheless, when they discuss the situation further it emerges that, at heart, these simple and predictable relationships are exactly the kind of assumption that lies at the centre of their dealings with issues of selection and maximizing performance at grades A*-to-C. Beyond superficial uncertainties lies an apparently deep-seated belief in the simple, unitary version of 'ability'/intelligence that many teachers appear to question but ultimately support through their actions. Hence, a head of year 11 can describe the association between school measures of 'ability' and outcomes as 'very loose', but go on to conclude that there are only 'the odd hiccups' where it does not work out and, at the next stage in the process, play a pivotal role in translating such criteria into differential expectations and treatment.

Second, both schools produce a range of detailed subject-by-subject predictions for the eventual GCSE results of every pupil. The schools use a range of criteria and adopt different procedures but, once again, the similarities are clear. In both schools the underlying view of 'ability' as fixed and measurable informs the production of GCSE predictions that involve a range of criteria beyond the pupils' actual performance in 'mock' examinations. Judgements about 'ability', effort and the best way to motivate pupils all come into play as the schools produce their own forecasts of future performance. These predictions are presented with an air of authority and certainty that belies their production. Teachers admit to using 'gut feeling' and adopting different 'ploys'. There is clearly great scope for such predictions to reflect assumptions based on pupils' gender, class and ethnic origin; we noted, for example, that a faculty head viewed Black pupils' concerns about low predicted grades as a 'challenge' and 'threat' rather than evidence of high aspirations and motivation to succeed.

Third, these notions of 'ability' and the predicted grades are combined to identify pupils who are 'under-achieving'. In both schools a particular and divisive notion of 'under-achievement' is mobilized. Here two pupils may be predicted exactly the same GCSE grades but only one might be identified for special treatment, where her/his predicted grades do not match the school's idea of appropriate performance for their level of 'ability'. In Taylor Comprehensive an Achievement Initiative has been launched, involving staff mentoring and special classes. In Clough GM the response has a sharper disciplinary edge, with elaborate surveillance of staff and pupils' performance meant to bolster effort through target setting and self-motivation. The latter includes the production (and regular update) of a public league table of pupil performance based on GCSE predictions. In many respects this can be seen as the ultimate working through of the internal logic that has driven British educational reform for the last two decades: the glorification of academic results above all else, the individualization of competition and the philosophy of 'naming and shaming' are all present here, encapsulated for all to see on a league table of pupils.

It is here, as the schools seek to generate one last push towards maximum success in terms of the GCSE higher grades so central to the A-to-C economy, that we can see most clearly the operation of educational triage. In both schools the particular definition of 'under-achievement' is mobilized to allow the targeting of additional support and resources on to a limited pool of pupils where the most reward is expected: these are the suitable cases for treatment in the final rationing of education. At either extreme there are safe/non-urgent pupils, who can be relied upon, and 'hopeless' cases whose teachers believe that five higher-grade passes is simply not a credible aim. In both schools white pupils and those not in receipt of free school meals are over-represented among the 'safe' group. At the other extreme, Black pupils and those in receipt of free school meals (a proxy for poverty) are over-represented among those believed to be beyond help.

The attempt to target resources and draw maximum benefit might have been expected to redress some of the previous inequities in the system. Afterall, since Black pupils and those in receipt of free school meals are less likely to be considered a safe bet, we might reasonably have assumed that they would be over-represented in the treatment group and draw considerable benefit. The opposite is the case. Not only are Black pupils and those in receipt of free school meals most likely to be condemned to the group of lost causes, even when they gain entry to the 'treatment' group, there is evidence that they do not draw equal benefit. In both schools, Black pupils in the 'treatment' group were markedly less likely to achieve five or more higher-grade passes than their white peers.

In Chapter 2 we discussed the dominant linked trends of changes in achievement and educational reform in contemporary Britain. We noted that as overall 'standards' have improved, so the relative inequalities between groups (especially those related to 'race' and social class) have widened. Here, in microcosm, we see those trends under construction in the myriad decisions, selections and interactions between teachers and pupils. Some Black pupils and their peers in receipt of free school meals *do* gain entry to the treatment groups and a very small number draw tangible benefits: but overwhelmingly the processes provide a second chance for those already predicted success. Pupils thought to posses 'ability' (on the basis of a previous test score and/or in relation to social criteria) are given a second chance to fulfil their privileged destinies through the mobilization of higher teacher expectations and additional resources. In Taylor, for example, the whole time-consuming machinery of the Achievement Initiative seems actually to provide an elaborate insurance policy for those already predicted to attain the all-important benchmark of five or more higher-grade passes. In all of this, as we have shown, pupils are positioned as passive recipients: recipients of others' judgements about their 'ability', motivation and the treatment best suited to their needs. But pupils are not passive. They experience the pain and uncertainty of these processes as much as, if not more than, any teacher. As we show in the next chapter, pupils understand their education in different ways but the processes of selection and differentiation do not pass them by. Pupils see triage at work; they perceive some of the principles and inequalities that shape the process; and, on occasion, they seek actively to resist and reshape the dominant labels and processes.

7

Pupils' experiences and perspectives

living with the rationing of education

Up to this point we have been concerned to understand the changing nature of secondary education within our two case-study schools. We have sought to identify how the demands of the A-to-C economy are perceived and responded to in the daily life of our schools and to analyse the consequences of these changes, especially for issues of equity and achievement. The account has been dominated by teachers' perspectives because the processes themselves, at the school level, are dominated by teachers. The demands of managers, the fears and expectations of subject teachers and the changing role of those with pastoral responsibilities have all featured as we seek to represent and understand the new realities of educational triage in Taylor Comprehensive and Clough GM. At each point we would have liked to accompany the teachers' voices with those of their pupils, the people who bear the heaviest burden as a consequence of the reforms. The limitations of space, however, are such that to do so would have risked trivializing the pupils' perceptions, experiences and desires. Young people do not passively receive the actions of teachers; they may often feel like objects, but they live a range of experiences to which they bring meaning and which, on occasion, they seek actively to resist and reshape. In this chapter we want to place the pupils centre-stage.

The chapter begins with pupils in year 9, a point at which selection is becoming increasingly widespread. At this stage some of our pupils have already been selected to different teaching groups that are 'set by ability' or marked as 'fast'. Additionally, all pupils experience the less formal, but no less real, selection involved in the options process, where the shape of Key Stage 4 curricula are manipulated by teachers with a view to the A-to-C economy. As we will see, pupils are well aware of the pressure exerted by the published school league tables. Their understanding of these forces, and their perceptions of selection, become sharper as they progress through their secondary schooling into year 11. We consider these issues and focus on the underlying question of equity and unfairness. Many pupils feel that they and/or their peers have not been dealt with fairly. Their accusations are not simple blanket rejections of the school or excuses for their own shortcomings. The final section of the chapter examines these perspectives in detail. In particular, we explore the interrelated notions of 'ability' and 'behaviour' and identify how class, gender and 'race' work through the various discourses.

Year 9: 13- and 14-year-olds

By year 9 the majority of pupils have been in their secondary school long enough to build a strong sense of the institution and their place within it. Although some pupils change school during their secondary years, most of our cohort entered their school as 11-year-olds in year 7. During their first two years of secondary education the pupils receive various messages about their supposed 'ability' and the school's expectations for them. The frequency and intensity of these messages increase to new levels in year 9. During this year the pupils are prepared for the different paths that their teachers think appropriate during the final stage of their secondary schooling (Key Stage 4, years 10 and 11) when they will undertake different GCSE examination courses. For all pupils, therefore, year 9 raises a series of issues that concern the school's view of them and the interface between school and the outside world, not least the world of (un)employment.

Selection and setting

In Chapters 3 and 4 we began our discussion of the selection and setting practices in the study schools. These practices were by no means transparent to pupils, although most of them felt they understood something of what was being done. Not surprisingly, this understanding developed between year 9 (our first pupil cohort) and year 11 (our second pupil cohort). In Chapter 4 we detailed Clough's selection and setting practices in the lower school (Key Stage 3). Clough year 9 pupils in the 'fast' groups tended to be aware of their set/stream position and the meaning of this within the 'ability' hierarchy.

Liam:	I'm in the top group.
Stuart:	So am I.
Researcher:	What does being in the top group mean?
Liam:	Like the *fast* group.
Stuart:	He's in the top group, I'm in the express group.
Tete:	It means your capable.
Stuart:	Like in English and maths, express.
Liam:	It's fast groups, working at a faster pace.

Similarly, these 'fast'-group pupils also assert an understanding of the lower positions, beneath them in the hierarchy:

Stuart: and then there's mixed ability and then there's, like, not dumb, but . . .
Tete: Slow people.
Liam: Slow people.
Tete: They can, like, learn at a slower pace.
Stuart: Learn slower. Because if they got put into an express group it would hold down the whole class.

These pupils, near the top of the hierarchy, have clearly understood the structure of the setting system and accept the school's rationale for it. Other pupils find the structure less clear. There is generally agreement about which groups are at the 'top' and the 'bottom', but the differentiation becomes less obvious between the extremes:

it's easy when you're in the bottom or the top. Not in between.
(Emma, Clough GM, year 9)

In both our case-study schools there are pupils who believe that movement between sets is possible, both upwards (promotion) and downwards (demotion):

Researcher: Can you move between groups?
Kofi: Yeah, if you speak up early enough, yeah, or if you, if you're working up to a higher standard then they'll put you up into a higher level.
Jason: Or if you want to move down you can move down if you're – [interrupted]
Vijay: If you want to move down a class you can if you want to.
Jason: You swap with someone.
(Clough GM, year 9)

For these pupils, set movement is seen being driven by pupils themselves. In a reading of the process that would surprise many of their teachers, they believe that promotion can be achieved so long as a request to do so is made 'early enough' and combines with their performance in class. Demotion is also viewed as within the pupils' own power. These perspectives do not accord with the way teachers operate setting and are not agreed by all pupils. In particular, there seems growing awareness that promotion is difficult to attain in practice. During small-group interviews, with two to four pupils at a time, we discussed their knowledge of a very small number of pupils who had actually moved between sets. Disagreement emerges about the reality of set movement (as opposed to the story teachers tell): some pupils strongly assert that set movement *is* possible while others express upset and resignation that, in reality, this does not happen. It is also interesting to note that while pupils do not challenge the notion of 'ability' *per se*, a number do feel that their own ability has been underestimated by teachers:

Richard: Sometimes I get upset 'cause sometimes like I'm in a lower class than what I think I should be in. I should be higher.
Researcher: And can you get to change?
Simon: If you work hard.
Richard: Well, no. They don't change you, do they?
Simon: Yeah, if you work hard and you get gooder marks and stuff they move you up.
Richard: I don't think they change you.

                                        (Taylor Comprehensive, year 9)

Irrespective of whether or not these pupils feel that set movement is a reality, they are at least clear that such decisions are the domain of teachers and that their own desires and beliefs have little or no bearing on set placements and movements.

The responses to setting by pupils in our study reflect the understandings of differentiation and polarization developed in early qualitative studies concerned with selection within schools (cf. Ball 1981; Hargreaves 1967; Lacey 1970). Just as Colin Lacey's study of Hightown Grammar identified the impact of differentiation on high-attaining pupils' social and academic relations, so pupils in our study who are positioned in the upper regions of the setting hierarchy vie for recognition of their relative positioning and subsequent status:

Tete: I'm just in the *top* group, I ain't in the express group.
Stuart: No, you're not in the top group.
Tete: Yes I am, *you're* in the express group.
Stuart: Yeah, I know.
Tete: And I'm in the top group, you're in the express group.

                                                    (Clough GM, year 9)

Here the set labels 'express' and 'top' are strategically deployed and battled over in order to enable the pupils respectively to assert and blur the ranking of the sets and their own positions within the hierarchy. Early understandings of polarization and the development of 'anti-school' pupil cultures (cf. Ball 1981; Hargreaves 1967; Woods 1979) and assertions of the negative effects on attainment of low set placement (CRE 1992; Hallam and Toutounji 1996) can also be seen in the responses to low set placement of pupils in our study:

> It makes you give up. 'Cause like you try your hardest all this time and then you're not getting nowhere so you think, 'What's the point? Is it worth it?' So you just slip down.

                                            (Terry, Clough GM, year 9)

A range of perspectives, therefore, can be seen among our year 9 pupils. For those at the top of the hierarchy the practice seems mostly trouble-free, although there are still arguments about the relative merits of the different groups at the top (witness the debate above about the 'top' group versus the 'fast'/'express' group). Such concerns, however, are as nothing compared to the views of the majority of pupils who find themselves in lower classes and sets. For these young people, selection is a process dominated by the perspectives of teachers. In some cases the pupils feel short-changed by official evaluations and, aged 13 and 14, are seriously questioning the point of further effort in a system that seems unwilling to acknowledge or reward their efforts and achievements.

Choice and the options process

As we discussed in Chapter 4, the options process in year 9 (when pupils' upper school curriculum is decided) offers a series of opportunities for interventions designed to maximize higher-grade passes. In many respects the National Curriculum makes the term 'options' something of a misnomer. The timetable share of compulsory subjects means that, in practice, pupils have very few options at GCSE. The move to compulsory modern foreign languages, double award science and the recommendation that core subjects receive a greater timetable share (Dearing 1994), at the time when these year 9 pupils were deciding on their GCSE subjects, reduced this further in comparison to existing Key Stage 4 pupils. Much of the choice that did exist was constrained within certain subject areas. Furthermore, the need to prioritize compulsory subjects in staffing decisions, along with the need to ensure minimum group sizes for financial and practical reasons, meant that relatively few non-compulsory subjects were on offer. After their 'choices' were made, we invited pupils to discuss the process and reflect on their role in it. Pupils in both schools are well aware of how limited their 'options' really are:

Ian: There wasn't a lot of choice.
Jason: There wasn't enough.
Vijay: There was limited options.

(Clough GM, year 9)

they gave us a list of which ones are compulsory and which ones are options. There wasn't really much to choose from. You had seven in the bottom, so you had seven and you can only choose two. You had the third and fourth choice but that's only if you didn't get into the two top ones that you chose.

(Marcella, Taylor Comprehensive, year 9)

The basis on which these limited choices were made differed markedly between the two study schools. As we saw in Chapter 4, in Clough consideration of future employment opportunities and aspirations was identified by teaching staff as central to pupils' decisions within the options process. Given the emphasis on future employment in personal, social and health education and careers classes, and in the options interviews themselves, it is not surprising that pupils identified this as a central factor in choosing between subjects. For some pupils, this meant missing out on favoured subjects because they perceived them to be irrelevant to their chosen area of employment:

Researcher: Was there anything that you dropped that you really liked?
Terry: Yeah, art, music and drama, I like but . . . That was a disappointment . . . but I couldn't choose it because of the job that I want to do now. So I took the lessons that help me.
(Clough GM, year 9)

Other pupils found it difficult and/or unnecessary to consider what work they might want to do in several years' time. Some were also concerned that they might be constrained by the employment preferences they had indicated, for instance, in relation to their work-experience placements. In addition to the perceived requirements of future employers, pupils in Clough also followed official advice by identifying their relative ability in and enjoyment of subjects, as well as how easy they perceived subjects to be as key factors in making options decisions.

In contrast to Clough, however, future employment aspirations were much less often identified as pertinent factors by pupils in Taylor Comprehensive. The explanation below was typical of those provided by pupils in the school:

Mridula: it isn't really hard, it's just according to what you want to do basically, if you're good at it or not.
Lisa: Which ones you're good at, that's the question.
Avtar: Whether you like it.
Lisa: They just told us don't choose it because you like the teacher or you hate [the teacher] or because of your friend. They just gave us a simple rule and the rest is up to you.
(Taylor Comprehensive, year 9)

In Taylor, although the job market was less prominent, the other sanctioned choice criteria were very familiar: the emphasis in decision making was on relative 'ability' in subjects, that is, ensuring the highest possible GCSE outcomes. Related to this, although remaining a secondary factor, was pupils' enjoyment of particular subjects. These criteria have been emphasized by schools during options processes for some time (cf. Gillborn 1987; Woods 1977; 1979) and are now given additional weight because of the A-to-C economy.

This emphasis on relative 'ability', and ensuring the highest possible GCSE outcomes, indicates where the investments of teachers and the school might lie in relation to the options process. As we saw in Chapter 4, pupils are 'warmed up' and 'cooled out' of subjects in relation to their perceived likelihood of attaining (or not) higher-grade passes. While high-attaining pupils in both schools report that they have been canvassed by a number of their subject teachers, this is most pronounced in Clough where, as we saw in Chapter 6, targets for the number of higher grades have been set at individual teacher, subject and department level. Year 9 pupils in Clough describe the talks they were given by subject teachers and heads of departments as part of the options process:

Researcher:	Did they want anybody from the whole room to take their subject?
Vijay:	Anybody.
Ian:	No.
Kofi:	No, clever people.
Jason:	Yeah, clever people.
Researcher:	What gave you that impression?
Kofi:	The way they were speaking.
Jason:	And they were looking at certain people in the group.
Kofi:	Just that they gave you hints, right.
Jason:	They had an expression on their face.
Vijay:	I thought they were talking to everybody.

(Clough GM, year 9)

Most of the pupils in this group have identified a series of subtle and sometimes non-verbal strategies through which subject teachers are said to identify who in particular they are directing their appeals towards. However, one pupil has understood these recommendations as generalized and is concerned to learn that his peers see things differently. Another pupil speaks of the 'pressure' he experienced from teachers who were keen for him to choose their subject:

Well, most people have been experiencing some pressure [from teachers] and it's not really up to them. I was fed up with every subject. I don't know. In the end I chose what I liked and that was it. There was one teacher, she said 'You shouldn't give this up 'cause you're good at it', and she really kept on forcing me and I didn't take it in the end because I didn't like the subject really.

(Arun, Clough GM, year 9)

Despite the time and effort that both schools invested in the options process, a number of pupils feel that the whole exercise was of limited significance. This is based on their assessments of the relatively low status of those subjects that are available to choose between. These pupils are aware both of the formal hierarchy of compulsory subjects within the National Curriculum and the informal hierarchy between 'academic' and 'arts' subjects:

Researcher:	What difference do you think it's going to make next year?
Lisa:	Not much. Because they're like, the subjects that are our choices, they're not really all that important.

Mridula: It's just something like one less sort of subject than we do now.

Lisa: Yeah, they're not really important, it's like music and art and that.

(Taylor Comprehensive, year 9)

Despite all the official pronouncements and staff time spent preparing formally (and canvassing informally), therefore, pupils see the options process largely as a disappointment. For a minority there is the experience of being 'pressured' to choose between competing subjects. For most there is a chance to express preferences between subjects that they do not view as particularly important in any case. In this sense the motivational aspect that teachers view as central to the options process (see Chapter 4) is lost on most pupils. Indeed, for some the process has the opposite effect, bringing home the fact that whatever preferences they express, once again it is teachers who usually have the final say in deciding on 'appropriate' choices.

Expectations of GCSE courses

In both study schools year 9 pupils anticipate that GCSE courses will bring about changes in the nature of their classroom work, with increased independent study and more essay writing. They also envisage an increased workload with greater levels of homework coupled to GCSE coursework and 'mock' examinations. Most assume that the work will be academically far more challenging. As a result, many pupils do not look forward to GCSE courses, which they expect to be stressful and to restrict the amount of free time they have available. For these reasons, a few pupils suggest that they would prefer not to follow GCSE courses. However, the majority assert that not only are GCSEs extremely important, but that 'good marks' and 'high grades' are essential:

If you get a good mark you're more likely to get a good job.

(Simon, Taylor Comprehensive, year 9)

They give you like a higher chance of getting a job, like, and you want to have high grades to get a high job.

(Robert, Taylor Comprehensive, year 9)

Not all pupils, however, share the perception of higher-grade GCSE passes as the route to a 'good' job. A small number of pupils express concerns about the employment market and recognize that even the highest-grade passes at GCSE do not guarantee employment:

Well sometimes they can help you get a job but the way life is these days there aren't that many jobs going. Sometimes it can just be a waste of time getting the best results when you can end up getting or not getting a job.

(Christopher, Taylor Comprehensive, year 9)

This range of views is common to both our case-study schools. However, more variation emerges when we probe pupils' understandings of GCSE tiering. In Clough GM the term is rarely recognized at all by year 9 pupils. More pupils recognize the word in Taylor, but in both schools only a handful of pupils seem aware that tiering brings with it implications for possible GCSE grades. Even here, these relatively 'knowledgeable' pupils are unclear about what the implications might be or how they might actually operate.

In discussing the difference between 'fast' and other groups, for example, two year 9 girls in Clough suggest that at GCSE non-'fast' groups will be 'working for another C' while the 'fast' groups will be 'working for an A'. One pupil in Taylor says:

> I heard if you're in a lower group you have to try really hard just to get C. But if you're in a medium or high group that means you don't have to study so hard to get an A or a B.

These pupils seem aware that some sort of relationship exists between tier/ set placement and the GCSE grades that might ultimately be attained. They are unsure of the processes but they seem to recognize clearly that their peers in the higher groups are somehow destined for greater things. It is notable also that the grades discussed are the higher-grade passes, with the all-important grade C being positioned centrally as a sort of minimum acceptable limit.

Pupils' understandings of GCSE courses, therefore, are somewhat hazy as they complete their third year of secondary education and prepare for the courses that will dominate their last two compulsory years in the school. Most of them view GCSE passes as important and they have already adopted the routine privileging of the higher grades (A*-to-C). Additionally, some pupils already recognize a relation between GCSE grades and position within selective teaching groups (sets and 'fast' groups). They seem unclear about the processes involved but know that those in higher groups are most likely to achieve the highest grades. So far as the internal structure of GCSE courses is concerned, the majority of pupils have no firm understanding of issues such as tiering. As we will see when we turn to look at year 11 pupils' perceptions in the next section, by their final year of compulsory education these vague ideas about GCSE tiers have been largely replaced by more detailed, but not necessarily more accurate, understandings of tiering.

Year 11: 15- and 16-year-olds

For many pupils the last year in compulsory schooling is the most traumatic. This is when they must 'prove' themselves in a series of examinations that they have been told (for example, during the options process) could influence the course of their future career and life chances. For some there is the increasing realization that the targets they have set themselves are unlikely (or even impossible) not least because of decisions that others have made about them.

The pressure to achieve within the A-to-C economy

In both our study schools, year 11 pupils share a tacit understanding of the demands of the A-to-C economy. They are acutely aware of the increased pressure on schools to deliver ever higher 'standards' in terms of the proportion of pupils achieving A*-to-C grade passes at GCSE:

> Anything below a C is failing to them lot, to the teachers.
>
> (Lyn, Clough GM, year 11)

> You have to get A-to-C otherwise it's a fail.
>
> (Bob, Taylor Comprehensive, year 11)

> As-to-Cs, that's all they want (. . .) they don't want no one to get below C.
>
> (Jenny, Clough GM, year 11)

> If you get marks from A-to-C, if you get C or above, then that's good.
>
> (Barry, Clough GM, year 11)

The emphasis on higher-grade passes is recognized by most pupils, though they do not always agree on teachers' motivations. In fact, pupils often identify several factors that they believe impact upon their teachers' concern for ever increasing achievements. These include the need to match or exceed previous cohorts; the status of the individual teacher or department within the school; and, ultimately, the status accorded to the annually published 'league tables' of school performance:

> *Researcher*: Why is it so important to the teachers?
> *Darren*: 'Cause they don't want to look bad.
> *John*: No, I don't think it is actually. (. . .)
> *Darren*: We've got very different views on that (. . .) it just looks like they try and make themselves look good, if you get higher or the same exam results as last year's. 'Cause last year it was quite good, all the exam results and that. And they just say, 'Oh, you've got to do as well as them or even better', just to make themselves look good.
> *John*: They're not going to look good to anyone though are they?
>
> (Taylor Comprehensive, year 11)

> I think all of the pressure the teachers are putting on us, I think they're doing it because last year, like, last year's year 11, they did really, really badly, and so we're, 'cause they want us to do well in this so their league tables are all right. They don't seem to care about what we want to do for ourselves. Just seem to care about us on the league table.
>
> (Samantha, Clough GM, year 11)

Pupils may disagree on the reasons for teachers' acute concern for GCSE pass grades but they are united in identifying higher grades as of crucial importance for staff. Furthermore, they explicitly identify the annually published GCSE performance tables (the so-called school 'league tables') as a major factor. The A-to-C economy touches pupils and teachers alike. As we have already noted, the imperative to produce year-on-year improvements is built into the tables; it is experienced by teachers who are held accountable for the results of 'their' pupils; and it is passed on to the young people themselves as teachers seek constantly to reinforce the importance of success in terms of 'benchmark' indicators. For some pupils, however, the repeated exhaltation to GCSE success is tainted by a recognition that they have effectively been sorted by the school and treated second-best in comparison to some of their peers.

Selection and pupils' sense of their own worth

A common concern when pupils are separated into hierarchies is that those at the lower end will tend to become disaffected.[1] As in the case of year 9 pupils, our findings show this concern to be well founded. However, some previous work (notably among early ethnographic school studies in the British sociology of education) has described a process of sub-cultural polarization, where young people at either extreme of the selective hierarchy come predominantly to accept or reject the official values of the school (cf. Ball 1981; Hargreaves 1967; Lacey 1970). While our data confirm that rejection of the school's values is most pronounced among those in the lower 'ranks' of the selective hierarchy, our conversations with pupils also suggest that unease, even anger, at their treatment is more generally shared among the young people in Taylor and Clough. 'Disaffection' is a slippery term, often assumed to describe open rebellion. We found more general (though less pronounced) disaffection to be fairly common: in this sense disaffection ranged from more or less open resistance at one extreme to deeply felt, but less obviously displayed dissatisfaction at the other. It seems that as the drive to 'raise standards' translates into ever increasing pressure on pupils, so young people may be becoming increasingly unhappy with their treatment and their position in the pecking order of teaching groups.

In our data it is clear that pupils experience set placements and/or tier allocations as a distinct hierarchy in which they are treated and valued differently. They view this as an extension of a more generalized preference and prioritization of pupils who are seen by the school as being both high attaining and well behaved. Where teaching groups are set, pupils in lower groups (and tiers) believe that, in line with the A-to-C economy, those in higher groups are valued more highly and allocated the most skilled teachers. This feeling is not restricted to the lowest sets within the hierarchy. Even those pupils placed in relatively high groups reflect negatively on their relationship with the top groups. This is most pronounced where setting is long established and used for all pupils. In Clough, for example, in interview the children in the second maths set describe themselves as 'cast-offs' from the top set. The introduction of GCSE tiering means that, even in mixed-ability teaching groups (where such distinctions were previously not formalized), pupils are increasingly made aware of their teachers' differential evaluations of them:

Maria: For pupils they get like Foundation [tier] or something, they feel a bit dumb or something. But then the teacher will sit and praise the higher-level people and say, 'Oh, we've got this person and we want to make an A* out of them' and you feel a bit stupid. Not that you are but you feel . . .
Mamdi: It's like your mentality level has just totally gone down.
Joclyn: It's like, for science yeah, we've got a modular test and they only do revision for the higher people.
Melisa: We don't even get a chance.

(Taylor Comprehensive, year 11)

This is an important development. First, our data suggest that the familiar dangers of disaffection linked to selective grouping (usually associated with the lower reaches of hierarchies) may now be extending further up the scale. Second, these problems seem most pronounced in environments where the selection is most clearly established and extensive. Third, even where schools resist the push for greater use of setting, and retain mixed-ability approaches, the introduction and extension of GCSE tiering may be acting to provide new bases for selection and differentiation *within* teaching groups. In this way, GCSE tiering may present an additional source of conflict and disaffection in schools.

GCSE tiering

Our interviews with pupils reveal that GCSE tiers are a common concern, especially as pupils near their final examinations and try to come to terms with the consequences of tiering in relation to their final grades. By the time they begin their final year of compulsory schooling most pupils have a working understanding of tiering. The tier to which pupils are allocated, however, is associated with clear differences in how pupils experience their allocation and make sense of the system. Pupils in the Higher (and, where available, Intermediate) tier are most likely to display an understanding of the tiering system as a whole and convey a sense of having an active role in this decision making. A number of these pupils report discussions, and even negotiations, with subject teachers regarding their tier of entry. For example, a group of girls in Taylor discuss with us the possibility of choosing between the Higher and Intermediate mathematics tiers. They argue that, given a choice, they will sit the Intermediate paper, thereby closing off access to the highest-grade passes (A* and A) but retaining access to the all-important C grade while minimizing the danger of dropping through the grade floor.

These pupils' calculations of risk are remarkably close to the terms in which their teachers approach the same dilemmas (see Chapter 5):

Jamila: some teachers talk it through with you, like my maths teacher, she did. To see which one she thinks I should be in and which one I think I should be in (. . .)
Helen: I think I'd do the Intermediate.
Diane: Play safe.
Jamila: Yeah.
Helen: Some teachers have said it's easier to get a B in the Intermediate than it is in the Higher (. . .) if you know that you're not going to get an A you might as well just do the Intermediate (. . .) I don't mind not getting an A, I just want to get sort of above a C in most things.
Diane: Yeah.
Helen: 'Cause that's sort of the known pass, A-to-C.

(Taylor Comprehensive, year 11)

By far the majority of year 11 pupils understand the implications of *their own* tier allocation, if not the entire tiering system. These variations in breadth of knowledge may be explained, at least in part, by pupils' different sources of information. Higher tier pupils identify teachers as a major source of information concerning tiering. In contrast, Foundation tier pupils are often unclear about where they have found out most about tiering. Nevertheless, misunderstandings seem rare. Where misunderstandings do occur it is significant that they often focus on the consequences of tiering for Foundation level pupils. Specifically, some pupils simply cannot believe that the exam system itself would disqualify them or their peers from attaining certain grades, especially the all-important grade C. In the following extract, for example, it seems that the grade ceiling in Foundation papers in the three-tier model (where D is the highest possible attainment) is literally unbelievable to a group of pupils in the Higher and Intermediate tiers:

Daniel: Tiers are important because say, if John wanted to get a C, like he needs a C in maths, English and science, it would be best if he took the Foundation in maths because it's easier to get a C in the Foundation than it is in the Higher.
Marcus: But in the Foundation you can't get a C.
Bob: What the fuck are you on about?
Marcus: The highest you can get is . . . [interrupted]
Daniel: Yeah, is a C.

(Taylor Comprehensive, year 11)

Similarly, in our other case-study school, the following Foundation tier pupils unknowingly reinvent the entire tiering system in order to retain the possibility of attaining grade C. While this understanding of tiering is wholly inaccurate, it at least offers some measure of comfort:

Paul:	if a person has got the same as, a person who's done a Foundation, and an Intermediate, just the Intermediate's done a lot better haven't they 'cause it is a harder paper. So it'll look better when you show people and that.
Researcher:	So do you get the same grade though? You say if somebody's got the same grade off two papers . . .
Paul:	Yeah, you'll probably get a C with, like, a 'Foundation' next to it [on the GCSE certificate], just written or something like that.
Phillip:	Yeah.

(Clough GM, year 11)

Although these cases are significant and revealing, such 'misunderstanding' is rare. Most other Foundation tier pupils are not party to such comforting myths: they are only too aware of the grade ceiling that will render imposs-ible exactly those higher-grade passes that they have been continually told are the only things worth attaining in the A-to-C economy. Some respond with a little hope, for example, the following pupil seeks to improve his posi-tion by rising to the Intermediate tier (unlike the Higher- and Intermediate tier girls noted above, this African Caribbean young man is aware that the decision is not his, but the teacher's):

'Cause in maths I'm in the Foundation and it means if I was to get all marks all right the highest grade would be a D. So in the mock I got a D and I got really high, well, quite high marks. (. . .) But hopefully I'm going to get into Intermediate, I'm not sure if I'm allowed.

(Sharma, Taylor Comprehensive, year 11)

For others, placement in the Foundation tier removes any last hope of success within the terms most often encouraged by the school (attainment of grades A*-to-C). Their response often includes anger and disillusionment:

Maths, yeah, he said the highest I can get on the Foundation is a D, so I was thinking there's no point in trying in maths if I'm going to get a D.

(Jenny, Clough GM, year 11)

Within the two-tier examination model, which applies to most GCSE subjects (see Chapter 5), Foundation tier pupils *can* still attain a C grade at the grade ceiling for their tier. This is small comfort, however, to many children who are faced during their final year with a depressing list of relatively low 'predicted grades'. In this context, it is unsurprising that pupils generally identify A*-to-C grades as those that they are personally aiming for, with only a minority of pupils acknowledging that such an outcome is highly unlikely for them. This recognition is expressed in a variety of ways and seems to bring with it a range of responses. One group of girls, with mixed aspirations and expectations, respond to the A-to-C economy by asserting the importance of continued effort in the context of the official pass criteria, including all grades from D to G. Yet while such assertions mobilize an alternative framework within which the opportunity to 'pass' is retained, the continued dominance of the A-to-C economy is undeniable:

Researcher: What counts as sort of having done well in the GCSEs? What are you aiming for?
Emily: Cs? A-to-Cs really.
Beverly: Yeah.
Jessie: Or Ds really, as long as it ain't unqualified [grade U, ungraded] then I ain't too bothered.
Beverly: I'll just do as well as I can.
Jessie: As long as they ain't unqualified and just do the pass, if I literally failed them, that's one thing! I'd rather get a D than fail. So A-to-C ain't really, 'cause I ain't getting no A-to-Cs.
Researcher: Everyone seems to talk so much about A-to-Cs . . .
Beverly: Mmm, I know, that's what gets up my nose.
(Clough GM, year 11)

We saw in Chapter 6 that some teachers use predicted grades as a motivating device. A head of faculty told us of one 'ploy' where 'although you've got a kid that you think might get a grade C, you think if you tell him he's going to get a C he'll sit back and won't do any more work. So you give him a D in the hope . . .'. Such an approach seriously underestimates pupils' own level of motivation and can backfire. Where pupils are told that their teachers do not expect them to attain higher-grade passes this can act to lessen their motivation. Having spent their secondary education being repeatedly told of the importance of grades C and above, to be informed that such grades are 'unrealistic' can feel depressing, even insulting:

Researcher: So how does that make you feel then if people go on about you've got to get A-to-C and then you aren't expecting A-to-C?
Stephen: It's a bit degrading and stuff like that.
Jim: 'Cause the point is that they try and get the middle C don't they? Or 50 per cent get C so that all the other 50 per cent get below. It's not cussed but . . .
Sharma: Some try to put that message across but other say the average is E.
Jonathan: Mmm, D or E.
(Taylor Comprehensive, year 11)

To understand these pupils' feelings it is important to realize that 'cussing' (the use of verbal abuse and insults) is taken very seriously within contemporary youth culture. A 'cuss' is not banter and it is not a joke. To be 'cussed' is to be insulted in the most personally derogatory and hurtful way. This quotation, therefore, signals something of the pain and hurt caused by tiering and related grade predictions. For these pupils, 15-year-olds preparing for their final GCSE exams, the negative impact of the predictions is clear: 'It's a bit degrading', 'It's not cussed but . . .'.

At this stage in the process, during the final preparations for GCSE examinations, some teachers try to reassure pupils that grades below C still retain importance and can be useful in the labour market. For many pupils, however, these reassurances are unconvincing:

Hamdi: I really can't be bothered, 'cause teachers, I mean every predicted grade for me is E, F, G, E, F, G. . . . I mean, what's the point? What am I going to bother for?

Researcher: Are they not worth having?

All: A-to-C is worth having. (. . .)

Lorna: No but, you know that F, F and above is average.

Maria: Well, that's what the teachers say to you, you know.

Hamdi: Please don't tell me. They're just trying to say that to make you feel better so you can just go 'Oh, it doesn't matter, I got a G'.

                                      (Taylor Comprehensive, year 11)

It is clear, therefore, that the introduction of GCSE tiering has produced a situation that many young people find worrying, often confusing and sometimes devastating. Assignment to lower tiers leads to disappointment and sometimes disaffection. For a few it is not an exaggeration to say that tiering decisions can lead to despair. It is important to bear in mind that, just as Black pupils are disproportionately over-represented in the lower tier (in both our case-study schools: Chapter 5), so they are in turn more commonly found to express such disillusionment. In the midst of these processes, pupils' often sense that they may not all have been given the same chances. In particular, young people sometimes suspect the process to be racialized: we will return to this issue in greater detail later in this chapter. At this point, however, it is useful to continue our account of pupils' perspectives by moving from the experience of tiering and predicted grades to the related issues raised by the schools' D-to-C conversion strategies.

Pupils and the D-to-C conversion

In the previous chapter we looked at how our case-study schools try to meet the demands of the A-to-C economy through realizing D-to-C conversions. Pupils in both schools are aware of the special initiatives that have been established and they understand that these are specifically aimed at improvements within the terms of the A-to-C economy where five or more higher-grade passes is the key performance indicator. In Taylor Comprehensive, for example, year 11 pupils know that membership of the Achievement Groups is restricted to those whom teachers' perceive as being potential D-to-C converters who might, in turn, attain the all important five higher-grade passes. Likewise, pupils are clear about who is excluded from the initiative.

Helen: they're trying to get you to get more than five A-to-C grades. But there's people that have, won't definitely get them, but they haven't bothered with them.

Jamila: Yeah, they're saying that they've only sort of done the groups of people they think they can push on a bit more.

(Taylor Comprehensive, year 11)

Pupils in Clough GM suggest that the establishment of various new school rules and the energetic implementation of existing rules (concerning punctuality, attendance and homework) are a direct attempt to improve the school's GCSE outcomes. In particular, 'achievement interviews' conducted by the headteacher (as a form of one-off mentoring) are seen as an attempt to improve individual students' grades. However, many pupils resent the 'achievement interviews' and are sceptical as to their usefulness:

Benzir: If the teacher thinks you are under-achieving in class they send you down to [the headteacher] and you have to explain yourself to him.

Fiona: Explain yourself to him! How nice!

Benzir: Why you are under-achieving . . . 'Oh yeah, I know why I'm under-achieving because, um, well . . .'.

Cath: Well if you knew then you wouldn't do it!

Benzir: Yeah, it's so stupid.

(Clough GM, year 11)

Pupils in year 11 in Clough see the school's 'pupil league table' (see Chapter 6) as an attempt to give teachers greater knowledge of pupils' performance and to motivate them to further efforts. Pupils are not generally concerned about the *existence* of this table, tending to view it as part of the machinery of monitoring built up around GCSE achievement. However, many are angered by the fact that the table is displayed in a public place. In addition, they express concern about the impact of the league table on their peers near the bottom and those omitted from it altogether:

Researcher: I heard there was a chart put up on the wall? With everybody's name and that on?

Emily: Yeah, and that was embarrassing.

Beverly: In a way it's a good thing 'cause I mean it got people saying 'Oh yeah, I know I've got to do better now'.

Emily: Yeah, but then surely they should have showed us where we were in private.

Beverly: It's embarrassing as well, yeah.

Jessie: Putting it up on the wall where everyone can see it.

Emily: Right, where everyone can see it and people's names at the bottom, they must have felt so stupid. People's names at the top, do you know what I mean (. . .) But the people at the bottom felt really stupid.

Researcher: Weren't there some people whose names weren't on?
Emily: Weren't even on the list.
Beverly: But there was a list that had all the names for the whole year in the office but they only put the top 150 up on the wall. So I don't know on that issue. More or less, everyone knew that you weren't on that list and it was embarrassing.

(Clough GM, year 11)

The omission of the lowest-performing pupils from the league table is seen as yet more evidence of the premium placed on higher passes, and correspondingly, an apparent disregard for those pupils not expected to attain at this level. A pupil who is himself omitted from the league table suggests the following rationale:

Well, from 150 to 190 they weren't in it 'cause there was no point showing is there really – probably didn't get no A-to-Cs, probably didn't.

(Paul, Clough GM, year 11)

To this point we have seen that pupils' perspectives reflect the range of experiences, activities and priorities that are presented to them during their secondary education. There are sometimes differences between those placed in the higher reaches of hierarchies and those in the lower ranks (whether through setting, tiering or even, in Clough GM, in a 'pupil league table'). Most notably, those near the peak seem better informed about selection strategies while those in the lower positions are more likely to be demotivated by their treatment and apparent lack of success. Nevertheless, there are also strong similarities, not least in the pupils' recognition of the A-to-C economy and its reflection in the priorities and actions of their schools and teachers. Across the range of achievement, for example, pupils are generally clear about the special status accorded GCSE passes of grade C and above – a factor that makes especially painful some pupils' realization that they are unlikely or (in the case of the maths foundation tier) certain to fall short of such attainments. Additionally, we have seen that the heightened concern with selection and differentiation (through the extension of setting and tiering) means that even those in relatively high sets (including second in the rank order) can feel devalued and treated as 'cast-offs'. In this way, GCSE examinations are a source of uncertainty, stress and danger for many pupils. A further dimension to this situation concerns some pupils' sense that not all are treated equally. It is to this issue that we now turn.

Inequality and pupil perspectives

In the little world in which children have their existence,
whosoever brings them up, there is nothing so finely perceived
and so finely felt, as injustice.

(Charles Dickens, *Great Expectations* 1861)

Pupils are among the most perceptive of all classroom observers. Their reading of situations is by no means infallible, and their own interests and biographies are no less important in shaping their perceptions than are those of any other participant. Nevertheless, children and young people's understandings of life in school are often no less nuanced and complex than those of adults. Indeed, on certain issues research suggests that pupils are somewhat *more* sensitive than their teachers; a particular example of this is equity. Pupils are especially sensitive to any differences in treatment and will often seek official justifications for action they perceive to be unfair (see, for example, Hammersley and Woods 1984; Woods 1990). In this section we want to consider in some detail the various ways in which pupils speak about fairness and equity in their experience of Clough GM and Taylor Comprehensive.

For year 9 pupils, experiences and perceptions of inequality centre around three key areas: ability, behaviour and 'race'. These categories are neither clear nor discrete and these discursive constellations constitute pupils, and their experiences of schooling, in complex and multiple ways. In many instances, for example, it appears that ability and behaviour act as proxies for *social class*. Furthermore, social class is frequently implicitly assumed in relation to 'race' (see, for example, Chapter 6; also Mac an Ghaill 1988; 1989). Ability, behaviour and 'race' are intimately linked: assumptions about each category feed into, sustain and produce assumptions about the others. In addition, pupils' narratives of inequality are frequently cross-cut by particular notions of gender and sexuality.

Inequality and 'ability'

Young people in both schools are certain that teachers prefer some pupils over others and that this has a number of implications:

> Sometimes there's teachers who like children more than others (. . .) because maybe some of them they really annoy them so that they don't like them and some are like really interested in the lesson and they help them a lot and things like that.
>
> (Rupert, Taylor, year 9)

Rupert's observation of the significance of pupils' 'interest' in a lesson begins to identify one locus of inequality, that is, *ability*. Across the case-study schools, pupils feel that peers who attain highly are favoured by teachers. This is seen to have its greatest impact in terms of the distribution of teachers' time and attention. High-attaining pupils are judged to be prioritized by teachers, seen in their disproportionate share of teachers' attention. A corollary is that other pupils, who may feel more in need of teachers' time, then feel neglected:

> if there's a clever person, and like you're not that clever and the clever person wants to know something, like they [teachers] tend to go to them first (. . .) but it should be round the other way.
>
> (Emma, Clough GM, year 9)

Such perceptions are not restricted to pupils who feel in particular need of teachers' attention and support. A group of pupils who are themselves seen as relatively high attainers, for example, nevertheless identify this differential treatment in terms of relative levels of attainment:

Mridula: Like all the teachers like them [high-attaining pupils] and they always work. And if we show a teacher a really, piece of good work, that's really good to us –
Avtar: What we think to us, took a long time.
Mridula: – they come along with a big piece of work and everything and we just get shoved aside.

(Taylor Comprehensive, year 9)

Even in such a short quotation we can begin to glimpse some of the muliple factors at work. These high-attaining pupils are complaining about what they perceive to be teachers' preference for another group of high-attaining pupils. It is interesting that *this* group of girls includes only Asian pupils and that they are comparing their treatment with that of a group of *white* girls all of whom come from professional backgrounds. Although 'race' and class are not explicitly posited in the quotation, therefore, these factors may be in play. Certainly research into the school experiences of Asian pupils suggests that assumptions based on ethnicity may be significant here: in the past South Asian young women have often complained that they seem invisible to white teachers (cf. Brah and Minhas 1985; Gillborn 1990a; 1998c; Mac an Ghaill 1988; Taylor and Hegarty 1985). This extract also begins to identify the intersection of constructions of ability and behaviour – the pupils that are perceived to enjoy preferential treatment are not marked only by their high attainment, but also by effort/behaviour; they are said to 'always work'.

The labels accorded to different categories of people and activity are often hugely significant. Research with pupils has produced a long list of names thrown at those accused of working too hard or attaining too highly. One of the most celebrated examples is the term 'ear'ole', applied by a group of working-class young men to their conformist peers in a 1970s comprehensive; the term nicely captures the conformists' supposed lack of appeal and passive receptivity to the wishes of teachers (Willis 1977: 14). In our schools the pupils most frequently identified by their peers as 'clever' and favoured by teachers are often referred to as 'bods' or 'boffins', terms that clearly appeal to popular views of cerebral insularity and may also reveal something of their peers' assessments of their social class origin as middle-class/professional. In addition, it is interesting to note that a pupil who is identified by several of his peers as being a particularly high attainer and, therefore, favoured by teachers himself suggests that it is not ability but 'eagerness' (a behavioural characteristic) that leads teachers to favour particular pupils.

Inequality and behaviour

In both Clough GM and Taylor Comprehensive, pupils argue that teachers' perceptions of individual pupils' behaviour can lead to differential treatment. Perceptions of ability and social class are again seen to play a part in this. Many pupils say that 'clever', middle-class and favoured pupils receive much lighter punishments than themselves (or even no punishment at all) for minor disciplinary issues such as lateness, forgotten equipment or chewing gum. Furthermore, it is felt that these favoured pupils are allowed to speak to teachers in a way that is not tolerated from other pupils:

> they're rather cheeky but in a posh way, cheeky to the tutor but in a posh way, and their work's good.
>
> (Lisa, Taylor Comprehensive, year 9)

On the other hand, pupils argue that the behaviour of some of their peers is disciplined in a disproportionately harsh manner. Similarly, it is felt that teachers often assume that certain individuals have misbehaved or are responsible for incidents when in fact they are innocent. Such assumptions on the part of teachers are generally seen as both a consequence of, and a contributory factor to, the establishment of certain pupils having a distinctive 'reputation':

> *Jenelle*: Some of them [teachers] were like, they love seeing pupils getting in trouble. 'Cause like if a pupil's been expelled [fixed term exclusion] more than three times or whatever, you know, you're timing a fight and they think you've got something to do with it.
> *Crystal*: Like me.
> *Jenelle*: Yeah, she's got in trouble a few times. Whenever like other people are having a fight she's there and the teacher says, 'Yeah I expected you to be there' (. . .) Some teachers get completely the wrong thing about you. If they see you doing something more than once they think this is the sort of person that . . .
>
> (Clough GM, year 9)

In reflecting on Crystal's poor reputation, these girls do not explicitly cite her ethnicity (mixed race) as a contributing factor. Nevertheless, there is a growing body of research that suggests strong links between 'race'-specific stereotypes and teachers' interpretations of pupils' behaviour. As we will see below, these issues are complex and often difficult to identify with complete certainty. For many young people, however, there is no doubt that their ethnic origin has been a factor in their treatment at the hands of teachers.

Inequality and 'race'

Accusations of racism are a serious matter. Often researchers must build rapport with young people before such potentially explosive charges can be shared, especially where researchers share the same ethnic origin as the majority of teachers. In Taylor Comprehensive, for example, it was notice-able that as the fieldwork progressed pupils became progressively more willing to share their experiences across a wide range of issues, including racism. There is little doubt that this aspect of our work benefited from the more informal style of fieldwork that was possible in Taylor (see Chapter 1): readers should be careful, therefore, not to misinterpret the fact that the majority of pupil testimony in this section relates to Taylor. We believe that the situation was at least as bad in Clough but that the school's insistence on a rather formal and prearranged style of fieldwork mitigated against building such strong rapport with pupils.

During the early part of our fieldwork pupils were extremely hesitant about identifying explicitly the racialized nature of their experience. During an early interview with a group of African Caribbean, mixed-race and white pupils (in year 9) the following exchange took place:

Marcella (African Caribbean): Personally I feel this school isn't fair. They have 'equal opportunities' in their Planner [diary and rule/conduct book for pupils] for no reason. I feel, sometimes I regret coming to this school.
Researcher: Who aren't they fair to?
Mark (African Caribbean): All of us.
Marcella: Then say it. Say it. I, no, no you see, I don't know.
Jasmine (mixed race): He knows.
Marcella: You know what I'm talking about, Mark?
Mark: Yeah.
Marcella: I don't know how to explain it but I just don't feel that they're fair, personally. If they've made a bed, if they've made a thing for you then you should sit in it.
(Taylor Comprehensive, year 9)

At this early stage in the fieldwork, when field relationships were just begin-ning to be established, these pupils were not prepared explicitly to name racism. Indeed, at the time of the interview it was not possible to be sure that this was what the pupils were actually alluding to. However, during later informal conversations some of these pupils and members of their friendship group began to speak about racism within the school and they later agreed to take part in an interview specifically to discuss this aspect of their experiences.[2] Early on in this discussion Marcella stressed the subtlety of racism in the school and the careful observation and reflection necessary to identify it. She said of racism in school:

It's not blatantly there. I mean, you can't, you wouldn't be able to just walk in the school and say 'Oh the school's racist'. You have to take time before you knew that.

In order to explain and illustrate their observations and personal experi-ences of racism and racialized practices within the school, the group outline a series of incidents and disciplinary responses. The first example concerns Marcella's own experiences of the school's disciplinary practices, which she perceives to be explicitly racialized:

> I've been excluded twice for no reason, and that's gone on my record and that, you know? (. . .) The 14th September. I remember the date because I see it every day in my planner, I was excluded and it was for watching a fight. And all the Black people got excluded. All the half-caste people and white people got to stay in school. And I thought that was out of order 'cause I did exactly the same thing Alice [a white member of the friendship group] did (. . .) I did exactly the same thing that the others did but I still got excluded.

A second example concerns the fixed-term and permanent exclusions of other African Caribbean pupils in the year group. Again, the group see these exclusions as racialized and embodying racist processes and practices:

Juliette (mixed race): Yeah but listen, yeah. Glyn [African Caribbean] yeah, he was excluded what twice or something and he couldn't come back. And Marcia's been excluded a third time . . .

Marcella: Be the third time (. . .) The thing is they just wanted to get rid of him, that's . . . sort of, and he's gone and appealed and everything but . . . Yeah, and one time, one time he got excluded was for hitting this other girl. But the fact is I understand why he hit her because she spat on him and I wouldn't like it if someone spat on me.

Su Lin (Chinese): I think they both should have been punished but . . .

Marcella: Yeah, only Glyn got punished.

Juliette: 'Cause he's a man and he hit a girl.

Molly (white): And that he's so tall.

Juliette: He's soft though, isn't he?

Marcella: They're scared of him.

(Taylor Comprehensive, year 9)

It is important to recognize that the group are not arguing that Glyn has done nothing wrong or that he did not deserve some form of punishment. They take issue with the severity of his punishment (permanent exclusion) and question the fact that the provocation has gone unrecorded and unpunished. The pupils note that, alongside 'race', gender was also a factor in this exclusion. By hitting a girl Glyn at once transgressed appropriate inter-gender behaviour and confirmed the particular fears and fantasies about black masculinity and sexuality that pervade dominant discourses of the 'Black macho lad' (Sewell 1998; see also Giroux 1996; Mac an Ghaill 1994; McCarthy 1998). Based on their knowledge of Glyn, these pupils argue that he was not at all the threat his teachers perceived; although Juliette describes him as 'soft', Marcella has no doubt that 'They're scared of him'.

This view strongly echoes previous research that has identified a wide-spread expectation among many white teachers that their Black pupils will represent both a more frequent and a more severe threat to order in school (cf. Gillborn and Gipps 1996: 54–6). This 'myth of a Black challenge to authority' (Gillborn 1990a) has been confirmed in subsequent research in both primary and secondary schools (Sewell 1997; 1998; Wright 1992). There has been considerable debate about this notion, with some observers refusing to accept that such teacher expectations are not simply a justified response to clear misbehaviour (see, for example, Foster 1992). In contrast, these pupils seem to have little doubt about the processes involved. We should also note that their discussions do not amount to simple, blanket accusations that might be dismissed as using 'racism' as 'a slogan to criticize the school' (Foster 1990: 135). They see the school's response as deeply racialized (see above) but they also see gender as a factor, and not in a simple way with Black boys as the only victims. On several occasions they also refer to a particular African Caribbean girl in the year group whom they see as 'having power' and whom they believe teachers in the school are 'scared' of.

As Marcella indicated early on, her perception of racism in Taylor Comprehensive is that it is subtle and complex; often difficult to pinpoint and define specifically. In their attempts to substantiate their experience of racism in the school, the pupils in this group offer numerous examples of racialized disciplinary responses to incidents involving Black pupils and peers from other ethnic groups:

Juliette: Oh Mr Flemming [the headteacher]'s racist.
Marcella: He's racist.
Researcher: Flemming is racist?
Marcella: Yes, he's racist.
Researcher: In what way? How?
Marcella: Just racist.
Researcher: How do see him do it? What's the kind of . . . ?
Marcella: Number one, excluding Glyn. Yeah, he don't listen to both sides. He picks on us.
Juliette: Oh yeah, and when Awad [African Caribbean] got beaten up!

It is not our belief that this is evidence of a 'rotten apple' (Henriques 1984) in the school management hierarchy. The pupils' assertion that the head-teacher 'don't listen to both sides' suggests that the racialized disciplinary practices perceived by the pupils may be imbued with the racialized beliefs, assumptions and expectations characteristic of *institutionalized* racism (cf. Gillborn 1990a; Mac an Ghaill 1988; Sewell 1998). As the senior manager of the school, with ultimate responsibility and authority for exclusions, it is not surprising that the pupils locate racialized exclusion practices in the person of the headteacher.

As already indicated, in our second interview, these pupils went on to list numerous examples that they see as racialized disciplinary events. To list each separately would be tedious and unnecessary in this context; suffice it to say that in each case the pupils see themselves or African Caribbean peers receiving disproportionate and/or particularized punishment where peers of other ethnic origins are treated more favourably. As a further example, we will take an incident already alluded to above. It is also noteworthy that the pupils see it as being particularly strong evidence of racism because this assessment was supported by the father of the Black pupil concerned:

Juliette: And Awad's dad came down and Awad's dad was going, 'Oh he [the headteacher] was so racist' and all that, he was swearing at him.
Marcella: It's true.
Molly: Yeah and he got really mad, he got really mad and he just drove away.
Juliette: Oh it was so funny. And he was going, 'Oh, he was so racist'.
Marcella: It's true though.
Researcher: What has he done, who's this, who's Awad?
Juliette: This boy, Martin [white] beat Awad up and they excluded Awad and let Martin come back into the school.

(Taylor Comprehensive, year 9)

The pupils have many such stories to recount, and it appears that such narratives of racialized and racist disciplinary responses circulate within sections of the pupil population. The pupils enjoy recounting their understanding of this particular incident, and the father's altercation with the headteacher seems to have achieved almost legendary status in the school. Any knowledge that the pupils have of this is possibly second-hand. This, however, does not negate the pupils' testimony. Rather it acts to demonstrate the rarity of a Black parent directly challenging the school institution and openly naming the processes and practices of the school as racist. Many (we have not interviewed the entire year and so we cannot say *all*) of the Black pupils share a tacit understanding of the school as acting in ways that systematically disadvantage Black pupils. Although this understanding is shared widely it is rarely articulated in public, and certainly not to teachers: it is the novelty and severity of the incident above (where a parent publicly breaks the silence on racism in the school) that has marked it out for special status in the pupils' eyes. For these pupils it is one more example of processes they know to operate at a deep but rarely acknowledged level. The pupils can recount example after example. Some critics will undoubtedly argue that there could possibly be many reasons for teachers' actions in each case and that we should not accept the accusation of racism without solid proof. And yet 'proof' of racism to one audience is 'supposition' to another (Gillborn

1998b; Troyna 1995b). In these pupils' experience racism is a powerful, recurrent but subtle force in their school lives. Juliette (mixed race) echoes Marcella when she says, 'It's not blatant'.

> *Marcella*:   'Cause me and my friend were supposed to go [on a school trip] but then half-way through we decided not to go and she [a teacher] said that the only way you can get your money [deposit] back is if you find people to replace you. We found people to replace us . . . but she didn't give us back our money. (. . .) We got Leslie and Owen to go, all she could have done is given Leslie and Owen's money and they wouldn't have known.
>
> *Researcher*: So they *did* get replacements for you but they still didn't give you your deposit?
>
> *Marcella*:   Never.
>
> *Researcher*: And you've asked them about it since?
>
> *Marcella*:   I have and she was just like, '*Tough*. The deposits aren't replaceable', and stuff like that. And that's a fact.
>
> (Taylor Comprehensive, year 9)

Like many of the examples offered by the pupils, this extract does not make explicit reference to ethnicity. Teachers here are not accused of using racist language or of explicitly positioning 'race' in their dealings with children. Rather, the Black pupils (and frequently peers of other ethnic origins) are convinced that African Caribbean young people are systematically and re-peatedly treated in ways that are different – more harshly disciplinary and exclusionary. The examples are simply too frequent and too clearly patterned for the pupils themselves to find any other explanation as credible as racism: it is not crude, 'It's not blatant', but it *is* racism.

Some of the examples given above are fairly dramatic: a parent accusing the headteacher of racism; a teacher withholding a deposit; and actions to bring about permanent or fixed-term exclusions. But the pupils also discuss more mundane and day-to-day interactions with teachers that they feel demonstrate racialized practices. This includes the types of relationships that pupils from different ethnic groups have with teachers and the racialized nature of teachers' perceptions of and responses to pupils. This is drawn out in relation to a discussion of the varied nature of group members' relationships with one particular teacher:

> *Marcella*: I mean sometimes Molly [white member of the friendship group] is so rude to her [the teacher], I mean. This is another thing with racism, and *I* wouldn't be able to do that because she'd just like refer me [sending the pupil to another room] or . . . Yeah, or give me to [a senior teacher]. I would never be able to say . . .
>
> *Juliette*: The way Molly speaks to them.

Molly: I'm not that rude.
Juliette: Yeah, you're really so rude.

(Taylor Comprehensive, year 9)

Here the African Caribbean and mixed-race pupils in the group identify the relative privilege enjoyed by their white friend in her interactions with the teacher. It is interesting to note that Molly (a white pupil who has to this point concurred with and contributed to the group's examples of racism) is alarmed by the assertion that her ethnicity allows her to engage with teachers in a way that is not possible for her friends. While she agrees that teachers' treatment of white pupils *in general* is superior to their treatment of Black pupils, she seems unwilling to consider that she might benefit from this personally and is eager to distance herself from this.

Such perceptions of racialized and racist disciplinary processes clearly underscore these pupils' wider experience of schooling. Even this group of year 9 pupils – who were prepared to speak openly about racism and able to articulate their experiences of racialized disciplinary processes and relationships with teachers – found it more difficult to identify how such racialized practice might impact on their *academic* experience and outcomes:

Researcher: Does any of this kind of translate into the classroom when you are learning, or supposed to be learning?
Marcella: Sometimes I suppose, not all the time.
Juliette: If you're being picked on by a teacher then you'll suffer, your work will suffer.
Marcella: Mr Morgan is the worst, he's always picking on me and Jasmine (. . .) I had this teacher called Hatchett and he didn't like me. And one time I went home and I told my mum and she said, 'Could you ever think that he would put down your grades because he doesn't like you?' I said, 'This man seriously doesn't like me'.

(Taylor Comprehensive, year 9)

Similarly, in Clough GM, despite the restrictions placed on our fieldwork (which prevented such close rapport with pupils) on occasion pupils did raise the issue of racism. Here, too, racism was not pictured as a crude and blatant process, but as a continual succession of differential treatment:

Jason (African Caribbean): Some of the classes are sexist or racist.
Researcher: How do they show that?
Kofi (African Caribbean): How they don't pick you [to answer in class], they pick on, like, particular people. Like you can put your hand up and they'll always pick the person next to you, the person on the side, the opposite side, they never pick you.

(Clough GM, year 9)

In year 9, therefore, many Black pupils are certain that they are treated less well by teachers as a direct result of racism. By the time they have entered their final year of compulsory schooling these understandings have been cemented still further. At this point the pupils are also clearer about the academic implications of the racism they perceive. As we have already shown, pupils often experience setting, tiering and the production of pre-dicted grades as a painful process. Many feel that they have been disadvant-aged within the school, that their experiences 'aren't fair'. Pupils from the range of ethnic and social class backgrounds sometimes accuse the school of unfairness. Nevertheless, it is clear that pupils from minority ethnic groups are most likely to feel that their low set and/or tier placement is unwarranted. This is not to say that all such pupils accuse teachers or the school itself of racism: every instance of perceived injustice is not assumed automatically to relate to ethnicity. Indeed, there is a sense in which many Black pupils refrain from quickly asserting the existence of racism, possibly fearful of seeming to resort to special pleading. Despite this, among minority pupils, especially those of African Caribbean ethnic background, there is a very real sense that all pupils are not afforded equal opportunities:

> *Maria (African Caribbean)*: There's no equal opportunities in this school.
> *Joclyn (African Caribbean)*: Because teachers prefer some other pupils to others. 'Cause they don't, they say they believe in equal opportunities, but they don't.
> *Researcher*: Who's not getting equal opportunities? Why are some peo-ple getting better treatment than others?
> *Melisa (mixed race)*: I don't know but sometimes it comes across as that some teachers are racist kind of thing. I'm not joking, but it's just that way.
>
> (Taylor Comprehensive, year 11)

In exploring these perspectives further it is useful to take one case and consider it in more detail. In this way, some of the different nuances in the process may become visible. We will focus briefly on the school career of an African Caribbean young man in one of our research schools: we will call him Stephen.

Stephen's case provides an illustration of the ways in which pupils under-stand inequalities to operate through teachers' negative expectations of Black young people. Stephen was admitted to Taylor following a permanent exclusion (expulsion) from his previous school. Subsequently, Stephen was given a fixed-term exclusion (suspension) from Taylor, a sanction that coin-cided with the mock GCSE examinations. Stephen's fixed-term exclusion, therefore, although brief, nevertheless threatened important consequences in that he would be prevented from taking 'mock' examinations – a chance for pupils to prepare for genuine examination conditions and for teachers to assess their performance.[3] The rights and wrongs of Stephen's suspension are not the issue here: of most significance is the way that other pupils, especially his Black peers, interpreted his treatment. Stephen's case was seen as symptomatic of a wider set of differential expectations that find expression in teachers' view that Black pupils will generally present disciplinary problems and that control and punishment will be placed before academic concerns. As one of Stephen's white friends argued:

> A lot of teachers don't like Stephen because he's been excluded from one school and he's come to this one, been in trouble a couple of times and tried making a new start and they just, they won't give him a chance.
>
> > (Jonathan, Taylor Comprehensive, year 11)

This assessment of Stephen's situation was echoed by another group of his classmates who describe his fixed-term exclusion as 'silly' and identify racism in their teachers' anticipation that he will behave badly.

Stephen's case is important, therefore, in providing a point around which Black pupils could focus their tacit understanding of how racism affected their chances of academic success. For some individuals, like Stephen, teachers' heightened anticipation of disruption from Black children can provide the basis for extreme disciplinary measures, even to the point of removing them from school. For many Black peers, this injustice was clear. As a mixed-race classmate commented:

> I think some people, like Stephen, he's not getting a chance at all. They all wanted him to fail.

More generally, however, the case provided an opportunity for Black and other ethnic minority pupils to reflect on the wider, but less obvious, ways in which differential expectations might impact on them. For these pupils the relationship between teachers' expectations and their own academic performance was not easy to identify and describe, but their sense of injustice was real:

> *Researcher*: Do you think it affects your chances in exams?
> *Hamdi (a classmate of Stephen's)*: In a way it might hurt some people, yeah, so to some people yeah because, I mean, you're getting lower down than your standards.

A week after this interview, one of the pupils volunteered a further example that seemed to her to provide concrete evidence of these usually hidden and uncertain processes. In her mock GCSE examination she had attained a grade C, the key benchmark of success/failure that is continually highlighted in so many contexts (from the Government's school league tables to the everyday concerns of teachers and pupils). Despite this 'success', her teacher had predicted a final grade of E, an act that the pupil perceived unequivocally as racist.

In understanding the operation of 'race' and racism in schools, therefore, it is important to recognize that the majority of Black pupils do not make such accusations lightly. This project supports and extends the findings of previous work in suggesting that teacher racism is not as simple and crude as some commentators might anticipate. Openly racist teachers and consciously discriminatory practices are rare. Yet widespread inequalities of opportunity are endured by Black children, seen in national achievement statistics and echoed in our case-study schools. This form of racism operates through multiple processes, especially via differential teacher expectations in relation to negative assumptions about Black children's' academic ability and behavioural standards. We have shown how selection to 'set' teaching groups and GCSE tiers provides an organizational means by which these expectations can be institutionalized and given further operational weight through the grade limits imposed on tiered GCSE examination papers. Our interview data suggest that many ethnic minority pupils have a clear sense of racialized injustice in relation to these processes. The pupils are certain that schools' rhetorical commitments to equal opportunities are not realized in practice: teachers' decisions about setting and tiering seem further to add to these negative, and sometimes disheartening processes. If schools are serious about social justice and inclusion, they must interrogate their selection approaches for any sign of bias. It is worrying that the inequalities are perceived so clearly by pupils (and not only those of minority origin) but do not feature in the schools' main concerns when addressing selection and achievement issues.

Conclusions

We have documented the successive selection strategies that schools apply to pupils (both formally and informally) as they move through their secondary education. These are practices that schools perform *on* pupils. Pupils do not passively receive these actions; they interpret, question and, on occasion, resist. Nevertheless, the scope for resistance is severely constrained, and pupils are clearly positioned as the subject of numerous organizational and disciplinary discourses in which the young people themselves play little active role.

Pupils' understandings of these practices vary considerably, sometimes in relation to their own treatment and position within the various hierarchies. Pupils in the highest sets, for example, are confident in their understanding of the hierarchy. Further down the order, however, their peers do not have a shared view of the mechanics of promotion and demotion, and often express anger and resignation that their efforts have gone so poorly rewarded by teachers. Similarly the options process failed to deliver the motivational boost that schools hoped for. Pupils in both our case-study schools identify the highly constrained nature of the curricular 'choices' they are invited to make. For some the process is marked by 'pressure' as a succession of teachers seek to ensure that, in the words of one 14-year-old, 'clever people' opt for their area in the upper school. For most, however, the process is again an opportunity to be reminded of the importance of five higher-grade passes within a system overwhelmingly shaped by the perspectives of teachers.

These feelings, of being subject to processes beyond their control, are reinforced for most pupils as they move through their GCSE courses. In year 9, when the examination courses still lie ahead, there is relatively little understanding of GCSE tiering and its consequences for grade ceilings and floors. These understandings change by year 11 as the pupils move through the examination courses and experience further selection into set teaching groups and/or different tiers (even within mixed-ability groups). For many these decisions are especially painful. They have been repeatedly told (throughout their secondary schooling) that a grade C is the minimum they should aim for. Now they find themselves being reassured that lower grades still have value and, on occasion, are placed in tiers that literally cannot attain grade C.

It is a cruel irony that the processes of selection and monitoring that have been adopted with the aim of heightening attainment are so frequently experienced as disempowering and demotivating by pupils. The use of setting, for example, results in a majority of pupils finding themselves in second-best contexts: just one place below the top set it can still feel like you have been 'cast off'. Similarly, even where a grade C remains possible, tiering provides another source of anxiety (in terms of the anticipated difficulty of different papers) and disenchantment (where teachers are seen to concentrate on those destined for the Higher tier). In this context the production of 'predicted grades' (intended partly as a motivational 'ploy' by teachers: see Chapter 6) can be experienced as personally insulting – akin to being 'cussed'. Similarly, schools' last-minute attempts to bring about grade D-to-C conversions provide further evidence of their inhumanity and patronizing self-interest in the eyes of some pupils. The pupil league table in Clough GM, for example, generates considerable discussion among pupils. The headteacher is correct when he argues that most pupils will be able to tell you where they feature in the table (Chapter 6), but they also see the publication of the table as at best unnecessary, at worst embarrassing and degrading. Many pupils are also clear that these moves have a direct relation to the school's concern for *its* place in the nationally published school league tables.

As if these feelings of disempowerment and closed opportunities are not bad enough, many pupils also believe that they (and/or their peers) have been treated unfairly. Some issues, such as social class and gender, feature as part of the pupils' accounts without being deployed as organizing principles. They believe that boys and girls are treated differently and they see connections between ability and other social classifications. Nevertheless, it is ability, behaviour and 'race' that feature most prominently in their accounts of inequality in school. Pupils argue that teachers privilege those with ability and seem to connect ability and social class in some of their talk. Similarly, behaviour is thought to bring about different teacher responses, with notions of acceptable behaviour being linked particularly to issues of gender, sexuality and 'race'. The latter is an especially complex issue. We have noted that pupils are not eager to raise 'racism' as an issue, possibly fearful of being accused of special pleading. Additionally, even once they are secure in the trustworthiness and understanding of the researcher, the pupils find it hard to pinpoint racism explicitly. This is because the racism they experience is complex and multifaceted: in their terms, it is 'not blatant'. It works through negative judgements of ability; harsh and particularized discipline; and a range of differential relationships with teachers.

Both Taylor Comprehensive and Clough GM have adopted statements of equal opportunities. After several years of living with differential treatment (through formal measures of selection and informal degrees of disciplinary and personal exclusion) pupils in both schools conclude that their teachers have failed to deliver on those promises.

8

Conclusions

rationing education

How do the league tables impact on us? It puts permanently more, more, more, more pressure on us, you know. Flog us to death, flog us to death, flog us to death. You do that anyway. But if at the end of the day you're going to be told, 'Hang on, we haven't got X per cent of A-to-Cs, so you must be bad teachers' – ah ah, no.

. . . they want us to do well in this so their league tables are all right. They don't seem to care about what we want to do for ourselves. Just seem to care about us on the league table.

These quotations are from a teacher and a pupil respectively, both engaged in surviving the new realities of school life in a context of published school league tables, heightened competition and unprecedented state surveillance. The league tables form the cornerstone of education reforms that have reshaped compulsory schooling in Britain. In this book we have examined the consequences of these reforms at the school level. Drawing on two years' qualitative fieldwork, we have sought to understand the multiple and sometimes conflicting constraints at work on teachers and pupils. We have studied two different London secondary schools: Taylor Comprehensive, a school that consciously exhalts an inclusive ideology and is generally against selective pupil grouping; and, Clough, a grant-maintained school that 'opted out' of LEA control specifically to expand its opportunities to select pupils and to heighten its reputation locally. Despite these differences, there are also strong similarities: both schools serve coeducational and multi-ethnic pupil populations; both perceive the reforms as threatening; both have embarked on new strategies to meet the demands of the reformed system.

In this chapter we wish to stand back a little from the minutiae of the school data and identify some of the broader issues arising from our study. We will reflect on the authoritarian nature of the education reforms that is in direct contradiction to the rhetoric (of diversification and decentralization) so beloved of both Conservative and 'New' Labour administrations. In fact, teachers and pupils in both case-study schools experience the reforms as overwhelmingly dictated from 'above'. Subsequent sections will then identify key aspects in the institutionalization of inequality that has been accomplished through the increased adoption of selection by 'ability'. We will argue that contemporary education policy and practice constitute a *new IQism*, whereby crude and regressive notions of intelligence (associated with hereditarian psychology and eugenicist politics) have been widely adopted as 'common sense'. In this way, and without debate, elitist and racist assumptions lie at the heart of the processes of selection and differentiation that dominate the system. The gross inequalities that arise from these processes are shielded from scrutiny by a perspective that stresses an *individualized* approach. 'Race' and social class factors, which operate relationally and reflect wider structural forces, are hidden from sight through the adoption of a blinkered perspective that is incapable of looking beyond individual instances. This perspective operates on an interpersonal level but is also evident in discourses that address 'appropriate' policy and research strategies. In our final section, we reflect on the nature of research and current educational reforms, and propose a series of measures that could provide the basis for a radical reimagining of education policy and practice – an approach that rejects the obsession with narrow, elitist and racist measures of 'standards' in order to pursue the realization of equal opportunities and social justice. We begin by examining the final attainments of the pupils in our case-study schools. Their results, like their experiences documented in earlier chapters, highlight the extent and nature of the rationing of education.

Educational triage and the A-to-C economy

Throughout this study the importance of GCSE grades A*-to-C has continually surfaced. They are the key performance indicator for schools, subject departments, individual teachers and pupils. Despite the continual addition of new measures to each successive version of the published school league tables, the proportion of final-year pupils attaining five or more higher-grade passes remains largely unchallenged as the central criterion of success and failure. It is this measure upon which schools are ranked by national and local newspapers; it is this measure that is first cited when schools are called to account for themselves; it is this measure that now drives work at the school and classroom level. We have argued that an *A-to-C economy* has developed, such that higher-grade passes have become the supreme driving force for policy and practice at the school level. In Chapter 3 we outlined the concept in greater detail and noted the suitability of the economic metaphor, with teachers and pupils all caught in a wider system, over which they exert little or no influence, that is shaped by forces of competition and experienced as depersonalized and disciplinary. Higher-grade passes are the currency of this economy, and secondary schools are increasingly geared to maximizing their performance in relation to this 'bottom line', whatever the cost elsewhere. In the A-to-C economy the needs of the school, so far as the league tables are concerned, have come to define the needs of pupils:

> the best thing that we can do for our pupils is to strive to get the greatest possible proportion achieving that five high-grade benchmark.
>   (Headteacher, memorandum to staff, Taylor Comprehensive)

Our case-study schools have responded by interrogating virtually every aspect of school life for its possible contribution to the all-consuming need to improve the proportion of pupils reaching the benchmark level of five or more higher-grade passes. The pastoral system, for example, has become a servant of the academic as both schools seek to identify individual pupils who, with additional support and resources, might change one or more predicted grade Ds into actual grade Cs. It is when attempting to engineer such *D-to-C conversions* that the underlying principles of *educational triage* are most clearly visible.

In medicine the principle of triage is followed as a means of sorting and prioritizing those in greatest need. The procedure is most extreme in emergency and crisis situations: here, the overriding goal is to identify those who require urgent treatment but are not so severely injured that survival is unlikely whatever aid they receive. Some injuries may be painful but not life-threatening: these cases have to wait. Some people have such severe injuries that, given the constraints of the situation (where there are insufficient resources to meet all needs) they are judged unlikely to survive even with additional attention: they may receive painkillers but they are not rushed into the operating theatre. In effect, they are allowed to die. These decisions would be unthinkable under normal circumstances, but are made in response to a prioritization of need in relation to current circumstances and finite resources. Comparable decisions are being made as teachers attempt to ensure their school's survival within the educational market place. The extraordinary demands of the A-to-C economy are such that both our case-study schools are seeking new ways of identifying suitable cases for treatment – pupils who will show the maximum return (in terms of higher-grade passes) from receipt of additional resources of teacher time and support.

It might be supposed that a push to extend achievement by adopting triage principles would begin to redress certain existing inequalities. Historically, pupils from some minority ethnic backgrounds, and those from working-class families, do not emerge from education with average attainments comparable to their middle-class and ethnic majority counterparts. By focusing extra resources on those 'in need', therefore, we might suppose that educational triage would raise the achievements of these groups. Unfortunately, the mechanisms of educational triage are informed by exactly the same assumptions that shape the wider system and result in the former inequalities of opportunity and attainment. Although Taylor Comprehensive and Clough GM adopt different methods, in search of D-to-C conversions, the overall results are similar. In both cases Black pupils and their peers in receipt of free school meals (a rough proxy for poverty) are significantly over-represented in the group of pupils deemed to be without hope.[1] Even when they do gain entry to the 'treatment' group, in comparison with their white peers and those not in receipt of free meals, these pupils are markedly less likely to emerge with five or more higher-grade passes.

This rationing of education is most deliberate and obvious in relation to the schools' attempts to effect D-to-C conversions (Chapter 6), but the same principles are present throughout the pupils' secondary schooling. We have detailed the various ways in which selection is becoming increasingly common in both case-study schools, despite their different ideologies on this matter. Clough GM seeks consciously and explicitly to extend the use of selection by 'ability', including limited selection on entry aged 11 (Chapter 3). Teaching groups in the lower school are increasingly differentiated and the options process operates as another system whereby pupils can be sorted into different groups with markedly different presumed educational careers (Chapter 4). In Taylor Comprehensive, a school committed to mixed-ability grouping, setting is becoming more widespread. Additionally, the introduction nationally of GCSE tiering is forcing teachers to differentiate pupils even where they are formally taught together in mixed-ability contexts (Chapter 5). At each stage there is the potential for teachers' judgements of 'ability' to be shaped by wider social forces such as gendered, classed and racialized notions of appropriate behaviour, motivation and attitude. Certainly many pupils look back on their schooling and feel a sense of injustice (Chapter 7): the statistics of success and failure in their schools suggest that they have a case.

Up to this point, despite our overwhelmingly qualitative approach, we have also drawn on numerous quantitative measures as an additional means of identifying and exploring the various processes at work in our case-study schools. Our final statistics concern the pupils' eventual attainments in their GCSE examinations. The inequities of rationing and selection to this point are clearly realized in the statistics. In both schools there is a clear pattern of inequality in the proportion of pupils attaining five or more higher-grade passes (A*-to-C) (see Figures 8.1 and 8.2). Overall levels of attainment are higher in Taylor, but the patterns of achievement by gender, class and ethnic origin are consistent. In both schools a higher proportion of girls achieve the benchmark level enshrined in the school league tables and valorized in the A-to-C economy. In both schools, however, this gap between the achievements of boys and girls is smaller than the inequalities associated with social class and ethnic origin. In Clough the greatest discrepancy is between those in receipt of free school meals (where 9 per cent attain the benchmark) and their peers not in receipt of free meals (39 per cent). This gap is considerably

Figure 8.1 Achievement of five or more higher-grade GCSE passes, by gender, class and ethnic origin (Clough GM)

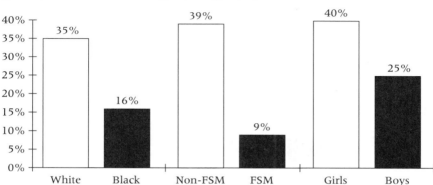

Figure 8.2 Achievement of five or more higher-grade GCSE passes, by gender, class and ethnic origin (Taylor Comprehensive)

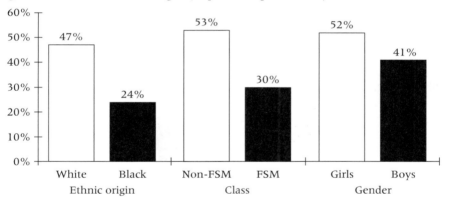

smaller in Taylor, but the gap between Black and white pupils is significant in *both* cases. In either school proportionately around twice as many white pupils attain the five higher grade benchmark compared with their Black counterparts.

We have shown that the National Curriculum 'core' subjects (mathematics, science and English language) enjoy greater status than other curricular areas. In the subject options process, for example, motivational attempts often begin by stressing the importance of these subjects as a basis for entry to key parts of the labour and post-compulsory education markets (see Chapter 5). Even greater inequalities of achievement emerge when we examine pupils' attainments with these subjects in mind. Figures 8.3 and 8.4

Figure 8.3   Pupils attaining at least five higher-grade GCSE passes that include maths, science and English language (Clough GM)

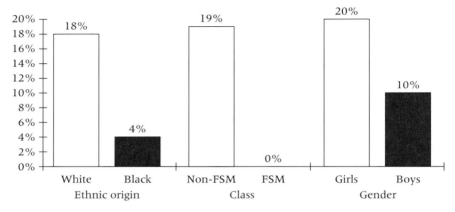

Figure 8.4   Pupils attaining at least five higher-grade GCSE passes that include maths, science and English language (Taylor Comprehensive)

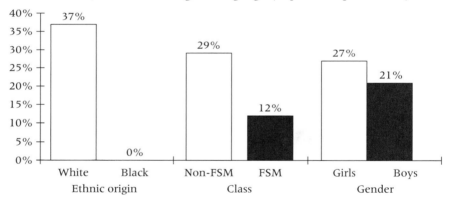

detail the proportion of pupils attaining the benchmark (five higher grade passes) where those passes include grades A*-to-C in each of the core subjects. Once again, girls perform rather better than boys. As with the benchmark level *per se* (regardless of the subjects involved), the inequalities associated with gender are smaller than those associated with class and ethnic origin. Indeed, in Taylor the gap between girls and boys attaining the benchmark including 'core' subjects is only six percentage points (Figure 8.4). In contrast, the inequalities associated with social class and ethnic origin are pronounced. In Clough no pupil in receipt of free school meals attains the benchmark level including all three core subjects (Figure 8.3). The situation is a little better in Taylor, where this level is attained by 12 per cent of pupils in receipt of free school meals. However, even here their peers not receiving free meals attain the benchmark (including 'core' subjects) at more than twice that rate (Figure 8.4). If anything, the situation is worst in relation to ethnic inequalities. In both schools white children account for the vast majority of pupils attaining the benchmark including all three core subjects. In Clough the proportion of white pupils achieving this level is more than four times the Black figure, with just 4 per cent of Black pupils appearing (Figure 8.3). In Taylor the inequality is even more striking: here almost four out of every ten white pupils attain the benchmark including all core subjects; not a single Black pupil attains a comparable level of success (Figure 8.4).

As we have seen, in terms of attaining the GCSE benchmark, girls fared slightly better than boys in both schools. The different outcomes for boys and girls signal the complex ways in which the processes of schooling are gendered. That girls are more likely overall to attain the benchmark grades does *not* imply, however, that concerns over the nature of girls' educational experience are obsolete, as is sometimes believed by those outside schools (see Chapter 2) and by teachers themselves (for example, the head of year quoted in Chapter 6). The options process, for example, proposes certain employment trajectories for girls that reinscribe traditionally gendered stereotypes (Chapter 4). Concerns about girls' inability to cope with some examinations, expressed by the head of mathematics in Clough, and the concentration of girls in the intermediate mathematics tier in Taylor (Chapter 5) may also be seen as underpinned by and reproducing particular versions of femininity. In this way girls are often perceived as compliant, motivated and hard-working – characteristics deemed necessary to attain the minimum benchmark standard. At the same time these characteristics are seen by teachers as being at odds with particular (especially Black and working-class) modes of masculinity (cf. Epstein *et al.* 1998a; Mac an Ghaill 1994). This does not mean, of course, that the gendered expectations always operate in a linear way or uniformly benefit any particular group. These same discursive formations position the majority of girls as being without the 'natural' ability required to genuinely excel and attain the very highest grades. The impact of these constructions of femininity and masculinity is clearly important and has implications well beyond the confines of GCSE examinations and education. However, within the confines of this study it is clear that the GCSE outcomes in Taylor and Clough are more obviously marked by social class and 'race' inequalities; for this reason our discussion has tended to focus more often on these dimensions and, therefore, it is these particular concerns that feature most strongly in this chapter.

Over time the rationing of education is happening earlier and with greater severity in each of our case-study schools. The adoption of various forms of grouping 'by ability' makes concrete previously hidden differences in teachers' expectations. Even where such overt differentiation is avoided, say by retaining mixed-ability groups, pupils are subject to similar processes through the options system, GCSE tiering and the push for D-to-C conversions. Our data clearly indicate that, far from redirecting resources to those in greatest need, this form of triage reinforces and extends existing inequalities, especially those associated with social class and ethnic origin.

Triage and league tables

One of the most important aspects of our analysis of educational triage concerns the relationship it exposes between national education policy and practices of selection at the school level. The schools' reactions are driven by the need to survive in the context of competition created and enforced by the school league tables. At present the central criterion is the proportion of pupils attaining five or more A*-to-C passes, hence the 'A-to-C economy'. However, simply tinkering with the tables – say, by substituting a different measure as the main criterion of success – will *not* remedy the situation. An innovation in the 1998 performance tables, for example, was the inclusion of an 'average points score' for each school.[2] It has been suggested that such an approach provides a fuller picture of pupils' attainments by giving credit for *all* pass grades, including those below grade C. This development was welcomed, for example, by the National Union of Teachers (the largest teaching union) (Pyke 1998a: 6). At present the 'average points score' has a long way to go before it challenges the status of the five A*-to-C passes criterion, which remains the most widely quoted statistic in the educational press and in policy statements. However, even if the latter were withdrawn and completely replaced by the average points score, triage would remain at the heart of schools' work. The particular goals would alter, but the overall nature of the process would be likely to remain as strong as ever.

We can hypothesize, for example, that under a 'points' economy, a critical issue would involve the definition of the relevant population to be counted in the calculations. The status of pupils designated as having special educational needs would be a widespread concern. If SEN pupils were not removed from the calculation schools might argue that they were being penalized for having an inclusive policy, possibly strengthening moves for separate provision outside the mainstream. Additionally, the government has already begun moves to encourage more 'work-related learning' in Key Stage 4 (DfEE 1997d). The initial consultation document included provision to disapply the National Curriculum for pupils involved in work-related schemes, which would involve time away from school in college or the work-place (QCA 1998).[3] It is likely that the inclusion of these pupils in the figures would also be contested. Furthermore, it is likely that some pupils predicted to achieve little or no exam success would be 'encouraged' to move elsewhere (for a 'fresh start'). There has been a suspicion that exclusions from school (both formal and informal) have already been used in this way and an emphasis on the average points score would do nothing to reduce this problem (cf. Bridges 1994; Gillborn 1996; Ofsted 1993; SEU 1998).

This is not to say that the creation of a 'points' economy would not bring about change. In Taylor Comprehensive, for example, a curriculum reorganization has led to fewer subjects enjoying a greater share of the timetable. This is justified in relation to the A-to-C economy as freeing pupils from stress and letting them concentrate on getting high grades in at least five subjects (Gillborn and Youdell in press). In relation to a points system, however, this is no longer a sensible strategy. Many schools, including Taylor, would undoubtedly re-evaluate their concern with five higher-grade passes, but the effects would not necessarily be any more egalitarian than the current rationing of opportunity. For example, it is likely that 'able' pupils would be encouraged to enter for the maximum number of subjects. The logic of educational triage would now reason that the effort expended in securing the highest grades (A* and A) might be used better elsewhere to get additional points. Rather than spending so long to get A* points in subject X, the argument might go, why not broaden your range and do an additional subject? In this way a 'predicted' A* might actually translate into a grade B (a 'loss' of two points), but the difference would be more than compensated for in an additional grade C or D (worth five and four points, respectively). Additionally, some subjects that currently have lower academic status (see Chapter 4) might find themselves a popular suggestion in options meetings if senior management thought that grades D and C could be gained relatively easily.

There are further ways in which schools might adapt to a 'points' economy, but the thrust of our argument is clear. The key issue concerns the publication of performance tables that can be translated into crude 'league tables', not whether the central criterion is the proportion of children attaining five higher-grade passes, average points score per pupil or average grade per pupil.[4] Whatever the main criterion, school league tables of exam success promote the rationing of education, with all the attendant inequalities that we have documented. We return to the role of league tables later in this chapter. At this point, however, it is useful to reflect on the authoritarian nature of the reforms that is embodied in the publication of such documents.

Authoritarian education

Qualitative research has sometimes been criticized for providing rich descriptive data at the expense of a wider critical perspective. In this, it has been argued, the detail of small-scale qualitative studies fails to engage with the 'bigger picture' of socio-political developments at the macro level (cf. Ozga 1990).[5] Our study suggests that any credible analysis of education policy and practice must address issues at both the macro and micro levels. The bulk of our analysis has been concerned with detailed qualitative data generated in two case-study schools; we have argued, however, that school-level developments can only be understood adequately in the wider context of changing policy priorities at a national level. The fetishization of 'standards' in public policy discourse, operationalized through a series of crude but remarkably powerful surveillant technologies, is central to the development of the A-to-C economy. This, in turn, lies behind the myriad decisions and interactions that make up the various forms of educational triage that we have documented. The school-level processes, therefore, must be understood within this 'bigger picture'. In isolation, however, the macro-sociological perspective is also inadequate. Our analysis shows the multiple and active ways in which teachers are engaged in the rationing of education: they do not do this because they want consciously to fail children from poor and/or minority backgrounds. Many teachers are passionately committed to challenging the very inequalities that they participate in reinforcing. It is only by identifying the multiple factors at work at the school level, including teachers' own interests and perspectives (located within wider dominant cultural contexts that are anti-working-class, sexist, homophobic and racist) that we can begin to understand how these factors come together through the daily, unremarkable but ultimately devastating processes of educational triage. It is this combination of macro- and micro-sociological processes that explains the simultaneous increase in inequality alongside the rise in 'standards' charted through the headline statistics (see Chapter 2).

One of our most striking findings is simply how authoritarian and effective the recent educational reforms have been. Before the 1988 Education Reform Act, and the multiple successive pieces of reforming legislation, schools were believed to be relatively sealed institutions, where practice was largely resistant to outside manipulation (cf. Rudduck 1991). Those days are gone. Despite the very significant differences in history and ethos between our case-study schools, the similarities between them have been overwhelming. Both are driven by the demands of the A-to-C economy, both have adopted forms of educational triage, and both actively remake familiar inequalities of achievement, especially those associated with social class and ethnic origin.

Although the bulk of our data focuses on two individual schools, it is striking how little sense of autonomy is displayed by any of the actors with whom we have engaged. Pupils feel largely powerless in a system that assesses them, labels them, tells them the 'appropriate' subjects to study and dictates the level of examination that is in their 'best interests'. Teachers feel caught within the conflicting demands of their pupils, their subject specialisms, their senior managers and their own desires as professionals with particular ideological and personal agendas. They are especially aware of the relentless push to maximize performance in terms of the A-to-C economy. This drive is uppermost in the minds of senior managers, and especially headteachers, who themselves feel trapped in a system that is increasingly punitive and sets ever higher targets with no understanding of the particular circumstances of individual schools.

At a time when the language of 'inclusivity' and 'partnership' is celebrated in policy texts as never before (see Chapter 2), it is interesting that so many of the processes have become dominated by top-down forces of surveillance and control. One of the most revealing developments concerns the introduction and extension of GCSE tiering. The GCSE examination was introduced in the late 1980s as a means of unifying the examination system and, in particular, was hailed as ending the inequities of the dual exam format. The GCE was widely seen as a superior qualification to the CSE, which the majority of pupils entered. However, we should not forget, first, that this division was widely understood by teachers, pupils and parents; and second, that pupils could enter *both* examinations simultaneously. The situation was far from perfect: schools frequently divided pupils into different GCE and CSE groups and, in any case, parents had to pay for one of the two examinations where they wished children to enter both: the situation was riddled with inequalities (cf. Abraham 1995; Ball 1981; Gillborn 1987). Nevertheless, it *was* possible for pupils to confound their teachers' expectations by entering the higher-status exam and passing despite advice to the contrary. This is no longer possible. In our case-study schools it appears that many parents know little about GCSE tiering and, in any case, have no formal say over the decisions which are placed in teachers' hands. Dual entry is simply no longer allowed by the system, and so pupils must accept the grade ceilings imposed by the exam tier that their teacher judges 'appropriate'. In this sense the GCSE, through the use of tiering, is now dominated by teacher assessments and closed to pupil and parent resistance. At a time of 'partnership' and 'inclusivity', and within a single 'unified' examination, therefore, there is even more scope for the institutionalization of inequality than in the dual system it replaced more than a decade ago.

Selection and the institutionalization of inequality

In an increasing number of schools, the marketization of British education has been associated with a return to selective practices, especially the adoption of setting and other forms of grouping pupils by 'ability' (cf. Boaler 1997a; Gewirtz *et al.* 1995). This trend has developed as schools seek to maximize their performance in terms of the A-to-C economy and has now been strengthened further as an element in official government policy (see Chapter 2) – all this despite a plethora of research studies showing the negative effects of such approaches, especially for working-class and minority pupils (Hallam and Toutounji 1996; Oakes 1990; Slavin 1996; Sukhnandan and Lee 1998). Our data on Taylor Comprehensive and Clough GM, illustrate the widespread and pervasive nature of selection. Despite sharp differences in ethos, for example, both schools have adopted selection, to varying degrees and with different levels of enthusiasm. The headteacher in Clough welcomes setting and wants to extend its use wherever possible; in contrast, the headteacher in Taylor seeks to retain mixed-ability grouping in most subjects. Regardless of these differences, however, both schools are now adopting setting at an earlier stage and in more curricular areas than at any time in their recent histories. In addition, we have seen that extensive academic differentiation takes place even in mixed-ability contexts, where, for example, the messages about 'ability' encoded in GCSE tiering decisions are generally well understood by pupils, many of whom are disappointed and dissatisfied with their treatment.

Our data not only record the growing use of selection, they also demonstrate its many negative effects. In particular, inequalities of opportunity seem to be fixed with greater certainty and to be most pronounced where selection is strongest. In general we have seen that, of our two case-study schools, Clough GM is the most supportive of selection and makes greatest use of formal differentiation where possible. This school also displays many of the greatest disparities in achievement between different groups of pupils. We noted (above) that overall levels of achievement were less in Clough, while many (but not all) of the 'gaps' associated with class background and ethnic origin were greatest in the same school. Earlier chapters have painted a similar picture: tiering decisions in Clough evidenced severe inequalities by 'race' and class (Chapter 5); while triage in that school also produced the largest group designated as 'without hope', where the benchmark level of five or more higher-grade GCSEs was unattainable even before a single exam was taken (28 per cent: see Chapter 6). The school, of course, would point to its 'long tail' of 'less able' pupils, a factor that teachers in Clough closely associate with its social class composition. The school has adopted selection, first, as a means of trying to improve the performance of its current pupils, and second, as a means of changing its composition over time (see Chapter 3). Our data suggest, however, that the school's preference for selection is part of its problem, not a solution. We have argued, in considerable detail, the many ways in which the school's view of 'ability' is exclusionary and regressive (a point we will expand on below). For the moment it is enough to recognize that both our case-study schools have a significant proportion of pupils in receipt of free school meals. Of these pupils 30 per cent attain five or more higher grades in Taylor, compared with 9 per cent in Clough. In Taylor just over one in ten pupils in receipt of free school meals achieved the benchmark *and* achieved higher grades in each of the three 'core' subjects; in Clough this was true for no pupils in receipt of free school meals (see Figures 8.1–8.4).

It is important to recognize, however, that the same kinds of inequality are produced within both our case-study schools, regardless of their support for mixed-ability or set teaching groups. In both schools Black pupils and those in receipt of free school meals are over-represented in the Foundation tier and least likely to be placed in the Higher tier (Chapter 5). These patterns are further entrenched and extended by the use of educational triage in the push for D-to-C conversions, where both schools are most likely to define these pupils as 'without hope'. Even where they do access the 'treatment' groups, which enjoy special support and additional resources, they are least likely to see benefit from them (Chapter 6).

We suggest that there are some important lessons to be learnt here. First, the debate about selection should not be conducted as if it were a simple matter of mixed ability versus setting. Both approaches reproduce all-too-familiar inequalities of opportunity associated with social class differences and ethnic origin. Even when pupils share the same classroom and are taught by the same teacher, there is a considerable body of qualitative research to show that they do not enjoy equal opportunities (for a summary of recent work, see Gillborn and Gipps 1996). Our data on Taylor, for example, show that in mixed-ability contexts pupils are still aware of differences in teachers' expectations and willingness to expend extra effort. Although the pupils identify 'ability' and 'behaviour' as key factors in these differences, their language is suffused with assumptions about class and sexuality, and some make explicit their belief that racism is involved (Chapter 7). The key difference between mixed ability and set environments is the *institutionalization* of separation that is frequently associated with the latter approach. Lower sets are taught different curricula and they are expected to cover less: witness the mathematics teacher who confirms that for some pupils their work in year 9 (with two more years still to study) is the hardest they will face (Chapter 5). The introduction of GCSE tiering takes this process still further, placing an impenetrable ceiling on the maximum grades certain pupils will be allowed to gain. Even as they enter the exam room, therefore, many pupils literally *cannot* attain the highest grades regardless of how well they perform in the coming examination. The situation is most pronounced in the three-tier model, currently used for mathematics: pupils in the Foundation tier cannot attain a grade C, constantly emphasized throughout 11 years of compulsory schooling as the basic grade they will need in competition for places in the labour market and/or post-compulsory education. The A-to-C economy has resulted in teachers continually reminding pupils of the need for grades of C and above, and yet the tiering system absolutely denies the possibility of such a grade to some. As we saw in the previous chapter, the situation is desperately painful and demotivating for some pupils. For others it is simply not credible:

Daniel: Tiers are important because say, if John wanted to get a C, like he needs a C in maths, English and science, it would be best if he took the Foundation in maths because it's easier to get a C in the Foundation than it is in the Higher.

Marcus: But in the Foundation you can't get a C.

Bob: What the fuck are you on about?

Marcus: The highest you can get is . . . [interrupted]

Daniel: Yeah, is a C.

(Taylor Comprehensive, year 11)

Selection to different teaching groups and different GCSE tiers, therefore, is part of a wider process of differentiation that separates pupils, exposes them to different curricula and different expectations, and ultimately enters them for different examinations. In mixed-ability groups, and especially where the GCSE subject is not tiered, it remains possible (though difficult) for pupils to confound their teachers' low expectations. The research literature offers several examples of this, especially concerning Black pupils, where children have recognized their teachers' lower expectations but struggled to succeed in spite of them (cf. Mac an Ghaill 1988; Mirza 1992). Setting makes this kind of success more difficult by formalizing differences in curricula and resources (cf. CRE 1992); tiering can remove the possibility altogether. Despite their many resident problems and inequalities, therefore, mixed-ability contexts do at least permit the possibility of pupils confounding the lower expectations that some teachers adopt, especially on the basis of class-related and racist stereotypes.

The new IQism

A distinction is drawn traditionally between intelligence and achievement tests. A naive statement of the difference is that the intelligence test measures *capacity to learn* and the achievement test measures *what has been learned.* But items in *all* psychological and educational tests measure *acquired* behaviour . . .

This quotation is taken from the Cleary Committee, appointed in the 1970s by the American Psychological Association's Board of Scientific Affairs (quoted in Kamin 1981: 94; emphasis added). The statement's central proposition, that there is no qualitative difference between 'IQ' tests, tests of 'cognitive ability' and *any* other test, has been repeated many times since. In Chapter 3 we noted one of the most recent attempts to clarify this same point, in Robert J. Sternberg's (1998) argument that 'abilities are forms of developing expertise'. The Cleary Committee described as 'false' the often repeated assertion that 'intelligence tests contain items that everyone has an equal opportunity to learn'. There is, the committee concluded, 'no merit in maintaining a fiction' (quoted in Kamin 1981: 95). Unfortunately, this very fiction has not only continued to be peddled by a wide array of psychometric testers and other self-proclaimed 'experts', but also passed into contemporary 'common sense'. As we have shown, this false notion (of 'intelligence' as an innate 'capacity') underlies the view of 'ability' that currently shapes national educational policy and the daily realities of school life in staffrooms and classrooms.

The debate about 'intelligence' and heredity seems periodically to spark into new life, most recently in the controversy surrounding *The Bell Curve* (Herrnstein and Murray 1994). As we noted in Chapter 3, for a book of its type *The Bell Curve* enjoyed unparalleled success as both a publishing and political intervention. The book was an international bestseller and propelled crude hereditarian perspectives into the spotlight of professional and public debate. The book restated the most narrow and regressive notion of 'intelligence' as a fixed and generalized intellectual capacity related to differences in the social class and 'racial' composition of groups. The authors took care to assert (wrongly) that their arguments were 'squarely in the middle of the scientific road' (Herrnstein and Murray 1994: 23) and alternated between different terms for the same construct; at times preferring 'cognitive ability' because of the 'political baggage' associated with the term 'intelligence' (Herrnstein and Murray 1994: 22). These niceties notwithstanding, Herrnstein and Murray were happy to offer bold opinions on the matter of apportioning blame and proposing policy solutions to the USA's supposed social ills.

As we have shown, the book provided an opportunity (on both sides of the Atlantic) for 'experts' and other commentators to reassert the inevitability, and indeed the justice, of inequality. Arguing simply that people are in poverty because of their own intellectual (genetically based) shortcomings, the book became part of a wider discourse that attacks any liberal compensatory programme as futile and anti-democratic. It is an approach that is anti-working-class, disablist, sexist, and racist:

> Putting it all together, success and failure in the American economy, and all that goes with it, are increasingly a matter of the genes that people inherit.
>
> (Herrnstein and Murray 1994: 91)

> A man's IQ predicted whether he described himself as disabled better than the kinds of job he had held. We do not know why intelligence and physical problems are so closely related, but one possibility is that less intelligent people are more accident prone.
>
> (Herrnstein and Murray 1994: 155)

> At lower educational levels, a woman's intelligence best predicts whether she will bear an illegitimate child.
>
> (Herrnstein and Murray 1994: 167)

> ethnic differences in cognitive ability are neither surprising nor in doubt. . . . the average white person tests higher than about 84 percent of the population of blacks . . .
>
> (Herrnstein and Murray 1994: 269)[6]

These kinds of perspective are repugnant to many people. Teachers, although not versed in the detail of the 'nature versus nurture' debates over IQ and heredity, are often aware of past controversies where testing has been found to discriminate against particular groups. Additionally, many working in the British system remember (having experienced it as pupils and/or professionals) the selective tripartite system that dominated after the Second World War, a system based on the hereditarian perspectives of Sir Cyril Burt[7] and ultimately abandoned in most LEAs because of its obvious inequities. Finally, of course, anyone even remotely aware of twentieth-century history needs little reminding of the atrocities carried out in the name of genetic superiority. These events are part of the reason for the furore that justifiably surrounds public interventions by those in the hereditarian camp. And yet our data suggest that the hereditarians have won. Without any genuine debate, the British education system is increasingly returning to policy and practice that takes for granted the assumptions proposed by IQists like Herrnstein and Murray.

Samuel Bowles and Herbert Gintis (1976: 119) described support for the hereditarian 'IQ theory of social inequality' as 'IQism'. This position is certainly *not* proposed as an explicit element in most policy discourse and, boldly stated (as above), we imagine that many (most?) teachers would reject such a perspective. However, exactly the same principles that underlie the IQist position *are* embraced and enacted within the detail of contemporary education policy and practice in Britain. We are not arguing that policy makers and teachers consciously accept the hereditarian position but that they *behave* as if they do. This is the *new IQism*, a situation where *hereditarian assumptions (and all the concomitant inequalities of opportunity that they produce and legitimate) are coded and enacted through the discourse of 'ability'*. Hence, education policy asserts that '[c]hildren are not all of the same ability, nor do they learn at the same speed' and uses this as the rationale for an extension in the use of 'setting by ability', so as to 'maximise progress, for the benefit of high fliers and slower learners alike' (Labour Party 1997: 7) (see Chapter 2). We have shown that both Clough GM and Taylor Comprehensive work with a view of 'ability' as a fixed and generalized intellectual potential: echoing the IQists' notion of 'intelligence' (cf. Herrnstein and Murray 1994: 19–24). We have shown also that this view of ability underlies multiple and complex selections that separate out the 'able' and the 'less able' within the schools: some decisions are explicit (such as the creation of separate 'sets' and 'fast groups': Chapters 3 and 4); some are camouflaged as advice on 'appropriate' courses (for example, during options processes and tiering decisions: Chapters 4 and 5); others are a mixture of public and private (including various D-to-C conversion strategies: Chapter 6). Regardless of the form taken, however, these decisions have a clear and discriminatory effect. Without exception our data show that Black pupils and their peers in receipt of free school meals are considerably more likely to be judged as lacking 'ability' and, therefore, find themselves in the lower sets, entered for the lowest tier of examination, and judged least worthy of additional support through the rationing of education in the A-to-C economy.

The new IQism informs, and is in turn strengthened by, contemporary policy and practice. The view of 'ability' that currently dominates education, from the heart of government through to individual classrooms, represents a victory for the hereditarian position, without debate and without conscience. At the school level this IQist notion of ability provides an opportunity for teachers (and especially senior management) to identify the winners and losers at the earliest possible stage, allowing continual checks to ensure that those predicted to achieve success 'fulfil' their potential. This perspective and the decisions it supports are serviced by a testing industry only too happy to tell schools what they want to hear. In Chapter 3, for example, we considered a popular test advertised nationally as a means of providing for 11-year-olds predictions of likely A*-to-C grade results when they are 16. On closer examination we raised concerns about the test's age (it was standardized before the recent reforms and the associated dramatic changes in attainment) and its suitability for multi-ethnic populations (basing GCSE predictions on work in areas of little minority settlement and making no allowance in individual calculations for pupils' ethnic origin). The latter is especially worrying in view of recent research that suggests differentially high rates of progress for some minority pupils during secondary schooling. This combination of factors could systematically discriminate against minority children by underestimating their likely attainments and, via apparently objective and 'scientific' means, offer yet another way in which Black pupils are failed by the system.

Writing in 1916, Lewis Terman, one of the most influential figures in the introduction of IQ testing, had this to say:

> The whole question of racial differences in mental traits will have to be taken up anew. . . . The writer predicts that when this is done there will be discovered enormously significant racial differences in general intelligence, differences which cannot be wiped out by any scheme of mental culture.
>
> Children of this group should be segregated in special classes . . . They cannot master abstractions, but they can often be made efficient workers.

The new IQism is ensuring that these same perspectives (usually unspoken, often unrecognized) are shaping the current reality of education in Britain. In case any readers are still in doubt about the dangers inherent in the new IQism and related perspectives, we offer a few more of Terman's words: 'There is no possibility at present of convincing society that they should not be allowed to reproduce, although from a eugenic point of view they constitute a grave problem . . .' (Terman 1916, quoted in Kamin 1981: 92). The eugenicist underpinnings of much education policy have gone largely unnoticed (cf. Selden 1999): this aspect of contemporary reform will continue so long as the new IQism is allowed to operate as a central component in policy and practice within an A-to-C economy.

Racism and blinkered vision: the individualization of inequality

racism is an ideology which is continually changing, being
challenged, interrupted and reconstructed, and which often
appears in contradictory forms. As such, its reproduction in
schools, and elsewhere, can be expected to be complex,
multifaceted and historically specific.

(Rizvi 1993: 15)

It's not blatantly there. I mean, you can't, you wouldn't be able
to just walk in the school and say 'Oh the school's racist'. You
have to take time before you knew that.
                                    (Marcella, Taylor Comprehensive, year 9)

We have seen that both our case-study schools are actively engaged in
reproducing racist patterns of inequality. In comparison with their white
peers, Black pupils are significantly less likely to achieve the benchmark
level of five or more higher-grade passes, a pattern that reflects their iniquitous treatment in the rationing of education through processes such as
setting, tiering and D-to-C conversion strategies. The inequalities are clearly
visible in the statistics we have produced; Black pupils often complain that
they have experienced racist treatment, and yet, in interview, they describe
the racism as 'not blatant' (see Chapter 7). The key to understanding how
such racist practices can survive, and remain hidden from public scrutiny,
lies in the increasing *individualization* of schooling discourses.[8]

We have already shown how education policy and practice, nationally
and at the school level, are adopting an increasingly disciplinary and
surveillant gaze. Individual schools are listed and ranked in the annual
league tables; individual subject departments and teachers are held accountable for their success in the A-to-C economy; and pupils are tested, ranked
and sorted individually. When these processes occur 'race' is eliminated from
public scrutiny. 'Race' is a category that only has wider meaning relationally.
The significance of 'race' as a social construct arises from historically specific
discourses that are applied to *individuals* as members of particular (socially
defined and identified) *groups*. When we look at the statistics of success and
failure (see, for example, Figures 8.1–8.4) their racialized character appears
obvious. And yet our case-study schools do not think they are systematically
failing Black pupils. Even the pupils themselves have difficulty identifying
the racist practices in any simple way. When pupils talk about the racism
they experience, they do so through a succession of examples (see Chapter
7). In isolation any of these events is open to multiple interpretation. During
this study we witnessed no occasion when a teacher could be described as
obviously racist in any simple, crude way (such as the use of racially derogatory slurs). And yet we witnessed, and the pupils experienced, numerous
occasions when they, as Black young people, were accorded second-rate
status and treated more negatively than their white peers. In isolation,
individually, the cases can be wished away as concerning a particular pupil
and/or some special circumstance, but *cumulatively* their importance as an
aspect of racist education is more apparent.

The individualization of education discourse, therefore, offers one more
way in which contemporary racism is taking new and complex forms. It is
racism through blinkered vision. By focusing on the individual, and block-
ing out the wider picture, these processes deny the validity and importance
of group identity and dynamics.[9] To illustrate the dangers of individualized

discourses in racist contexts, let us briefly consider a well-known example. The videotape of Los Angeles police officers beating up Rodney King was beamed around the world and provided a brutal and obvious example of racism. Certainly that is how many viewers saw it. Not so the original jury asked to decide on the officers' behaviour. The lawyers defending the police officers played the tape over and over, still-frame by still-frame. They took what appeared to be simple and irrefutable evidence of racism and, by reducing it to its smallest components, removed its force. They argued that at various points it looked as though Mr King was being 'aggressive', was refusing to be pacified. By taking the film a frame at a time the obvious and devastating power of the piece was lost. When you are being set upon by armed men with night-sticks your first reaction is not to lie motionless on the ground. But show the film frame-by-frame and, the lawyers argued, you could see King resisting arrest.[10] Relatedly, in cases of exclusion from school, Black pupils and their families often complain that the circumstances leading up to a 'flashpoint' are not taken into account by the authorities, even where an interaction has involved racist harassment by others and/or inappropriate action by teachers (see Blair 1994; Ofsted 1996). In this way the racialized nature of the processes, which have led the Black pupil to the point of expulsion, disappear from sight. The gaze of the excluding authority focuses on the individual and their supposed crime; the wider context and the things that brought about the situation are deemed irrelevant or beyond the scope of the hearing: they are beyond the field of vision.

The Los Angeles Police Department, like London's Metropolitan Police, has a very poor record on race relations. The statistics indicate that in Britain (as in the USA) Black people are more likely to be stopped, more likely to be convicted, and more likely to receive harsh sentences whatever the crime (cf. Skellington 1992). In the USA the ultimate sanction, the death penalty, is also used as an extension of the racism at the heart of the judiciary.[11] Like the police forces around them, the school systems of the USA and UK have an equally distressing record. Black youth are considerably more likely to leave school unqualified – a situation that has persisted for decades. In Britain, Black children are expelled from mainstream education at several times the white rate (cf. Gillborn and Gipps 1996), in some authorities they are up to 15 times more likely to be excluded (*Times Educational Supplement*, 11 December 1998). The situation has become so appalling that, as Sir Herman Ouseley (one of the few prominent Black voices in contemporary British politics) has warned, there is a danger of complacency when figures suggest Black youth are excluded at 'only' two or three times the white rate (Ouseley 1998).

The similarities between schooling and the criminal justice system, therefore, are striking: the systematic over-representation of Black youth; a professional culture that views Black people as 'other'; and a refusal to deal with the realities of institutionalized racism at the core of the professional consciousness. Part of the current refusal to address this situation, and an aspect of the processes that further extends the inequalities, is the individual-ization of the relevant discourses. By looking at each incident separately it is possible to ignore the wider picture. Just as in the Rodney King video, the full story is of clear racism, but the freeze-frame version is less certain, more open to debate and uncertainty. Similarly, the wider picture on exclusions and attainment appears clear; racism is the inescapable conclusion. But reduce the situation to individual cases and doubt is the only thing everyone will agree on.

The current emphasis on the 'ability' of individuals, for example, acts completely to remove wider structural inequalities from the picture. Our case-study schools are convinced that they are doing their best for each individual; it just so happens that many individual Black pupils are seen as lacking ability, acting in a disruptive way and displaying signs of being unmotivated. Ethnicity and racialized perspectives are deeply implicated in the processes (witness the head of faculty on Black pupils' complaints about predicted grades in Chapter 6) but the discourse is only ever about indi-viduals. The situation takes on even greater force in the formal tests of ability that are used. We have commented already on a commercially produced test that could systematically underestimate the results likely for minority chil-dren, all other things being equal (see Chapter 3 and the discussion above). The issue escapes scrutiny because the dominant perspective focuses on separate individuals: it is a failure to see the full picture. A similar situation is operating with regard to discipline and control in school. Teachers argue they are dealing with individuals – responding to each case – but their perceptions are frequently racialized. The negative expectations of Black failure, demotivation and a threatening 'attitude' are difficult to pin down conclusively in each individual case. It is only from the wider picture that the racism becomes clear.

By adopting an individualized perspective, therefore, education policy and practice are increasingly enshrining racism in a discourse that apparently removes 'race' from the picture, but simultaneously provides the perfect conditions for racist stereotyping to flourish. This is why ethnic monitoring (at a national, local and school level) is essential. It is only when we stand back and remove the blinkers (press 'play' and let the individual frames build into their more revealing plot) that we see most clearly the indications of the racism that operates at the individual level. There is an overwhelming case for more use of ethnic monitoring, therefore, as a first step in under-standing current patterns of experience and achievement, and as a precursor to the critical examination and reform of education policy and practice.[12] This also provides strong grounds for resisting further the individualization of discourse and its related technologies.

Following critical reviews of educational research in the late 1990s (Hillage *et al.* 1998; Tooley 1998), there have been calls for less work on equity issues and more research concerned with 'practical' and 'relevant' approaches and solutions, including more longitudinal studies and what the minister responsible for educational research terms 'randomly controlled trials' (Clarke

1998) (more on this below). Where such work fails to take ethnic origin seriously as a group characteristic the opportunity for racist processes to escape detection, and be further strengthened, is obvious. Perhaps one of the most persuasive reasons for resisting the individualization of policy and practice is the nature of its advocates:

> group differences in cognitive ability, so desperately denied for so long, can best be handled – can *only* be handled – by a return to individualism. A person should not be judged as a member of a group but as an individual. With that cornerstone of the American doctrine once again in place, group differences can take their appropriately insignificant place in affecting American life.
>
> (Herrnstein and Murray 1994: 550; original emphasis)

It is difficult to deny racism and reject calls for change when the statistics of inequality are as obvious as those currently produced by the British education system. By individualizing the discourse, however, race is taken out of the equation. Failure is constructed as a matter for the individual pupil, their family and community. This racism by blinkered vision is a potent and growing force in contemporary policy (in education and beyond). Its further spread and institutionalization represents one of the gravest challenges facing those concerned with equity in education.

Research, policy and equity

One of our main purposes in undertaking this study has been to explore the consequences of education reform at the school level. We have given prominent consideration to issues of equity and educational disadvantage, hoping that, by examining how current inequalities are produced, we might contribute to a process of future reform that strengthens the egalitarian possibilities of education. There is, however, no simple or definite relationship between educational research and practice.

Research and policy: whose agenda?

The late 1990s saw educational research being castigated in the popular press and by government. While headlines proclaimed 'school researchers "wasting £70m on irrelevant studies"'(*Daily Mail*, 23 July 1998), government ministers were quoted as having 'grave misgivings about the quality of research' (DfEE 1998) and sought to alter the funding mechanism so as to concentrate work in fewer institutions (Clarke 1998). The attacks were legitimized by two reviews of educational research; one funded by Ofsted (Tooley 1998), the other funded by the DfEE (Hillage *et al.* 1998).

The Tooley review was previewed in an article by the Chief Inspector of Schools, Chris Woodhead, whose organization had funded the study. Writing before the review was published, Woodhead launched an attack on academics in general, and the sociology of education in particular, as 'gone to seed' and producing 'badly written dross' (Woodhead 1998: 51). The review's author, James Tooley, is a prominent neo-liberal writer who has consistently championed the free market as a basis for educational reform. Additionally, as we noted in Chapter 3, in response to *The Bell Curve* (Herrnstein and Murray 1994) Tooley proposed that IQ tests be administered as a means of 'liberating' those with 'low IQs' from the 'egalitarian vision' (which he described as 'by assumption false') that 'they can do as well as anyone' (Tooley 1995a). On the question of racialized test bias, he suggested that '[p]erhaps there is something more objective lurking in these tests that cannot be so easily manipulated' (Tooley 1995b). In view of such a track record, it was no surprise when Tooley's review was especially critical of research concerned with equity. Relatedly, qualitative research was also singled out for particular criticism. Although he stated 'It would be wrong to assume that the discussion here reflects criticism of small-scale, qualitative studies *per se*', the very next paragraph began, 'The key problem here lies in the subjectivity of qualitative research' (Tooley 1998: 43). Qualitative research is always open to multiple interpretation and contestation. To seek proof 'beyond reasonable doubt' (Foster 1992; Foster *et al.* 1996) is superficially fair but flounders in practice because what is reasonable to one reader is wholly insufficient to another (cf. Gillborn 1998b; Troyna 1995b). In this way the new-found public concern with methodology is increasingly acting as a smokescreen to protect inequality from scrutiny. Hence, the Chief Inspector of Schools, and self-proclaimed champion of educational 'standards', dismisses sociological research, especially that based on qualitative approaches, as either unreliable or simply irrelevant:

> the sociology of education is a subject without a future. Its intellectual trajectory is doomed. On one hand, as I fear recent history shows, sociological researchers can go further and further down the ethnomethodological road, probing the interaction of everyday life in ever more minute detail; on the other, they can struggle to develop ever more complex and abstruse theories that purport to offer macro-explanations of what happens in our educational institutions. Neither possibility is likely to generate much that is of intellectual interest or, indeed, practical use.
>
> (Woodhead 1998: 52)

The Tooley review was most strident in its criticisms of alleged bias and irrelevance. The Hillage review was somewhat more measured in tone although it, too, was accused of repeating many of the flaws it found in others (cf. Goldstein 1998a; 1998b; Hammersley 1998). Based on a literature review and interviews with selected 'stakeholders', the report was criticized on several grounds. Harvey Goldstein has argued that 'There is no systematic attempt to define or evaluate quality' and 'no objective attempt to verify what their various respondents say' (Goldstein 1998b: 1). Despite noting the lack of any single 'objective definition of what actually constitutes "good quality" research', for example, Hillage *et al.* (1998) nevertheless proceed to report 'widespread concern about much of the quality of educational research'. Perhaps more significantly, they also recommended 'establishing a commitment to evidence-based policy development and approaches to the delivery of education'. This is important because it recognizes that such a relationship does not presently exist. This is in contradiction to official claims that 'Current Government policies are informed by research evidence' (Clarke 1998: 9) but accords with the reality of contemporary policy making where 'some of the research that is now being systematically ignored or derided by Labour Ministers was actually quoted by them with approval in Opposition' (Whitty 1998: 7).

We have noted that the specific discriminatory effects of selection by 'ability' have been well chronicled in both the USA and UK. Despite these clear and unambiguous findings, such approaches continue to shape policy and practice at a national and school level in Britain. It is not a question of inappropriate research topics, methods or dissemination, therefore, it is a matter of politics. The findings do not seem to fit with current priorities and so they are rejected or wilfully ignored. As we noted in Chapter 2, for example, the adoption of colour-blind policies has been widely condemned by practitioners, community activists and academics in the field of 'race' equality. This evidence has been reviewed and widely publicized by official bodies (see, for example, CRE 1992) and independent researchers (Gillborn and Gipps 1996). In the case of the latter, the study was commissioned and (eventually) published by Ofsted, quoted in formal policy documents (see Chapter 2), and even held up as an example of the kind of review that should be produced more frequently in the future (cf. Clarke 1998: 9). And yet every major government target continues to be colour-blind. By failing to require that pupils in particular social groups share equally in attaining the targets, these moves leave the way open for racialized and racist processes that simultaneously deliver improvements to the headline statistics while widening inequalities between different ethnic groups. This process can be detected in the national statistics (Chapter 2), and now this study has laid bare the school-based assumptions and decisions through which it operates as a component of the A-to-C economy.

There is, therefore, no certainty that any meaningful change will happen as a result of the growing influence of the A-to-C economy and the widening inequalities that it is producing. Nevertheless, on the basis of this study, it is possible to identify numerous ways in which the current processes could be addressed.

Education and equity: ways ahead?

This book raises some fundamental problems and challenges for everyone engaged in education. We have argued that although equity issues are now once again paid lip-service by government, dominant approaches to the policy and practice of education actively reproduce and extend existing inequalities of opportunity. This is especially so in relation to social class and 'race' inequalities that have increased significantly as a direct result of recent reforms. These inequalities are shaped by the daily routines of selection and differentiation in schools, a process that is deeply scarred by the racist and class-biased notions of intelligence and ability that have long been rejected by mainstream science but continue to shape 'common sense'. These views find powerful expression in the assumptions of teachers and policy makers alike. To challenge these processes will take concerted action on several fronts.

This study clearly points to the fact that processes at both the macro *and* micro levels are implicated in the current iniquitous status quo. The actions of individual teachers, and the policies adopted across our case-study schools, cannot be understood in isolation from the wider context of reformed education and public surveillance through league tables and the attendant tyranny of measurable, elitist 'standards'. In turn, however, the reforms themselves do not 'automatically' result in greater inequality. These outcomes can only be understood through a situated reading of the perceptions, interests, actions and beliefs of teachers who shape the implementation of the reforms at the school and classroom level. Consequently any attempt to combat inequality in the education system must address issues at both the macro and micro levels. This should be informed by an awareness of local complexities and subtleties but resist the individualized and colour-blind approaches that seek to remove 'race' and class from the picture.

It follows from the above that participants at every level of the system can affect change but, in isolation, only within certain limits. Equality policy statements and target setting at national level are worthless without mechanisms to translate them into changed activities at the school level. Similarly, we have seen that individual schools and teachers can work against the logic of national reform. Elsewhere we have noted schools trying to develop anti-racist education against the tide of national reforms (Gillborn 1995), and in this study we have seen a few individual teachers working to goals that are more or less in conflict with the logic of the A-to-C economy. Such individuals and institutions can achieve important results, but only within certain limits. The lesson of the last decade or so in the UK is that top-down reform can bring about startling results *if* other goals are sacrificed and the stakes are raised sufficiently to force schools to share the reformers' agenda. Hence, it is relatively easy to identify several decisive steps that government could take to reduce inequalities of outcome between groups. This would probably involve, for example, targeting greater resources to areas and schools currently lowest in the 'league tables', as opposed to the current system that subjects these schools to multiple penalties (even closure) and rewards those already at the top.

Similarly, the surveillant and disciplinary power of Ofsted inspections could be used to enforce equity priorities, such as adopting equality of outcome as a goal to be pursued with all the vigour previously focused on the bench-mark of five or more higher-grade passes. This would mean refocusing effort on to the wasted potential of those pupils currently short-changed by the system. Such a shift could not take place within the terms of the existing A-to-C economy.

We have seen how almost every aspect of schools' work is currently interrogated for its contribution to maintaining/improving performance in the headline statistics. Consequently, taking equity seriously means abandoning the publication of school performance tables in their current form. Such a proposal might seem naive, even ridiculous, amid the present political climate where education is a key battleground and each major party seeks constantly to outshout the other in its championing of 'standards'. As we have seen, however, the present debate trades on a spurious, elitist and ultimately racist interpretation of 'standards'. The performance tables are *the* driving force in the A-to-C economy and, given the dominance of the raw examination data, the tables are utterly inconsistent with the goal of equal opportunity. In this respect it is instructive to compare the British case with changes elsewhere. In the USA, for example, the *detracking* movement is involving increasing numbers of schools in attempts to move away from selective teaching groups. The process is complex and difficult, not least because of the resilience of IQist 'common sense' among educators, parents and pupils, but real progress is possible (Oakes *et al.* 1997). Meanwhile, the publication of school performance data and league tables is illegal in New South Wales, Australia.[13]

We have seen that the form and organization of the dominant public examination is also deeply implicated in the production of inequalities in our schools. Abolishing GCSE tiering, or at least radically amending the system, would make an important contribution to equalizing opportunity. Schools might also be challenged to demonstrate that equity is not comprom-ised by their approaches to assessment and pupil grouping. The current Ofsted inspection framework includes provision for schools to be made answerable for any undue differences in performance by gender or ethnic origin, but experience suggests that this is rarely addressed in practice (cf. Gillborn and Gipps 1996: 79; Ouseley in Pyke 1995).

Similarly, teachers and schools *can* work against the flow of top-down reforms. The scope for such subversion may be limited, but even an individual teacher can (over a course of years) make an enormous difference to the lives of hundreds of young people. This study illustrates how easily inequality can be remade at a mundane, day-to-day, routine level. The simple taken-for-granted assumptions that inform approaches to tiering, pupil grouping, the adoption of 'ability' testing, etc. are the unremarkable yet devastating detail of a machine (the education system) that creates enormous disparities of experience, achievement and esteem between young people. These differ-ences will impact on the life chances of many children for the foreseeable future. These inequalities often flow from the unintended consequences of policy and practice; this is perhaps the most important single point to arise from our research. Unless policy and practice address equity as a matter of concerted, conscious and deliberate attention, at all levels, existing inequalities will not only persist, they may worsen.

We started this book with a quotation identifying education systems as 'busy institutions' (Connell 1993: 27): the wider education system, policy makers, headteachers and teachers are currently remarkably busy remaking and reinforcing inequality, especially in relation to 'race' and social class (albeit that they are frequently unaware of these particular 'fruits' of their labours). It is time this level of activity was refocused toward the achievement of social justice.

Notes

Chapter 1 Education and equity

1 Although the United Kingdom is formally constituted of four countries (England, Northern Ireland, Scotland and Wales), education legislation is not common across the UK. Although there are strong similarities, education provision (and the detail of reform) vary between countries. Since our ethnographic data were generated in England, in this study our main concern is with the reforms as enacted in the English system.

2 We present these understandings of equal opportunity separately for ease of discussion. In different treatments authors do not always identify their perspectives clearly and/or consistently. These various understandings, therefore, are not exhaustive.

3 This perspective underlies, but is rarely made explicit in, some British approaches that stress substantive equity of *outcomes*.

4 Educational certification is no guarantee of access to post-compulsory education or the labour market. Surveys consistently reveal that people of minority ethnic background are more likely to be unemployed, for example, even when they are as highly qualified as their white counterparts (see Drew 1995; Modood *et al.* 1997). Nevertheless, while qualifications are not *sufficient* to gain access, they are often *necessary*: in relation to peers of the same ethnic origin, rates of unemployment are considerably less for minority young people with educational certification.

5 A related determination to refuse the taken-for-granted nature of 'race' talk lies in the convention of placing the term in inverted commas.

6 Some academics have argued that, because the new racism does not trade in conventional 'race' categories, *racism* is not the correct term (for discussions, see Cole 1998; Gillborn 1995; Miles 1993). Such a debate risks placing academic niceties before the realities of oppression and injustice as they are experienced in the real world. We believe the term to be wholly appropriate.

7 The original idea for the project was Desmond Nuttall's. It is revealing that, as a world-renowned quantitative researcher, he nevertheless saw the need for a qualitative study and approached a new and junior colleague in his institution with the idea. His support during the early planning discussions was crucial.

8 Because of the socially constructed nature of 'race' categories there is no consistent and universally agreed form of ethnic identification in Britain. Following common practice among the people so labelled we use the terms 'Black' and 'African Caribbean' interchangeably. In our statistics we include in this group all pupils categorized (by their schools) as Black, Black Caribbean, Black African and Black Other (cf. Gillborn and Gipps 1996: 8).

9 Our final report to the project's sponsors, the Nuffield Foundation, was submitted in early 1998. During 1997 and 1998 we discussed the project with numerous colleagues, including presenting preliminary ideas at seminars and international conferences. This book was completed during 1998 and early 1999.

10 The project included funding for a half-time researcher but (as is too often the case within the constraints of contemporary research funding) the demands of data collection and the particular social relations demanded by qualitative research could sometimes only be met through the researcher's own dedication beyond the funded time allowance.

11 GCSE results are graded A*, A, B, C, D, E, F, G and U (ungraded). Grades of G and above are described as 'pass grades', although most attention focuses upon grades of C and above, which are designated as 'higher-grade' passes. These 'higher' grades are generally considered to be roughly equivalent to passes in the former General Certificate of Education (GCE) O-level examinations, which the GCSE replaced in 1988.

12 Taylor and Clough are in different London boroughs.

13 Under reforms introduced by the new Labour government, elected in 1997, most GM schools assumed 'Foundation' status, allowing them to continue to own their buildings and assets and to act as their own admissions authorities (*Times Educational Supplement*, 23 April 1999 p. 1).

Chapter 2 Reforming education: policy and practice

1 In places this chapter draws on our earlier analyses of education policy and practice in the UK (cf. Gillborn 1997a; 1998a; Gillborn and Youdell in press). We would like to thank those who have commented on these pieces and acknowledge their original places of publication.

2 *Times Educational Supplement*, 18 April 1997: 6.

3 Within days of announcing the Social Exclusion Unit, for example, Labour moved to cut the welfare benefit available to single parents (a favourite scapegoat of conservative politics on both sides of the Atlantic).

4 GCSE and other examinations, for 16-year-olds, are used as the benchmarking tests at the end of the fourth and final 'key stage'.

5 Figure 2.1 shows the performance table for one London borough, as reproduced in a major national newspaper. We have chosen to present Hammersmith and Fulham because in many ways the LEA is similar to the one that houses Taylor Comprehensive, one of our case-study schools.

6 In 1998, Labour's first full year in office, the word 'standard' or 'standards' appeared in 2,272 articles in the *Times Educational Supplement* – almost a quarter of all items in the newspaper (*Times Educational Supplement*, 1 January 1999 p. 4).

7 Despite the year-on-year overall increases, the five A*-to-C benchmark is still not attained by half of pupils ending their compulsory schooling.

8 Most debate on exclusions from school focuses on permanent exclusion (expulsion), but the SEU also address 'fixed-term exclusions', otherwise known as suspensions.

9 Recent figures place the over-representation of Black pupils nationally at 3.4 times the white rate. One study suggested that nationally children of Black Caribbean ethnic origin were almost six times more likely to be expelled than their white counterparts (Gillborn and Gipps 1996: 52–3). In some LEAs the over-representation of Black pupils is up to 15 times the white rate (Thornton 1998).

10 The Social Exclusion Unit set an ambitious target for a one-third reduction in exclusions by 2002. Unfortunately, no 'race'-specific targets were set, meaning, first, that Black pupils are unlikely to share equally in any improvement (see the data on shares in improvements, later in this chapter); second, as a result the relative over-representation of Black pupils will in all probability worsen (see Gillborn 1999).

11 An official report on health inequalities, by Sir Donald Acheson (a former chief medical officer) recently catalogued a series of significant and growing health inequalities in Britain. The situation was so serious as to merit particular measures intended to close existing gaps by focusing on the poorest sections of society (Acheson 1998).

12 'Between 1980 and 1990 the bottom fifth of British households saw their share of disposable income fall from 10 per cent to 8 per cent' (Budge 1995).

13 In 60 LEAs there had been a pattern of 'overall improvement' between 1992 and 1995, that is, relatively more pupils had achieved the five A-to-C benchmark level, while proportionately fewer had left school completely unqualified. In 36 LEAs, however, there was increased polarization, with more achieving the five A-to-C level *and* more leaving without any pass grades (Hackett 1995).

14 In a letter to the *Times Educational Supplement* (12 January 1996: 23) Sir Tim Lankester (formally a senior civil servant at the DfEE), drew on official data to argue that lower-achieving schools had enjoyed the greatest improvements. He based this on the relative improvement in the percentage of pupils achieving at least five A*-to-C passes 'in schools around the bottom quartile point' and those 'around the top quartile'. The relative improvement was somewhat misleading, however, since improvement by those at the bottom quartile point was being compared with such a low starting point. In fact, the *gap* between the two sets of schools had widened: in 1993 the lower schools achieved 20.1%, the higher 55.05% (a gap of 34.95 percentage points); in 1995 the lower quartile achieved at 21.7%, the highest at 58.45% (a gap of 36.75 percentage points).

15 The research review called for ethnic monitoring of achievement as a matter of priority (Gillborn and Gipps 1996: 79), a recommendation that is now partly met by the DfEE's use of the school census (form 7) as a means of gathering some ethnically based data.

16 The YCS is funded by the Department for Education and Employment. Regular analyses of achievement by different ethnic groups have not been published in recent years (see Drew *et al.* 1992; Gillborn and Gipps 1996: 16–18). The data reproduced here are drawn from a reanalysis of archive material. We are grateful to Sean Demack, David Drew and Mike Grimsley for sharing these, as yet unpublished, data with us.

17 Data for 1985 are from YCS results quoted in Gillborn and Gipps (1996). Data for 1996 are drawn from YCS results made available to, and published by, the Commission for Racial Equality (CRE). In this analysis South Asian groups were collapsed into a single category, making more detailed comparison across these groups impossible (CRE 1998).

18 In 1985, 7 per cent of Black pupils in the YCS attained five or more higher-grade passes; the figure for white pupils was 21 per cent – a gap of 14 percentage points (Drew 1995: 76). In 1996, this hurdle was achieved by 23 per cent of Black pupils and 45 per cent of whites – a gap of 22 percentage points (CRE 1998).

19 The social class categories cited here are derived from Demack *et al.* (1998). Employment data were collected for each parent and an approximation created for each household using the Registrar-General classification. Social class I (professional) includes, for example, judges, medical practitioners, engineers, university academics; social class II (managerial/technical) journalists, headteachers, marketing and sales managers, hotel/restaurant managers, publicans, farm managers; III(N) (skilled non-manual) shop sales assistants, police, firefighters, receptionists; III(M) (skilled manual) ambulance drivers, bus drivers, chefs, travel stewards, hairdressers; IV (partly skilled manual) bar staff, postal workers, hotel porters, farm workers; V (unskilled) cleaners, labourers, refuse collectors, car park attendants.

Chapter 3   Ability and economy: defining 'ability' in the A-to-C economy

1 In referring to an 'A-to-C' economy we have not forgotten that the highest grade possible is, in fact, an A*. Rather, we are deliberately echoing teachers and pupils who, in their talk about grades, rarely mention the 'starred' grade explicitly.

2 The last Conservative Education Bill (1996) sought to extend to all GM schools the right to 'select pupils by ability or aptitude' for up to half their intake (DfEE 1996). Although this proposal was never realized, a circular issued in June 1996 signalled a relaxation in the interpretation of existing legislation such that 'Selection of up to 15 per cent of the intake is likely to be possible without the need to publish proposals' (Dean 1996b).

3 The term 'institutional racism' was often applied in a lazy catch-all way during the 1980s, which severely weakened the nature of the concept and was rightly criticized (cf. Carter & Williams 1987; Cohen 1992; Rattansi 1992; Troyna 1988; Troyna and Williams 1986). Nevertheless, properly applied and interrogated, the concept retains considerable importance as a tool of critical analysis.

4 In this quotation Robert J. Sternberg is describing the most extreme and fixed notion of intelligence common among certain psychometricians – a view he characterizes as a 'myth'. We return to Sternberg's critique later in this chapter.

5 The continual demands for more and more higher-grade passes might logically be assumed to promote a view of 'ability' as mobile or pliable. As we show in Chapter 6, however, the schools' notions of 'ability', though robust and simple, owe little to logic.

6 For more detailed reviews of these issues, see Fraser (1995), Gould (1981), Kamin (1974), Kohn (1996) and Richards (1997). For a challenging perspective on the place of intelligence and hereditarian assumptions in everyday thought, see Mirza (1998).

7 Signatories include Hans Eysenck, Robert A. Gordon, Linda S. Gottfredson, Lloyd G. Humphreys, Arthur R. Jensen, Alan S. Kaufman, Richard Lynn, J. Philippe Rushton, Julien C. Stanley and Robert M. Thorndike. Herrnstein and Murray are not included.

8 The technical appendix also notes that in the predictions by GCSE subject categories the 80 per cent figure includes the predicted grade plus or minus one or two GCSE grades. For the summary predictions '80 per cent are likely to achieve the predicted *number of GCSE grades A to C*, plus or minus *three GCSEs*; 80 per cent of pupils are likely to achieve the predicted *total of GCSEs*, plus or minus *two GCSEs*' (Thorndike *et al.* 1986: 91; original emphasis).

9 The 1997 data have the advantage of being more recent than the Census, but it should be noted that the figures only include pupils in LEA-maintained schools – excluding, for example, GM schools.

10 In 1997, across England white children accounted for 88.7 per cent of primary pupils and 89.2 per cent of secondary pupils. In Lancashire the figures were 90.7 per cent primary and 90.8 per cent secondary; in East Sussex the respective figures were 97.1 per cent of primary and 97.8 per cent of secondary pupils (DfEE 1997c).

11 Despite repeated requests (to the headteacher and to the senior teacher responsible for administering the test in Clough) we were never supplied with details of the test itself. We were not actually refused the information – on several occasions we were assured that a copy would be found and sent to us. More than a year (and several reminders) later, we have yet to receive the promised materials.

12 The CAT does not gather information on pupils' ethnic origin: there is no possibility within the test, therefore, of generating separate projections for pupils in different ethnic groups.

Chapter 4 Selection 11–14: fast groups, 'left-over' mixed ability and the subject options process

1 When we use phrases such as 'most' and 'least able' in this way, we are relating official assessments of pupils. These judgements are made in line with the dominant understanding of 'ability' that we have already identified and critiqued (see Chapter 3).

2 These quotations are transcriptions taken from TV coverage of Blair's speech on *Channel Four News* and BBC's *Newsnight*.

3 It is revealing that these groups are known among staff as 'fast' groups – a term that seems to reflect, and in turn reinforce, common-sense notions of pupils learning at different speeds (see Chapters 2 and 3).

4 Streaming and setting are both forms of selection that give institutional force to assessments of 'ability'. In *streamed* environments pupils are placed in a teaching group that stays together regardless of different curricular subjects. In *sets*, however, teaching groups are constructed separately for each curricular area.

5 In view of current best practice in the field we refer to pupils with 'English as an additional language' (EAL); in Clough such pupils are described as having 'English as a second language' (E2L).

6 This literature is summarized elsewhere (Gillborn 1997a). Among the most important studies are Ball (1981), Delamont (1990), Measor and Sikes (1992), Pratt *et al.*

(1984), Riddell (1992a), Tomlinson (1987), Tomlinson and Tomes (1986) and Woods (1979).

7 Once again the relative value of particular grades is signalled in the ranges made available for selection.

8 In the words of an SMT member, the 'special option' is designed to provide 'a basic sort of life skills course' for two main groups of pupil. The first are those deemed to be the 'least able': 'kids who are unlikely to get, they'll be the F's and G's, and it's better to identify them at this stage, and have them working towards something, rather than they go into the main block and it's *another* area where they can't succeed'. The second group are 'pupils for whom English is their second, third or even fourth language. And who need support in their other subjects – language support. So for four lessons a week, rather than doing a GCSE course they will have support and follow-up work in whatever courses they're doing'. Once again, therefore, EAL pupils are approached organizationally in a similar way to those with learning difficulties (see Chapter 3).

9 Before the restrictions imposed by the National Curriculum, girls tended to 'opt out' of science given the chance, or to overwhelmingly choose biology, where at least one science was required by the school. Boys tended to be over-represented in physics and chemistry. Girls were significantly more likely to continue to study a modern foreign language. In technology subjects, a gendered division was common such that girls dominated domestic and commercial subjects while boys were the majority in woodwork, metalwork and computer studies (cf. Measor and Sikes 1992; Pratt *et al.* 1984).

10 One of us, Youdell, is currently engaged in a more detailed investigation of gendered roles, sexuality and youth cultures in one of our case-study schools.

Chapter 5   Selection 14–16: sets, tiers, hidden ceilings and floors

1 For details of the early background discussions on differentiated schemes of entry and assessment in GCSE, see Gipps (1987) and Kingdon and Stobart (1988).

2 This does not mean, of course, that pupils must be entered for the same tier in every subject.

3 The announcement was given little coverage in the educational press: a short item on page 5 of the *Times Educational Supplement* (22 May 1998) was the smallest article on the page, dwarfed by a picture of Tony Blair and an advertisement for personal loans.

4 Jo Boaler's (1997a; 1997b; 1998) case-study work on mathematics teaching provides an interesting complement to our project. Boaler focuses in particular on mathematics and gender equity. Our findings support her view that the more highly selective environments are associated with greater inequality. However, our work takes a rather different perspective on certain issues by extending the range of relevant questions. First, mathematics is not our only concern: we also draw direct comparisons with selection and attainment in English, another core subject. Second, we give equal weight to 'race' inequalities. Third, we adopt a more critical notion of 'ability' as a socially constructed and divisive classification.

5 Clough follows NEAB syllabuses in English. Before 1998 these tiers were given different names by NEAB, such that the Higher tier was labelled 'Tier Q', the

lower was 'Tier P'. To minimize confusion, in the body of the text we refer to these tiers using the post-1998 nomenclature.

6 This kind of motivation to succeed *despite* the system, but in terms that the system itself must acknowledge (educational certification), seems especially strong among certain ethnic minority pupils (cf. Mac an Ghaill 1988; Mirza 1992).

7 Of course, not every teacher of English and mathematics shares an identical reading of the tiering process. Our aim here has been to identify the main trends within the departments, and we have consequently chosen to draw most heavily on interviews with the heads of department. They have a good overview of actions in their subject, take overall responsibility for tier/examination entry and are broadly representative of the dominant positions taken up by close colleagues.

8 All calculations of tier entry in this chapter are based on GCSE examinations taken in the summer of 1997.

9 The size of our pupil sample is such that it is not appropriate to carry out numerous cross-tabulations to make statistical judgements of the interaction of gender, class and 'race' factors. However, in Taylor and Clough there was not a significant difference in the proportion of Black and white pupils in receipt of free school meals. It is not possible to explain away 'race' differences, therefore, as artefacts of social class inequalities in the pupil population.

10 Because of the relatively small numbers involved we have combined the equivalent maths sets from each half of the timetable.

11 In Clough for mathematics, tier of entry was: Higher, 3% of boys and 2% of girls; Intermediate, 45% of boys and 43% of girls; Foundation, 52% of boys and 55% of girls.

12 Our analysis of tier allocations in English is based on allocations for English language examinations. Data pertaining to English language cover the greatest part of the cohort as some pupils, specifically the 'least able', are entered for English language but are not entered for English literature. Pupils who are entered for both language and literature are entered for the same tier in both examinations.

13 Since English exams use a two-tier system of entry, where distributions can be described easily in the text, it is not necessary to include as many illustrations as in the section on mathematics (above).

14 In Taylor, 29% of FSM pupils are entered at Foundation level in English, compared with 13% of their non-FSM peers.

Chapter 6   Educational triage and the D-to-C conversion: suitable cases for treatment?

1 We recognize that the use of such a metaphor might be considered masculinist, but we feel that it accurately captures both the nature and severity of the relevant processes. Educational triage is a process by which schooling does violence to the opportunities afforded different groups of pupils: it is systematic, deliberate and inequitable.

2 A phrase used by a member of the school's Equality and Achievement Working Party and echoed by several colleagues.

3 See Chapter 2 for a discussion of these debates in public policy and educational discourses.

4 See Power (1996) for a full exploration of the historically competing, yet shifting, relationship between the pastoral and the academic. In the instance discussed here, the pastoral can be seen to have shifted into a position where it is not merely subordinate to the academic, but actually colonized by it.

5 This is not to say that these pupils have not *already* experienced favourable treatment. On the contrary, as we saw in Chapter 5, various selection and setting practices are used by some subject departments in Taylor, each associated with differential educational expectations, experiences and opportunities.

6 This may well be attributed to the year head's explicit attempt to ensure a gender balance in the groups.

7 Of pupils included in the Achievement Initiative, 20 per cent (n = 12) of white pupils attained the benchmark in comparison to 9 per cent (n = 1) of Black pupils. Similarly, 25 per cent (n = 14) of pupils not in receipt of free school meals attained the benchmark in comparison to 14 per cent (n = 4) of pupils in receipt of free school meals.

8 This would require that the pupil not meeting the benchmark nevertheless went on to attain pass grades (of G and above) in a greater number of subjects.

9 See Chapter 3 for a detailed discussion of how these different cases are explained within the school's dominant conception of 'ability'.

10 As with our analysis of Taylor (above), here we apply the language of triage to the school's own classification and hierarchization of pupils. The terms are ours but the distinctions are the schools'.

Chapter 7 Pupils' experiences and perspectives: living with the rationing of education

1 There is an extensive research literature on this issue. For a review of relevant work in the USA and UK respectively, for example, see Slavin (1996) and Hallam and Toutounji (1996).

2 This development in Deborah Youdell's field relations (with teenagers in Taylor in the 1990s) almost exactly mirrors David Gillborn's experiences (when beginning doctoral research in City Road Comprehensive during the 1980s). In both cases the white researcher was taken fully into the confidence of Black pupils only after they had been around the school some time and proved themselves trustworthy (cf. Gillborn 1987: 27–9). When pupils know that a researcher will be in the school for months (possibly years in some ethnographic research) it seems that they take time to reassure themselves that confidential interview data are not shared with other participants in the setting.

3 In the event, Stephen was permitted to sit the mock exams, after his mother visited the school to complain at the timing of the suspension.

Chapter 8 Conclusions: rationing education

1 As we noted in Chapter 5, there are too few pupils in our sample to merit the production of cross-tabulations in an attempt statistically to isolate the separate influence of factors such as gender, class and ethnic origin. We noted, however, that receipt of free school meals was not significantly different between the white

and Black pupils: this means that the ethnic inequalities cannot be explained as artefacts of social class interactions.

2 This is created by assigning a different value to each grade attained by pupils (from 8 points for an A* down to 1 point for a grade G) and then calculating an average for the school.

3 The consultation document included no explicit provision to monitor (by 'race', class or gender) whether certain pupils are over-represented in the scheme.

4 Average points per pupil was reportedly chosen as an indicator in preference to average grade per pupil because the latter could have encouraged schools to restrict entry to cases where success was viewed as most likely: 'It would also have brought about the strange situation in which a pupil with one A-grade scored higher than one with nine B-grades' (Pyke 1998b: 2).

5 For a particular response to these criticisms, see Power (1995).

6 Herrnstein and Murray's views on 'race' inequality are extended in the appendices to their book where, for example, they describe the work of J. Philippe Rushton. Rushton (1995: xiii) proposes 'a gene-based evolutionary theory' that stratifies people by 'race' such that 'Mongoloids, Orientals' are most advanced, then 'Caucasoids, whites', with 'Negroids, blacks' at the lowest end of the spectrum. Rushton (1995: xiii) claims a clear relationship between 'race' and numerous attributes including 'brain size, intelligence, reproductive behaviour . . . speed of physical maturation, personality, family stability, law-abidingness, and social organization'. Herrnstein and Murray note that Rushton's writings have been heavily criticized, but they respond that 'Rushton's work is not that of a crackpot or a bigot' but 'is plainly science' (Herrnstein and Murray 1994: 643). To give a taste of this 'science', in his recent work Rushton draws on a reanalysis of the Kinsey study of sexual behaviour (Kinsey *et al.* 1948; 1953). In support of his evolutionary thesis on the ordering of the 'races', Rushton (1995: 176) argues that 'race is more important than social class in determining sexual behaviour'. He cites various items that support his view, that is, where 'the white college-educated sample was more sexually restrained than the white noncollege-educated sample, which, in turn, was more sexually restrained than the black college-educated' (Rushton 1995: 176). Among the items proposed as evidence are responses to the following: 'measured length of erect penis', 'angle of penile erection', 'average length of menstrual flow', 'age hymen broken' , 'frequency of cunnilingus in foreplay in first marriage' and 'frequency of fellatio in foreplay in first marriage' (Rushton 1995: 176–8). Herrnstein and Murray are not alone in their judgement of the scientific basis of Rushton's work. In an article by Arthur Jensen (1998) the same study is described as one of few '[f]airly comprehensive and scientifically respectable treatments' of 'race' differences. Jensen's article appears in a collection coedited by Robert J. Sternberg (Sternberg and Williams 1998) and, incredibly, contains the only reference to 'racial differences' in the book's index.

7 Cyril Burt was the leading British hereditarian psychologist, knighted for his services to education, whose ideas exercised considerable influence over the shape of the selective post-war education system. In the early 1970s Leon Kamin raised serious doubt over the authenticity of Burt's work, noting that in view of his published sample descriptions, the statistical correlations claimed by Burt were literally incredible (Kamin 1974). The issue made front-page headlines (after Burt's death) when Oliver Gillie, of the *Sunday Times*, discovered that two 'research associates' who had supposedly gathered the data for some of Burt's most famous

work had, in all likelihood, never existed. Initially the charge of fraud was vehemently defended by Burt's supporters, such as Hans Eysenck, who complained of 'character assassination'. Later, however, Burt's authorized biographer (Leslie Hearnshaw) unearthed further evidence and Burt's supporters began to accept publicly that he had behaved 'in a dishonest manner' (Hearnshaw 1979; for an account, see Kamin 1981: 98–105). The late 1980s, however, witnessed an attempt to rehabilitate Burt's reputation (Joynson 1989) every bit as flawed and selective in its evidence as was Burt himself (cf. Hearnshaw 1990). Nevertheless, the attempt to reconstruct Burt as victim rather than fraud was partially successful. Reviewing the Joynson book for the *Guardian* newspaper, for example, Clare Burstall (then director of the National Foundation for Educational Research) declared that 'Burt stands exonerated', a conclusion that she reached with obvious relief:

> I found it impossible to accept anyone who could write as Burt did, and who had for so long, and with such obvious justification, been held in such high esteem by so many of his contemporaries, could possibly be the confidence-trickster, liar and fraud that he was now being made out to be.
>
> (Burstall 1989)

8 We are not suggesting that the blinkered vision of individualized discourse is the only, or principal, form of racism in contemporary politics and education. Racist discourses can take multiple and apparently contradictory forms. As we noted in our introduction, the 'new racism' (Ansell 1997; Barker 1981) stresses 'culture' rather than 'colour' and speaks of 'difference' not 'superiority'; but it is no less racist in its consequences than more overtly racialized discourse. The importance of the new racism is that it offers an alternative discourse, suited to different contexts and issues. The new and old racisms are complementary (cf. Gillborn 1997a). Similarly, the blinkered vision of individualism works through particular discourses and can complement both 'crude' and 'new' culturalist forms of racism.

9 In many respects a similar dynamic can also be seen in operation regarding social class.

10 One of the most long-standing and powerful racist stereotypes associates Black people, and especially Black men, with notions of aggressive (often hypersexualized) physicality (cf. McCarthy 1998; McClintock 1995; Mirza 1997). For further analyses of the school-based processes that reproduce such a view, see Gillborn (1990a; 1995) and Sewell (1997; 1998).

11 Amnesty International (1998) described it as 'applied in an arbitrary and unfair manner' that 'is prone to bias on the grounds of race'.

12 For examples of schools using ethnic monitoring in this way, see Blair and Bourne (1998) and Gillborn (1995).

13 The Education Reform Regulation 1996, under the Education Reform Act 1990, states that results in a range of tests (including School Certificate and Higher School Certificate) 'must not be publicly revealed in a way that ranks or otherwise compares the results of particular schools'. Our thanks, in particular, to Harvey Goldstein and Roger Slee for their assistance on these issues.

References

Abraham, J. (1995) *Divide and School: Gender and Class Dynamics in Comprehensive Education.* London: Falmer Press.

Acheson, D. (1998) *Independent Inquiry into Inequalities in Health.* London: The Stationery Office.

Amnesty International (1998) *Rights for All: Report on the USA.* London: Amnesty International.

Angus, L. (1993) The sociology of school effectiveness, *British Journal of Sociology of Education,* 14(3): 333–45.

Ansell, A.E. (1997) *New Right, New Racism: Race and Reaction in the United States and Britain.* London: Macmillan.

Apple, M.W. (1993) *Official Knowledge.* New York: Routledge.

Apple, M.W. (1996) *Cultural Politics and Education.* Buckingham: Open University Press.

Apple, M.W. and Zenk, C. (1996) American realities: poverty, economy, and education, in M.W. Apple, *Cultural Politics and Education.* Buckingham: Open University Press.

Arnot, M., Gray, J., James, M., Rudduck, J. with Duveen, G. (1998) *Recent Research on Gender and Educational Performance.* London: The Stationery Office.

Bagley, C.A. (1992) *Back to the Future: Section 11 of the Local Government Act 1966: LEAs and Multicultural/Antiracist Education.* Slough: National Foundation for Educational Research.

Ball, S.J. (1981) *Beachside Comprehensive: A Case Study of Secondary Schooling.* Cambridge: Cambridge University Press.

Ball, S.J. (1987) *The Micro-Politics of the School: Towards a Theory of School Organization.* London: Methuen.

Ball, S.J. (1994) *Education Reform: A Critical and Post-Structural Approach.* Buckingham: Open University Press.

Ball, S.J. and Lacey, C. (1980) Subject disciplines as the opportunity for group action: a measured critique of subject sub-cultures, in P. Woods (ed.) *Teacher Strategies.* London: Croom Helm.

Ball, S.J., Maguire, M. and Macrae, S. (1998) Race, space and the further education market place, *Race Ethnicity and Education*, 1(2): 171–89.

Banks, J. (1995) Address as part of the symposium 'Teaching culturally different students: political assumptions of the educational research', annual meeting of the American Educational Research Association, San Francisco, April.

Banton, M. (1988) Race, in E.E. Cashmore (ed.) *Dictionary of Race and Ethnic Relations*, 2nd edition. London: Routledge.

Barber, M. (1997) Why simply tackling poverty is not enough, *Times Educational Supplement*, 12 September, p. 17.

Barker, M. (1981) *The New Racism: Conservatives and the Ideology of the Tribe*. London: Junction Books.

Beane, J. and Apple, M.W. (1995) The case for democratic schools, in M.W. Apple and J. Beane (eds) *Democratic Schools*. Alexandria, VA: Association for Supervision and Curriculum Development.

Blair, M. (1994) Interviews with Black families, in R. Cohen and M. Hughes, with L. Ashworth and M. Blair (1994) *Schools Out: The Family Perspective on School Exclusion*. London: Family Service Units with Barnardo's, Ilford.

Blair, M. and Bourne, J., with Coffin, C., Creese, A. and Kenner, C. (1998) *Making the Difference: Teaching and Learning Strategies in Successful Multi-ethnic Schools*. London: Department for Education and Employment.

Blum, J.M. (1978) *Pseudoscience and Mental Ability: The Origins and Fallacies of the IQ Controversy*. London: Monthly Review Press.

Blunkett, D. (1997) Speech to the annual conference of the National Association of Head Teachers, Scarborough, May. Press release 123/97, Department for Education and Employment.

Blunkett, D. (1998) Speech to the Labour Party Conference, 1/10/98. London: Labour Party.

Boaler, J. (1997a) *Experiencing School Mathematics: Teaching Styles, Sex and Setting*. Buckingham: Open University Press.

Boaler, J. (1997b) Setting, social class and survival of the quickest, *British Educational Research Journal*, 23(5): 575–95.

Boaler, J. (1998) Mathematical equity – underachieving boys or sacrificial girls?, *International Journal of Inclusive Education*, 2(2): 119–34.

Bowe, R. and Ball, S.J. with Gold, A. (1992) *Reforming Education and Changing Schools: Case Studies in Policy Sociology*. London: Routledge.

Bowles, S. and Gintis, H. (1976) *Schooling in Capitalist America: Educational Reform and the Contradictions of Economic Life*. London: Routledge & Kegan Paul.

Bradley, H. (1992) Changing social divisions: class, gender and race, in R. Bocock and K. Thompson (eds) *Social and Cultural Forms of Modernity*. Oxford: Polity Press.

Brah, A. and Minhas, R. (1985) Structural racism or cultural difference: schooling for Asian girls, in G. Weiner (ed.) *Just a Bunch of Girls: Feminist Approaches to Schooling*. Milton Keynes: Open University Press.

Bridges, L. (1994) Exclusions: how did we get here?, in J. Bourne, L. Bridges and C. Searle (1994) *Outcast England: How Schools Exclude Black Children*. London: Institute of Race Relations.

Budge, D. (1995) Cold shouldered in a polarised country, *Times Educational Supplement*, 3 March, p. 12.

Burgess, R.G. (1984) *In the Field: An Introduction to Field Research*. London: George Allen & Unwin.

Burstall, C. (1989) Boffin passes new IQ test, *The Guardian*, 15 August.

Burstall, E. (1996) Parent anger at London's last bastions of banding, *Times Educational Supplement*, 15 March 1996, p. 9.

Butler, J. (1990) *Gender Trouble: Feminism and the Subversion of Identity*. London: Routledge.

Butler, J. (1993) *Bodies that Matter*. London: Routledge.

Byrne, E.M. (1978) *Women and Education*. London: Tavistock.

Carrim, N. (1995) From 'race' to ethnicity: shifts in the educational discourses of South Africa and Britain in the 1990s, *Compare*, 25(1): 17–33.

Carter, B. and Williams, J. (1987) Attacking racism in education, in B. Troyna (ed.) *Racial Inequality in Education*. London: Tavistock.

Cassidy, S. (1998a) Labour moves the GCSE goalposts, *Times Educational Supplement*, 23 October, p. 1.

Cassidy, S. (1998b) GCSE safety net created, *Times Educational Supplement*, 22 May, p. 5.

Clarke, C. (1998) Resurrecting educational research to raise standards: statement from the new minister responsible for research, *Research Intelligence*, 66 (October): 8–9.

Cohen, P. (1992) 'It's racism what dunnit': hidden narratives in theories of racism, in J. Donald and A. Rattansi (eds) *'Race', Culture and Difference*. London: Sage.

Cole, M. (1998) Racism, reconstructed multiculturalism and antiracist education, *Cambridge Journal of Education*, 28(1): 37–48.

Commission for Racial Equality (CRE) (1992) *Set to Fail? Setting and Banding in Secondary Schools*. London: CRE.

Commission for Racial Equality (CRE) (1993a) *Comments on Proposed Changes to the Admission Arrangements to the Watford Grammar Schools*. London: CRE.

Commission for Racial Equality (CRE) (1993b) *Comments on Proposed Changes to the Admission Arrangements to Parmiter's School*. London: CRE.

Commission for Racial Equality (CRE) (1993c) *Comments on Proposed Changes to the Admission Arrangements to Rickmansworth School*. London: CRE.

Commission for Racial Equality (CRE) (1998) *Education and Training in Britain*. London: CRE.

Connell, R.W. (1993) *Schools and Social Justice*. Philadelphia: Temple University Press.

Connolly, P. (1995) Racism, masculine peer-group relations and the schooling of African/Caribbean infant boys, *British Journal of Sociology of Education*, 16(1): 75–92.

Connolly, P. (1998) *Racism, Gender Identities and Young Children: Social Relations in a Multi-Ethnic, Inner-City Primary School*. London: Routledge.

Curtis, S. (1998) Geographies of social exclusion and health inequality. Presentation at the 'Social Exclusion and the City' conference, organized by the Royal Geographical Society with the Institute of British Geographers, London, October.

D'Souza, D. (1995) *The End of Racism*. New York: Free Press.

Dean, C. (1996a) Review GM escape route, ministers advised, *Times Educational Supplement*, 20 December, p. 7.

Dean, C. (1996b) Anger as two Surrey GM schools go for selection, *Times Educational Supplement*, 11 October, p. 12.

Dearing, R. (1994) *The National Curriculum and its Assessment: Final Report*. London: School Curriculum and Assessment Authority.

Delamont, S. (1990) *Sex Roles in the School*, 2nd edition. London: Routledge.

Demack, S., Drew, D. and Grimsley, M. (1998) Myths about underachievement: gender, ethnic and social class differences in GCSE results 1988–93. Paper presented at the British Educational Research Association annual conference, Belfast, August.

Demaine, J. (1989) Race, categorisation and educational achievement, *British Journal of Sociology of Education*, 10(2): 195–214.

Department for Education and Employment (DfEE) (1996) Education Bill launched. DfEE Press release 364/96, DfEE.

Department for Education and Employment (DfEE) (1997a) Primary performance tables. Press release 60/97, DfEE.

Department for Education and Employment (DfEE) (1997b) *Excellence in Schools*, Cm. 3681. London: HMSO.

Department for Education and Employment (DfEE) (1997c) Minority ethnic pupils in maintained schools by Local Education Authority area in England – January 1997 (provisional). Statistical Press Notice, DfEE.

Department for Education and Employment (DfEE) (1997d) £3.5m to 'turn on' children through work-related learning. Press release 311/97, DfEE, 6 October.

Department for Education and Employment (DfEE) (1998) Quality of educational research needs improvement – Howells. Press release 376/98, DfEE, 22 July.

Doe, B. (1995) They also can achieve who live in the lower ranks, *Times Educational Supplement*, TES 2, 27 October, p. 6.

Dorn, A. (1985) Education and the Race Relations Act, in M. Arnot (ed.) *Race and Gender: Equal Opportunities Policies in Education*. Oxford: Pergamon.

Drew, D. (1995) *'Race', Education and Work: The Statistics of Inequality*. Aldershot: Avebury.

Drew, D. and Gray, J. (1991) The black–white gap in examination results: a statistical critique of a decade's research, *New Community*, 17(2): 159–72.

Drew, D., Gray, J. and Sime, N. (1992) *Against the Odds: The Education and Labour Market Experiences of Black Young People*. England and Wales Youth Cohort Study, Report R&D no. 68. Sheffield: Employment Department.

Epstein, D., Elwood, J., Hey, V. and Maw, J. (eds) (1998a) *Failing Boys? Issues in Gender and Achievement*. Buckingham: Open University Press.

Epstein, D., Maw, J., Elwood, J. and Hey, V. (1998b) Guest editorial: Boys' 'under-achievement', *International Journal of Inclusive Education*, 2(2): 91–4.

Eysenck, H.J. (1971) *Race, Intelligence and Education*. London: Temple Smith.

Eysenck, H.J. (1973) *The Inequality of Man*. London: Temple Smith.

Eysenck, H.J. (1994) Much ado about IQ, *Times Higher Education Supplement*, 11 November, pp. 18–19.

Flew, A. (1986) Clarifying the concepts, in F. Palmer (ed.) *Anti-Racism – An Assault on Education and Value*. London: Sherwood Press.

Foster, P. (1990) *Policy and Practice in Multicultural and Anti-Racist Education*. London: Routledge.

Foster, P. (1992) Equal treatment and cultural difference in multi-ethnic schools: a critique of the teacher ethnocentrism theory, *International Studies in Sociology of Education*, 2(1): 89–103.

Foster, P., Gomm, R. and Hammersley, M. (1996) *Constructing Educational Inequality: An Assessment of Research on School Processes*. London: Falmer Press.

Foucault, M. (1991) *Discipline and Punish: The Birth of the Prison*. London: Penguin.

Fraser, S. (ed.) (1995) *The Bell Curve Wars: Race, Intelligence and the Future of America*. New York: Basic.

Gardner, H. (1983) *Frames of Mind: The Theory of Multiple Intelligences*. New York: Basic.

Gewirtz, S., Ball, S.J. and Bowe, R. (1995) *Markets, Choice and Equity in Education*. Buckingham: Open University Press.

Ghouri, N. (1998) Clarke backpedals on primary setting, *Times Educational Supplement*, 11 September, p. 18.

Gillborn, D. (1987) The negotiation of educational opportunity: the final years of compulsory schooling in a multi-ethnic inner city comprehensive. Unpublished Ph.D. thesis, University of Nottingham.

Gillborn, D. (1990a) *'Race', Ethnicity and Education: Teaching and Learning in Multi-ethnic Schools*. London: Unwin Hyman.

Gillborn, D. (1990b) Sexism and curricular 'choice', *Cambridge Journal of Education*, 20(2): 161–74.

Gillborn, D. (1994) The micro-politics of macro reform, *British Journal of Sociology of Education*, 15(2): 147–64.

Gillborn, D. (1995) *Racism and Antiracism in Real Schools: theory · policy · practice*. Buckingham: Open University Press.

Gillborn, D. (1996) *Viewpoint, 5: Exclusions from School*. London: University of London Institute of Education.

Gillborn, D. (1997a) Racism and reform: new ethnicities/old inequalities?, *British Educational Research Journal*, 23(3): 345–60.

Gillborn, D. (1997b) Race and ethnicity in education 14–19, in S. Tomlinson (ed.) *Education 14–19: Critical Perspectives*. London: Athlone.

Gillborn, D. (1998a) Racism, selection, poverty and parents: New Labour, old problems?, *Journal of Education Policy*, 13(6): 717–35.

Gillborn, D. (1998b) Racism and the politics of qualitative research: learning from controversy and critique, in P. Connolly and B. Troyna (eds) *Researching Racism in Education: Politics, Theory and Practice*. Buckingham: Open University Press.

Gillborn, D. (1998c) Race and ethnicity in compulsory schooling, in T. Modood and T. Acland (eds) *Race and Higher Education: Experiences, Challenges and Policy Implications*. London: Policy Studies Institute.

Gillborn, D. (1999) 50 years of failure: 'race' and education policy in Britain, in R. Majors (ed.) *The British Education Revolution: The Status and Politics of Educating Afro-Caribbean children*. London: Falmer Press.

Gillborn, D. and Gipps, C. (1996) *Recent Research on the Achievements of Ethnic Minority Pupils*. Report for the Office for Standards in Education. London: HMSO.

Gillborn, D. and Youdell, D. (in press) 'Raising standards' and deepening inequality: selection, league tables and reform in multiethnic secondary schools, in J. Demaine (ed.) *Sociology of Education Today*. London: Macmillan.

Gilroy, P. (1987) *There Ain't No Black in the Union Jack*. London: Hutchinson.

Gipps, C. (1987) Differentiation in the GCSE, *Forum*, 29(3): 76–8.

Gipps, C. and Murphy, P. (1994) *A Fair Test? Assessment, Achievement and Equity*. Buckingham: Open University Press.

Giroux, H.A. (1996) *Fugitive Cultures: Race, Violence, and Youth*. New York: Routledge.

Glaser, B.G. and Strauss, A.L. (1967) *The Discovery of Grounded Theory: Strategies for Qualitative Research*. Chicago: Aldine Press.

Goffman, E. (1952) On cooling the mark out, *Psychiatry*, 15: 451–63.

Goldberg, D.T. (1993) *Racist Culture: Philosophy and the Politics of Meaning*. Oxford: Blackwell.

Goldberg, D.T. (1997) *Racial Subjects: Writing on Race in America*. London: Routledge.

Goldstein, H. (1987) *Multi-level Models in Social and Educational Research*. London: Griffin.

Goldstein, H. (1997) From raw to half-baked, *Times Educational Supplement*, 18 July, p. 15.

Goldstein, H. (1998a) How can we evaluate educational research? Unpublished paper available on the internet at *http://www.ioe.ac.uk/hgoldstn/*.

Goldstein, H. (1998b) 'Excellence in Research on Schools' – a commentary. Unpublished paper available on the internet at *http://www.ioe.ac.uk/hgoldstn/*.

Gore, J.M. (1993) *The Struggle for Pedagogies: Critical and Feminist Discourses as Regimes of Truth.* New York: Routledge.

Gould, S.J. (1981) *The Mismeasure of Man.* New York: W.W. Norton.

Grant, C. (1989) Equity, equality, teachers and classroom life, in W. Secada (ed.) *Equity in Education.* Philadelphia: Falmer Press.

Gray, J., Reynolds, D., Fitz-Gibbon, C. and Jesson, D. (eds) (1996) *Merging Traditions: The Future of Research on School Effectiveness and School Improvement.* London: Cassell.

Hackett, G. (1995) A flawed spur to improve, *Times Educational Supplement*, 15 December, p. 12.

Hallam, S. and Toutounji, I. (1996) *What Do We Know About the Grouping of Pupils by Ability? A Research Review.* London: University of London Institute of Education.

Halsey, A.H., Heath, A.F. and Ridge, J.M. (1980) *Origins and Destinations: Family, Class, and Education in Modern Britain.* Oxford, Clarendon Press.

Hammersley, M. (1998) Who questions the questioners?, *Times Educational Supplement*, 9 October, p. 25.

Hammersley, M. and Atkinson, P. (1995) *Ethnography: Principles in Practice*, 2nd edition. London: Routledge.

Hammersley, M. and Woods, P. (eds) (1984) *Life in School: The Sociology of Pupil Culture.* Milton Keynes: Open University Press.

Hargreaves, D.H. (1967) *Social Relations in a Secondary School.* London: Routledge & Kegan Paul.

Harris, S., Rudduck, J. and Wallace, G. (1996) Political contexts and school careers, in M. Hughes (ed.) *Teaching and Learning in Changing Times.* Oxford: Basil Blackwell.

Hatcher, R. (1997) New Labour, school improvement and racial inequality, *Multicultural Teaching*, 15(3): 8–13.

Hatcher, R. (1998) Social justice and the politics of school effectiveness and improvement, *Race Ethnicity and Education*, 1(2): 267–89.

Hawkins, M. (1997) *Social Darwinism in European and American Thought 1860–1945: Nature as Model and Nature as Threat.* Cambridge: Cambridge University Press.

Hearnshaw, L.S. (1979) *Cyril Burt, Psychologist.* London: Hodder & Stoughton.

Hearnshaw, L.S. (1990) The Burt Affair – a rejoinder, *The Psychologist*, 3(2): 61–4.

Henriques, J. (1984) Social psychology and the politics of racism, in J. Henriques, W. Hollway, C. Urwin, C. Venn and V. Walkerdine (1984) *Changing the Subject: Psychology, Social Regulation and Subjectivity.* London: Methuen.

Herrnstein, R.J. and Murray, C. (1994) *The Bell Curve: Intelligence and Class Structure in American Life.* New York: Free Press.

Hillage, J., Pearson, R., Anderson, A. and Tamkin, P. (1998) *Excellence in Research on Schools.* London: Department for Education and Employment.

Hugill, B. (1998) The male liberator's sit-down protest, *Times Educational Supplement*, 30 October, p. 11.

Hurman, A. (1978) *A Charter for Choice: A Study of Options Schemes.* Windsor: NFER.

Irigaray, L. (1977) *Ce sexe qui n'est pas un.* Paris: Éditions de Minuit.

Jensen, A.R. (1969) How much can we boost IQ and scholastic achievement?, *Harvard Educational Review*, 39(1): 1–123.

Jensen, A.R. (1972) *Genetics and Education.* London: Methuen.

Jensen, A.R. (1991) Spearman's *g* and the problem of educational equality, *Oxford Review of Education*, 17(2): 169–87.

Jensen, A.R. (1998) The *g* factor and the design of education, in R.J. Sternberg and W.M. Williams (eds) *Intelligence, Instruction, and Assessment: Theory into Practice.* Mahwah, NJ: Lawrence Erlbaum Associates.

Johnson, P. (1994) Gone is the time when Americans led the world in saying what they thought, *The Spectator*, 26 November.

Jollife, J. and South, H. (1997) Policy for funding the learning of minority ethnic pupils, *Multicultural Teaching*, 15(3): 16–17.

Joynson, R.B. (1989) *The Burt Affair.* London: Routledge.

Kamin, L.J. (1974) *The Science and Politics of IQ.* Harmondsworth: Penguin.

Kamin, L.J. (1981) Contributions to the volume *Intelligence: The Battle for the Mind. H.J. Eysenck versus L.J. Kamin.* London: Pan Books.

Kamin, L.J. (1995) Behind the curve, *Scientific American*, February, pp. 82–6.

Kelly, A., Whyte, J. and Smail, B. (1984) *Girls into Science and Technology: Final Report.* Manchester: University of Manchester Department of Sociology.

Kingdon, M. and Stobart, G. (1988) *GCSE Examined.* Lewes: Falmer Press.

Kinsey, A.C., Pomeroy, W.B. and Martin, C.E. (1948) *Sexual Behaviour in the Human Male.* Philadelphia: Saunders.

Kinsey, A.C., Pomeroy, W.B., Martin, C.E. and Gebhard, P.H. (1953) *Sexual Behaviour in the Human Female.* Philadelphia: Saunders.

Kohn, M. (1996) *The Race Gallery: The Return of Racial Science.* London: Vintage.

Labour Party (1997) *New Labour: Because Britain Deserves Better* (The Labour Party Manifesto). London: Labour Party.

Lacey, C. (1970) *Hightown Grammar: The School as a Social System.* Manchester: Manchester University Press.

Lacey, C. (1977) *The Socialization of Teachers.* London: Methuen.

Lepkowska, D. (1998) Opted-out schools accused of stealing the cream, *Times Educational Supplement*, 2 January, p. 4.

Levačić, R. (1995) *Local Management of Schools: Analysis and Practice.* Buckingham: Open University Press.

Mac an Ghaill, M. (1988) *Young, Gifted and Black: Student–Teacher Relations in the Schooling of Black Youth.* Milton Keynes: Open University Press.

Mac an Ghaill, M. (1989) Coming-of-age in 1980s England: reconceptualising Black students' schooling experience, *British Journal of Sociology of Education*, 10(3): 273–86.

Mac an Ghaill, M. (1994) *The Making of Men: Masculinities, Sexualities and Schooling.* Buckingham: Open University Press.

Mason, D. (1995) *Race and Ethnicity in Modern Britain.* Oxford: Oxford University Press.

Mayer, J.D. (1997) Emotional intelligence. Paper presented at the annual meeting of the American Educational Research Association, Chicago, March.

McCarthy, C. (1998) Educating the American Popular: suburban resentment and the representation of the inner city in contemporary film and television, *Race Ethnicity and Education*, 1(1): 31–47.

McClintock, A. (1995) *Imperial Leather: Race, Gender and Sexuality in the Colonial Context.* London: Routledge.

Measor, L. (1983) Gender and the sciences: pupils' gender-based conceptions of school subjects, in M. Hammersley and A. Hargreaves (eds) *Curriculum Practice: Some Sociological Case Studies.* Lewes: Falmer Press.

Measor, L. and Sikes, P. (1992) *Gender and Schools.* London: Cassell.

Miles, R. (1993) *Racism after 'Race Relations'*. London: Routledge.

Mirza, H.S. (1992) *Young, Female and Black*. London: Routledge.

Mirza, H.S. (1997) *Black British Feminism*. London: Routledge.

Mirza, H.S. (1998) Race, gender and IQ: the social consequences of a pseudo-scientific discourse, *Race Ethnicity and Education*, 1(1): 109–26.

Modood, T. (1992) *Not Easy Being British: Colour, Culture and Citizenship*. Stoke-on-Trent: Runnymede Trust and Trentham Books.

Modood, T. (1996) The changing context of 'race' in Britain, *Patterns of Prejudice*, 30(1): 3–13.

Modood, T., Berthoud, R., Lakey, J., Nazroo, J., Smith, P., Virdee, S. and Beishon, S. (1997) *Ethnic Minorities in Britain: Diversity and Disadvantage*. London: Policy Studies Institute.

Mortimore, P., Sammons, P. and Thomas, S. (1994) School effectiveness and value added measures, *Assessment in Education*, 1(3): 315–32.

Mortimore, P. and Whitty, G. (1997) *Can School Improvement Overcome the Effects of Disadvantage?* London: University of London Institute of Education.

Murphy, P. and Elwood, J. (1998) Gendered experiences, choices and achievement – exploring the links, *International Journal of Inclusive Education*, 2(2): 95–118.

Myers, K. (1990) Review of 'Equal Opportunities in the New Era', *Education*, 5 October, p. 295.

Nehaul, K. (1996) *The Schooling of Children of Caribbean Heritage*. Stoke-on-Trent: Trentham.

Newsam, P. (1996) Take the terminology to task, *Times Educational Supplement*, 22 March, p. 13.

Northern Examinations and Assessment Board (NEAB) (1997) *GCSE Examinations 1998 and 1999: New GCSE Tiering Arrangements*. Manchester: NEAB.

Northern Examinations and Assessment Board (no date) *GCSE Syllabus for 1995, 1996 and 1997: English*. Manchester: NEAB.

O'Connor, M. (1996) Appalled by some unnatural selection, *Times Educational Supplement*, 22 March, p. 12.

Oakes, J. (1990) *Multiplying Inequalities: The Effects of Race, Social Class, and Tracking on Opportunities to Learn Mathematics and Science*. Santa Monica, CA: Rand Corporation.

Oakes, J., Wells, A.S., Jones, M. and Datnow, A. (1997) Detracking: the social construction of ability, cultural politics, and resistance to reform, *Teachers College Record*, 98(3): 482–510.

Office for Standards in Education (Ofsted) (1993) *Exclusions: A Response to the Department for Education Discussion Paper*. London: Ofsted.

Office for Standards in Education (Ofsted) (1996) *Exclusions from Secondary Schools 1995/6*. London: The Stationery Office.

Ouseley, H. (1998) Black exclusions scandal, *Times Educational Supplement*, 18 December, p. 13.

Ozga, J. (1990) Policy research and policy theory: a comment on Fitz and Halpin, *Journal of Education Policy*, 5: 359–62.

Padilla, A.M. and Lindholm, K.J. (1995) Quantitative educational research with ethnic minorities, in J.A. Banks and C.A. McGee Banks (eds) *Handbook of Research on Multicultural Education*. New York: Macmillan.

Payne, J. (1995) *Routes beyond Compulsory Schooling*. England and Wales Youth Cohort Study, Report no. 31. Sheffield: Employment Department.

Phillips, R. (1996) History teaching, cultural restorationism and national identity in England and Wales, *Curriculum Studies*, 4(3): 385–99.

Power, S. (1995) The detail and the bigger picture: the use of state-centred theory in explaining education policy and practice, *International Studies in Sociology of Education*, 5(1): 77–92.

Power, S. (1996) *The Pastoral and the Academic: Conflict and Contradiction in the Curriculum*. London: Cassell.

Power, S., Halpin, D. and Fitz, J. (1994) Underpinning choice and diversity? The Grant Maintained schools policy in context, in S. Tomlinson (ed.) *Educational Reform and its Consequences*. London: Institute for Public Policy Research/Rivers Oram Press.

Power, S., Whitty, G. and Youdell, D. (1995) *No Place to Learn: Homelessness and Education*. London: Shelter.

Pratt, J., Bloomfield, J. and Seale, C. (1984) *Option Choice: A Question of Equal Opportunity*. Windsor: NFER.

Pyke, N. (1995) Inspections 'neglect' racial equality, *Times Educational Supplement*, 3 February, p. 3.

Pyke, N. (1996) Male brain rattled by curriculum 'oestrogen', *Times Educational Supplement*, 15 March, p. 8.

Pyke, N. (1998a) Welcome for value-added table, *Times Educational Supplement*, 13 March, p. 6.

Pyke, N. (1998b) New tables threaten quality, *Times Educational Supplement*, 24 April, p. 2.

Qualifications and Curriculum Authority (QCA) (1998) *Statutory Consultation: Work-Related Learning at Key Stage 4*. London: QCA.

Rampton, A. (1981) *West Indian Children in Our Schools*, Cmnd. 8273. London: HMSO.

Rasekoala, E. (1998) The black hole in science ranks. Paper presented at the American Educational Research Association annual meeting, San Diego, April.

Rattansi, A. (1992) Changing the subject? Racism, culture and education, in J. Donald and A. Rattansi (eds) *'Race', Culture and Difference*. London: Sage.

Reay, D. and Ball, S.J. (1997) 'Spoilt for choice': the working classes and educational markets, *Oxford Review of Education*, 23(1): 89–101.

Reynolds, D., Bollen, R., Creemers, B. *et al.* (1996) *Making Good Schools*. London: Routledge.

Richards, G. (1997) *'Race', Racism and Psychology: Towards a Reflexive History*. London: Routledge.

Richardson, R. (1993) *Section 11 Funding: Troubled History, Present Campaigning, Possible Futures*. London: Runnymede Trust.

Riddell, S. (1992a) *Gender and the Politics of the Curriculum*. London: Routledge.

Riddell, S. (1992b) Gender and education: progressive and conservative forces in the balance, in S. Brown and S. Riddell (eds) *Class, Race and Gender in Schools: A New Agenda for Policy and Practice in Scottish Education*. Edinburgh: Scottish Council for Research in Education.

Rizvi, F. (1993) Critical introduction: researching racism and education, in B. Troyna, *Racism and Education: Research Perspectives*. Buckingham: Open University Press.

Rudduck, J. (1991) *Innovation and Change: Developing Involvement and Understanding*. Buckingham: Open University Press.

Runnymede Trust (1993) *Equality Assurance in Schools: Quality, Identity, Society. A Handbook for Action Planning and School Effectiveness*. Stoke-on-Trent: Trentham for the Runnymede Trust.

Rushton, J.P. (1995) *Race, Evolution, and Behaviour: A Life History Perspective*. New Brunswick, NJ: Transaction.

Rutter, M., Maughan, B., Mortimore, P. and Ouston, J., with Smith, A. (1979) *Fifteen Thousand Hours: Secondary Schools and their Effects on Children*. Shepton Mallet, Somerset: Open Books.

Sammons, P. (1995) Gender, ethnic and socio-economic differences in attainment and progress: a longitudinal analysis of student achievement over 9 years, *British Educational Research Journal*, 21(4): 465–85.

Sammons, P., Hillman, J. and Mortimore, P. (1995) *Key Characteristics of Effective Schools: A Review of School Effectiveness Research*. London: University of London Institute of Education.

School Curriculum and Assessment Authority (SCAA) (1996) *Tiering in GCSE Examinations*, ref. KS4/96/369. London: SCAA.

Selden, S. (1999) *Inheriting Shame: The Story of Eugenics and Racism in America*. New York: Teachers College Press.

Sewell, T. (1997) *Black Masculinities and Schooling: How Black Boys Survive Modern Schooling*. Stoke-on-Trent: Trentham.

Sewell, T. (1998) Loose canons: exploding the myth of the 'black macho' lad, in D. Epstein, J. Elwood, V. Hey and J. Maw (eds) *Failing Boys? Issues in Gender and Achievement*. Buckingham: Open University Press.

Sikes, P.J., Measor, L. and Woods, P. (1985) *Teacher Careers: Crises and Continuities*. Lewes: Falmer Press.

Skellington, R. with Morris, P. (1992) *'Race' in Britain Today*. London: Sage.

Slavin, R.E. (1996) *Education for All*. Lisse: Swets and Zeitlinger.

Smith, D.J. and Tomlinson, S. (1989) *The School Effect: A Study of Multi-Racial Comprehensives*. London: Policy Studies Institute.

Smith, I. and Woodhouse, D. (1982) Sorting Them Out. Unpublished interim report to the Social Science Research Council.

Social Exclusion Unit (1998) *Truancy and School Exclusion*, Cm. 3957. London: SEU.

Sternberg, R.J. (1985) *Beyond IQ: A Triarchic Theory of Human Intelligence*. New York: Cambridge University Press.

Sternberg, R.J. (1995) Interview with Skeptic magazine, *Skeptic*, 3(3): 72–80.

Sternberg, R.J. (1996) Myths, countermyths, and truths about intelligence, *Educational Researcher*, 25(2): 11–16.

Sternberg, R.J. (1998) Abilities are forms of developing expertise, *Educational Researcher*, 27(3): 11–20.

Sternberg, R.J. and Williams, W.M. (eds) (1998) *Intelligence, Instruction, and Assessment: Theory into Practice*. Mahwah, NJ: Lawrence Erlbaum Associates.

Stobart, G., Elwood, J., Hayden, M., White, J. and Mason, K. (1992) *Differential Performance in Examinations at 16+: English and Mathematics*. London: University of London Examinations and Assessment Council.

Strauss, A.L. (1987) *Qualitative Analysis for Social Scientists*. Cambridge: Cambridge University Press.

Sukhnandan, L. and Lee, B. (1998) *Streaming, Setting and Grouping by Ability*. Slough: NFER.

Swann, Lord (1985) *Education for All: Final Report of the Committee of Inquiry into the Education of Children from Ethnic Minority Groups*, Cmnd. 9453. London: HMSO.

Tate, N. (1996a) The role of the school in promoting moral, spiritual and cultural values, *Education Review*, 10(1): 66–70.

Tate, N. (1996b) *Curriculum, culture and society.* Text of speech by Dr Nick Tate, Chief Executive, School Curriculum and Assessment Authority. London: SCAA.

Taylor, M. and Hegarty, S. (1985) *The Best of Both Worlds . . . ? A Review of Research into the Education of Pupils of South Asian Origin.* Windsor: NFER-Nelson.

Terman, L.M. (1916) *The Measurement of Intelligence: An Explanation and a Complete Guide for the Use of the Standard Revision and Extension of the Binet–Simon Intelligence Scale.* Boston: Houghton-Mifflin.

Thatcher, M. (1993) *The Downing Street Years.* London: HarperCollins.

Thomas, S. and Mortimore, P. (1994) *Report on Value Added Analysis of 1993 GCSE Examination Results in Lancashire.* London: University of London Institute of Education.

Thomas, S., Pan, H. and Goldstein, H. (1994) *Report on the Analysis of 1992 Examination Results: AMA Project on Putting Examination Results in Context.* London: Association of Metropolitan Authorities.

Thomas, S., Sammons, P., Mortimore, P. and Smees, R. (1997) Differential secondary school effectiveness: comparing the performance of different pupil groups, *British Educational Research Journal,* 23(4): 451–69.

Thorndike, R.L. and Hagen, E. (1986) *Cognitive Abilities Test. Levels A to F. Pupil's Book,* 2nd edition. Windsor: NFER-Nelson.

Thorndike, R.L., Hagen, E. and France, N. (1986) *Cognitive Abilities Test. Levels A to F. Administration Manual,* 2nd edition. Windsor: NFER-Nelson.

Thornton, K. (1998) Blacks 15 times more likely to be excluded, *Times Educational Supplement,* 11 December, p. 1.

Tomlinson, S. (1987) Curriculum option choices in multi-ethnic schools, in B. Troyna (ed.) *Racial Inequality in Education.* London: Tavistock.

Tomlinson, S. and Tomes, H. (1986) Curriculum option choice in multi-ethnic schools. Unpublished project report to the Department of Education and Science.

Tooley, J. (1995a) Can IQ tests liberate education?, *Economic Affairs,* 15: 7.

Tooley, J. (1995b) A measure of freedom, *Times Higher Education Supplement,* 7 July, p. 18.

Tooley, J. with Darby, D. (1998) *Educational Research: A Critique.* London: Office for Standards in Education.

Troyna, B. (1988) The career of an antiracist education school policy: some observations on the mismanagement of change, in A.G. Green and S.J. Ball (eds) *Progress and Inequality in Comprehensive Education.* London: Routledge.

Troyna, B. (1991) Underachievers or underrated? The experiences of pupils of South Asian origin in a secondary school, *British Educational Research Journal,* 17(4): 361–76.

Troyna, B. (1993) *Racism and Education: Research Perspectives.* Buckingham: Open University Press.

Troyna, B. (1994) The 'everyday world' of teachers? Deracialised discourses in the sociology of teachers and the teaching profession, *British Journal of Sociology of Education,* 15(3): 325–39.

Troyna, B. (1995a) The Local Management of Schools and racial equality, in S. Tomlinson and M. Craft (eds) *Ethnic Relations and Schooling: Policy and Practice in the 1990s.* London: Athlone.

Troyna, B. (1995b) Beyond reasonable doubt? Researching 'race' in educational settings, *Oxford Review of Education,* 21(4): 395–408.

Troyna, B. and Hatcher, R. (1992) *Racism in Children's Lives: A Study of Mainly White Primary Schools.* London: Routledge.

Troyna, B. and Siraj-Blatchford, I. (1993) Providing support or denying access? The experiences of students designated as 'ESL' and 'SN' in a multi-ethnic secondary school, *Educational Review*, 45(1): 3–11.

Troyna, B. and Williams, J. (1986) *Racism, Education and the State*. Beckenham: Croom Helm.

Valli, L., Cooper, D. and Frankes, L. (1997) Professional development schools and equity: a critical analysis of rhetoric and research, in M.W. Apple (ed.) *Review of Research in Education, Volume 22*. Washington, DC: American Educational Research Association.

Van den Berghe, P.L. (1988) 'Race', in E.E. Cashmore (ed.) *Dictionary of Race and Ethnic Relations*, 2nd edition. London: Routledge.

Vincent, C. (1996) *Parents and Teachers: Power and Participation*. London: Falmer Press.

Vincent, C. and Tomlinson, S. (1997) Home–school relationships: 'the swarming of disciplinary mechanisms'?, *British Educational Research Journal*, 23(3): 361–77.

Walford, G. and Miller, H. (1991) *City Technology College*. Buckingham: Open University Press.

Wellman, D.T. (1977) *Portraits of White Racism*. Cambridge: Cambridge University Press.

Wellman, D.T. (1993) *Portraits of White Racism*, 2nd edition. Cambridge: Cambridge University Press.

Whitty, G. (1997a) Creating quasi-markets in education: a review of recent research on parental choice and school autonomy in three countries, in M.W. Apple (ed.) *Review of Research in Education*, Volume 22. Washington, DC: American Educational Research Association.

Whitty, G. (1997b) Social theory and education policy: the legacy of Karl Mannheim, *British Journal of Sociology of Education*, 18(2): 149–63.

Whitty, G. (1998) New Labour, education and disadvantage, *Education and Social Justice*, 1(1): 2–8.

Whitty, G., Edwards, T. and Gewirtz, S. (1993) *Specialisation and Choice in Urban Education: The City Technology College Experiment*. London: Routledge.

Whitty, G., Power, S. and Halpin, D. (1998) *Devolution and Choice in Education*. Buckingham: Open University Press.

Willis, P. (1977) *Learning to Labour: How Working Class Kids Get Working Class Jobs*. Farnborough: Gower.

Woodhead, C. (1996) Boys who learn to be losers, *The Times*, 6 March, p. 18.

Woodhead, C. (1998) Academia gone to seed, *New Statesman*, 20 March, pp. 51–2.

Woods, P. (1976) The myth of subject choice, *British Journal of Sociology*, 27(2): 130–49.

Woods, P. (1977) How teachers decide pupils' subject choices, *Cambridge Journal of Education*, 21–32.

Woods, P. (1979) *The Divided School*. London: Routledge & Kegan Paul.

Woods, P. (1983) *Sociology and the School: An Interactionist Viewpoint*. London: Routledge & Kegan Paul.

Woods, P. (1990) *The Happiest Days? How Pupils Cope with School*. Lewes: Falmer Press.

Wright, C. (1986) School processes – an ethnographic study, in J. Eggleston, D. Dunn and M. Anjali, *Education for Some: The Educational and Vocational Experiences of 15–18 Year Old Members of Minority Ethnic Groups*. Stoke-on-Trent: Trentham.

Wright, C. (1992) *Race Relations in the Primary School*. London: David Fulton.

Name index

Subject index